DATE DUE			

GAYLORD M-2   PRINTED IN U.S.A.

private and
public planning

private and
public planning

NEIL W. CHAMBERLAIN
Professor of Economics
Yale University

McGraw-Hill Book Company
New York St. Louis San Francisco Toronto London Sydney

Private and Public Planning

preface

In the period since World War II there have been two remarkable but seemingly unrelated developments in Western economies—the refinement and proliferation of planning-budgeting programs within the private corporation, and experimentation with national (public) planning and budgeting programs. The first developed without the second in the United States, in the United Kingdom, and to a lesser extent in Germany. The second developed without much of the first in France, Belgium, and Norway. Sweden and the Netherlands had something of both; Italy had little of either. These are admittedly only approximate and rather gross characterizations, but they suggest the unsystematic relationship between the two lines of development.

If an historical relationship was largely absent, a functional relationship was not. This has been most apparent in those countries which emphasized public planning programs initially. In these the broader, firmer, and usually expansionary basis provided by the public plan stressed the importance and value of investment and production planning within the major business units on which the national plan depended. Trade associations have found national planning a welcome ally in encouraging a more serious interest in corporate planning.

In countries not given to public planning, the functional relationship between the private and public spheres has received less attention. In the United States, in particular, top managements remain strongly opposed to government "programming," even though they have brought their own planning systems to probably as high a stage of perfection as is to be found in any economic unit in the world. But even here the tie between planning in the private sector and some more systematic economic management by the national government has begun to impress itself on planning staffs in the large corporations. The casting up of both short- and long-run plans in the corporation depends so heavily on what is likely to be happening in the economy at large that at least some corporate planners are beginning to recognize—in private conversation if not public statement—the value of having a more reliable base on which to project their own futures.

This study attempts to analyze the relationship between planning in the two sectors. Actually, the distinction is less between public and

v

private than between macro and micro, between system and subsystem. Local governments, though "public," belong in the same category with private business firms in this respect—they are both subunits of a larger (national) system.

There are a few ideas which are central to the analysis and which perhaps may be said to constitute whatever contribution this study makes. Among the most important of these are the conception of planning as the systematic management of assets; the inescapable conflict of objectives between system and subsystem, and the consequent dependence not only on technical-economic but also organizational-political coordination; the ongoing nature of the planning process, with a continuing interplay between intent and event, and the significance of the distinction between what are here called specific and categorical social objectives.

To catalogue all those to whom I am indebted for information and insights in the United States, England, Sweden, Norway, Denmark, France, Belgium, the Netherlands, Germany, and Italy would be too monumental a task and would expose me to the embarrassment of an inadvertent omission. The same is true of those who have been of assistance in the Organization for Economic Cooperation and Development and the United Nations Economic Council for Europe. To one person I am especially grateful, Mr. Joseph Slater, associate director of the International Affairs Program of the Ford Foundation, whose deep interest in the subject area and whose involvement with economic developments in Europe provided the encouragement for the writing of this book.

NEIL W. CHAMBERLAIN

contents

1...
the planning process

In the last few years the West has witnessed a revival of interest in economic planning. In the depression-ridden thirties the subject had had a widespread vogue. Even the citadels of business conservatism had contributed their quota of models of a new planning order, complete with councils and administrators and advisory bodies. The economic system was to be remade in a new image, and there were many prophets, of varying persuasions, who with ingenuous immodesty wrote as though that image had been revealed to them. Planning was a popular panacea for ills that were too evident for anyone to disregard.

World War II brought planning as a matter of necessity, without the need for disputation over doctrine or dogma. It was thrown up under urgent pressure to meet specific purposes, with every intention that the jerry-built structure would be dismantled as soon as possible. The intention was made good, in North America more rapidly than in Europe. Reconversion was relatively less of a problem than reconstruction.

In the fifties a few Western economies flirted with planning—France, the Netherlands, Norway, perhaps Sweden could be included. To some extent these were efforts to deal with problems left by the war, using controls which were abandoned as the problems were met. But following the "shakeout" of these temporary measures, and building on an accumulating experience, the planning procedures in these few countries gradually became more comprehensive, more systematic, and more sophisticated.

It was not until the decade of the sixties, however, that the bumpy progress of the United States and the United Kingdom, backgrounded by pressing balance-of-payments problems in both countries and highlighted by a politically inspired growth race, led to official interest in what the continental economies were doing, particularly France. A visit to the French Commissariat du Plan became almost an essential status symbol in upper business, government, and academic echelons. Le plan, which until 1960 and even a little later had been practically unknown outside France, suddenly became one of the most frequently encountered topics in business journals.

The interest in planning of the sixties is different from that of the thirties, however. Although prompted by economic malaise, the suffering is far less acute, so that the search for a remedy is not so pressing. But more important, the discussions of the sixties are less ideological and more technical. The old and admittedly important problems of centralization of power and infringement of individual economic liberties, while still the subject of earnest debate, are now discussed with more subtlety. Crude notions that economic liberty is directly opposed to economic planning, so that more of one necessarily means less of the other, have not wholly disappeared, but they are used less categorically. There is more curiosity about the procedures and techniques of planning, the administrative relationships between business and government, the elements of private discretion and public sanction, the basis for collaboration between the two sectors, and the technical feasibility and reliability of economic forecasting.

This partial shift from the ideological to the technical plane of discussion is probably due to a number of causes. For one thing, corporations with European subsidiaries have learned that doing business under the newer forms of planning has not been markedly more painful. Their European colleagues, with whom they feel a business rapport, seem to approve and even to champion the new programs—sometimes even participating in them.

As another consideration, comprehensive corporate planning and budgeting, which had just been picking up steam in the period prior to World War II, spread with a rush in the years after, so that most businessmen in medium- to large-size corporations became personally involved in the often elaborate budget-planning programs in their own company. Corporate planning, particularly in the United States, has become one of the most fully articulated forms of planning to be found in any economic unit in the world today. Nor are such exercises inconsequential in size and scope: the plans of such giants as General Motors and General Electric involve annual budgets as large as those of some governments. The development of planning in these nongovernmental units has produced greater familiarity with, interest in, and appreciation of the role of planning generally than had been true in the thirties.

Less evident but perhaps no less effective in stirring an interest in the technical aspects of planning has been the advent of systems analysis. The technological revolution of which automation and cybernetics are the verbal symbols heightened an interest in production processes (and organizational activity generally) as *systems*—the integration of numerous contributing parts to an overall process.

Of course this is scarcely a new concept. It can be traced back explicitly at least as far as Adam Smith, one of the greatest exponents of systems analysis of all time, who, in an essay on astronomy written long before his *Wealth of Nations*, had epitomized a system as neatly as has ever been done: "A system is like a little machine." With all its parts fitting together to produce a desired motion, a system is judged by its effectiveness or ineffectiveness.

As Smith had sought to show, an economy too is a system. If his conception of the nature of that system is no longer valid, an economy nevertheless remains some kind of system—working well or poorly. If poorly, it is the engineer or the scientist, not the ideologue, who becomes fascinated with unraveling the mysteries of the myriad economic relationships which must be integrated to explain how it works or why it fails to work.[1] Once the notion takes hold, and the economy is conceived as such, interest in planning is almost certain to follow.

The present inquiry is prompted by these newer lines of interest. While philosophical questions obviously cannot be laid aside as being less important, emphasis here is on an understanding of planning not as something which grows out of an ideology, but as something which grows out of the requirements of any economic system, as something which may be enlisted in the service of differing, perhaps conflicting, ideologies. Planning is not the property of the Socialists or the Communists, as U.S. business planning clearly demonstrates.

PLANNING CONCEPTS

Little would be gained by cataloguing the numerous definitions of planning which are to be found in the literature. Instead, let us start with our own definition and try to establish its conceptual usefulness.

Planning is the systematic management of assets. This is a generic definition, applying to any economic unit from the individual to international "communities" or associations. The theme of the planned use of assets will recur throughout this study; it is the central concept.

The management of assets involves numerous supporting activities, but we shall identify only the most important. First is the identification of the primary objectives in the pursuit of which assets will be managed. The assets on which any economic unit can draw—individual, company, city, nation—are limited; for effective use they must be directed to the ends which are most desired. The economic notion of opportunity cost enters here: the cost of using up assets in one way, or for one objective, *is* the other uses to which those assets might have been directed.

Second, the management of assets involves the integration of the several strategic streams of decisions which are necessary if assets are to be converted to the achievement of the objectives posed. The stra-

[1] At the level of the firm, one of the best-known advocates of this approach is Prof. Jay Forrester of M.I.T., formally untrained as an economist and coming to his present interest in "industrial dynamics" via his earlier involvement with the development of computers and their applications. Summer seminars which he has conducted have been populated chiefly by businessmen. An abbreviated version of his *Industrial Dynamics* (Cambridge, Mass.: M.I.T. Press, 1961) appeared in the *Harvard Business Review*, July–August, 1958, and March–April, 1959.

tegic streams of decisions will differ depending on the nature of the economic unit. They are different for a household than for a business firm and different for a business firm than for an economy as a whole. But within every economic unit there are a limited number of strategic decisions which must be recurringly made and on which the gaining of its goals depends.

Third, since both objectives and strategic decisions are not one-time matters, but continue indefinitely throughout the life span of the economic unit and are subject to change due to a variety of easily catalogued influences, the element of time must enter. Assets are managed not only for the current income which they provide (the present achievement of objectives). There must also be decisions, in any economic unit, as to:

a   the preservation of existing assets for the production of future income (conservation of natural resources is the obvious example here)

b   the accumulation of further assets in a meaningful growth pattern, which involves net new investment out of current income

c   the transformation of assets, over time, to preserve their value, involving the appropriate reinvestment of assets as they become liquid

We have said that planning is the systematic management of assets and have identified three behavioral implications of that definition. Let us return for a moment to the second of these: management of assets involves the integration or coordination of the several strategic streams of decisions which determine the operations of the unit. In the case of a large corporation, each of its departments or divisions is involved in an intricate network of relationships, all of which must be jointly coordinated. The job of management—to produce a mosaic of interrelationships which has meaning in terms of some projected result—becomes highly demanding.

That this function can be performed over and over again, in numerous units scattered over the face of the globe, sometimes causes us to ignore its demanding character. It would almost appear that anyone can become a business manager, given a little luck and a little capital. At times we even talk of businesses which "run themselves," as though the managerial task of coordination had become superfluous.

But we can talk loosely in this manner only if we drop out of consideration any standards of excellence. It may be true—to put the proposition in exaggerated form—that almost anyone could learn to fill a manager's job; the parts of the system for which he assumes responsibility would get coordinated after a fashion. With heavy reliance on more experienced assistants, he might keep the unit operating. But to construe such amateur performance as professional management would require us to refrain from any judgments as to the quality of the result. Almost anyone can rhyme, but few are capable of being poets.

This insistence on the demanding character of the managerial function of coordination is not just a literary aside. It is intended to emphasize that coordination, if it is done well, involves a degree of specialist finesse. It can be performed at all levels of quality, with varying degrees of conscious attention to its requirements, but to be performed adequately—especially in complex units—requires procedures and techniques which must be designed for the purpose and used by specialists.

The coordination which is called for is basically of two sorts. We shall later have occasion to observe that failure to recognize the different and often conflicting nature of these two streams of coordinating activity is often the basis for misunderstanding the planning process. One coordinating activity deals with the purely technical aspects of operations. It involves the manipulation of technologies, machines and equipment, materials, schedules, accounts, symbols—*things*. In a business firm it calls for architects planning buildings, engineers developing processes, researchers spawning products and ideas, economists projecting product demand, accountants devising and maintaining the books of account. These are the matters which can be coordinated and integrated on paper, with blueprints and flow charts and mathematical formulas. They relate to the efficiency and internal consistency of the numerous parts which compose the organized whole.

But there is a second line of coordinating activity which is superimposed on the first—the coordination of the people on whom the functioning of the unit depends. If in some organization paper schedules were transposed to computer tapes which actuated production equipment whose output in turn was transmitted to delivery systems transporting the end product to consumers who accepted what they received, without any question of price or payment or quality or adequacy, there would perhaps be no need for this second stream of coordination. Efficiency and internal consistency through the manipulation of things would be all that were needed for the functioning of such a system. But even the most highly automated organizations do not come close to such a peopleless operation.

In order for a system to function, it must coordinate the activities of numbers of individuals, each of whom is self-serving in the sense that he seeks the advancement of his own objectives over those of his coworkers. All attempt to achieve their personal aspirations, in some degree, through the medium of the organization of which they are a part. This means that conflicting ideas as to how things should get done are bound to arise—even over relatively technical matters. Decisions about what marketing structure should be adopted by a business firm, the system of local real estate assessments in a city, or the depreciation rates to be permitted by the Federal government for income tax purposes often arouse differences and disagreements—not only among those people who are most directly involved (the salesmen who may be eliminated by a change in distribution policy, the householders and business firms affected by modification of tax measures), but also among the officials who are charged with deciding on policy. At stake may be such issues as whether the acceptance of one policy rather than another will lead to the preferment of one vice president over another, or the loss of organizational status in the case of a government department official or of constituent support in the case of a city councilman or of political patronage in the case of a congressman.

Within economic units depending on a number of people for their functioning, there are few policies which are so "technical," so independent of people's reactions, that they can be instituted without question. Most matters of any consequence involve discussion and compromise. The views of those on whom the functioning of the system depends cannot be wholly ignored unless the system is prepared to part with their services—in which case it must come to terms with their replacements. We shall not take the time to examine here the nature of the process by which differing views of individuals in an organization are compromised into a more or less compatible set of policies and practices.[2] It is enough for present purposes to recognize that this involves a rather complicated and continuing bargaining process, inter-

---

[2] I have tried to do this at some length in an earlier book, *A General Theory of Economic Process* (New York: Harper & Row, Publishers, Incorporated, 1955).

nal to the organization. These internal bargains must simultaneously be coordinated with the bargains which are external to the unit—involving its relations with other economic units, whether business firms, households, or governments. We sometimes think of the external bargains as setting constraints on internal bargains, or occasionally vice versa, but actually the whole complex of bargains is sufficiently inter-dependent that none has the finality of a firm constraint. Even relation-ships with "sovereignty," in the form of laws and administrative rul-ings, are often subject to compromise and negotiation.

This complex of bargains does not somehow arrange itself. To make it into a consistent and workable set of relationships requires the mana-gerial function of coordination. The reactions of people must be manipulated by whatever inducements are suitable and permissible. To secure an acquiescence which may be needed to settle a policy issue or to elicit a desired response, managements must be prepared to make concessions or invoke sanctions. This is a quite different type of co-ordination from the technical integration achieved through schedules and formulas. The efficiency of the latter process may have to give way to the "practical" requirements of integrating people into an or-ganization. A system of bargains among people must be contrived, and it presumably can be contrived more or less efficiently from the view-point of achieving the objectives of the system—that is, with varying degrees of sacrifice of system objectives to subsystem (individual) goals.

There has been some tendency to identify planning with only the first type of coordination, the technical manipulations. But if one takes the position that planning refers to the systematic management of assets, the managerial function does not end with symbols on paper but includes induced actions which must be compared with intended re-sults. The traditional effort to distinguish planning from execution marks not only an artificial but a misleading division, as will become clearer in future chapters. Perhaps for the moment it is enough to suggest that since planning in the sense used here is a continuing process, extending over an indefinite time stream stretching into the future, and since such continuous planning is necessarily influenced by the stream of ongoing activity of the unit, and if we regard the unit as a functioning system, with actions feeding back into plans, and plans influencing outcomes, systematically even though fallibly, then we cannot meaningfully cut into such an ongoing operation to isolate "plans" and "actions" as though these were independent of each other.

These definitional comments can perhaps be summarized as follows. There are three principal aspects of the planning process:

1   Ideological—the framing of objectives, both present and future, and the use of value systems to limit or prescribe instruments for achieving those objectives. This aspect is not confined to any particular ideology, certainly not to any of the *isms*. It involves the definition of the central goals of the unit, any unit, over time, guiding decisions on the use of its assets.

2   Technical and economic—the question of the most efficient hypothetical means of achieving the system's objectives. This involves, among other things, considerations of technology and factor proportions and the familiar economizing principles of economic theory.

3   Organizational and political—the manipulated or contrived coherence of the participants in the system. This coherence is not autogenetic but must be managed with the use of such inducements as the value orientation of the system permits. It leads to a system of bargains.

SYSTEMS AND SUBSYSTEMS

Let us focus our attention for the moment on the business firm as a planning system. We shall explore the characteristics of planning in the firm in greater detail in the chapter which follows, so that we can afford to slide over now much that will detain us later. Corporate objectives differ from those of the individuals or interest groups which compose it, such as workers and unions, supervisors and top management itself. Corporate objectives also differ from the goals of the corporation's own organizational subunits such as plants and departments. The objectives of a department may be to maintain a steadiness of workflow, a state of good day-to-day relations between workers and supervisors, a record of performance good enough to forestall intervention from higher authority, but targets that are not so demanding as to impose an uncomfortable tension and pace, and so on. These objectives need not be inconsistent with an overall corporate profit goal, but they are not the same, any more than the objectives of the individual worker in the shop are identical with the company's profit target.

These personal, group, and subunit objectives must be sufficiently satisfied to maintain the organization. This is indeed the managerial function of coordination which we have just noted. But the obverse is equally true. Each of the subunits must perform its functional role in the organization sufficiently well, facilitating the achievement of the overall corporate objective, if the people in that subunit are to be allowed to continue to occupy that role.

If we recognize that each subunit (a shop, a plant, a department) is itself a *planning unit*, involved with the systematic management of the assets which come under its control, we get the notion of systems and subsystems. Each plans within its own unit boundaries, and each must face the three principal planning questions which we have just summarized—but it cannot answer those questions independently, without respect to its relationship to any larger system of which it is a component or subsystem. Its ideological, technical-economic, and organizational-political aspects must not only satisfy its own (internal) requirements but they must be reasonably compatible with the ideological, technical-economic, and organizational-political characteristics of the larger unit if it is to retain its position in the overall system.[3]

A business unit is involved not only in sub and supra relations, as it looks up or down the organizational structure of which it is a part. It is also the center of a network of lateral relationships running to other units which are busily managing their own bundle of assets in the pursuit of their own objectives, the relationship relying on the striking of a bargain which sufficiently satisfies the purposes of both. Sub and supra relations involve an element of hierarchical authority which is absent from lateral relations. Lateral relations are relations of consent and contract, where nonconsent carries no organizational discipline or penalty. These lateral relations are of two types:

1   Some are internal to an organization. For example, two subunits may stand in different hierarchical systems or sequences, so that neither has organizational authority with respect to the other, but at some level above them their respective hierarchies merge into a single authority which can impose a decision on both or arbitrate their differences or make rules respecting their relationships.

[3] I take it that this necessity of satisfying the goals of subunits, without sacrificing unnecessarily the goals of the larger unit, is fundamentally what "suboptimization" is all about.

2 Some lateral relationships are wholly external to an organization, and no common hierarchical authority can impose a decision. Even the law does not touch their relationship affirmatively and cannot require joint action or prescribe terms, though it may enjoin or penalize certain behavior of one toward or with the other. Any rules respecting their relationship must be bargained out jointly, as between a union and a management, or between a firm and its suppliers.

At times what is formally a relationship between two independent units in practice takes on the aspect of system and subsystem, that is, having hierarchical rather than lateral relations. This is likely to be the case of a small supplier dependent on a large corporation for its market. Technically the relationship is one of consent and contract, but the unequal distribution of bargaining power converts it into a relationship of authority.

THE ECONOMY AS A SYSTEM

We have already identified the economy as a system. As a *planning* system, it, like the business firm, is concerned with the management of assets, in this case the nation's assets. But in this instance it is less clear what the managerial function entails or who exercises it. The economy too has its subsystems and in some instances is itself the subsystem of a still larger system, as is the case of the six countries composing the European Economic Community. It has its hierarchical and its lateral relations. But in this instance it is less clear than in the case of the firm what the "hierarchy" consists of.

While we shall seek to explore these questions more fully in subsequent chapters, let us attempt a tentative summary approach to them now, since it will help to clarify the general orientation of this study. In the public economy, the government must play the role of manager within the appropriate governmental limits, whether national, regional, or local. We focus for the moment on the national economy to simplify the discussion. Governmental authority is given by the constitution, whether written or not, and that same instrument also limits its hierarchical ("sovereign") powers. Its authority in such major areas as monetary and fiscal management, defense, foreign trade, and social security give it certain instruments for inducing behavior on the part of private economic units, such as households and business firms.

There is no country in the modern world which is without such powers. Even in those societies such as the United States and West Germany where opposition to "planning" is widespread, the federal governments enjoy very considerable powers to induce private responses. Tax reforms are debated in terms of their effects on investment and consumption and in turn on national income and employment. Public revenues are appropriated for retraining people and redeveloping areas through inducement by subsidies. Tariffs are raised or lowered to stimulate domestic competition, protect favored industries, promote exports and conserve foreign exchange, or provide assistance to developing economies. This is but the start of what could be a catalogue of fiscal measures by means of which governments—all governments—seek to influence the behavior of subsystems which are simultaneously independent and subordinate, which are "laterally" autonomous in most respects but "hierarchically" responsive in particular respects. All such actions are aspects of national management— efforts to coordinate people and organizations in a preferable set of relationships, efforts which are, however, necessarily limited and incomplete by reason of constitutional and legislative restraints on the manipulative powers of government.

How effective—even though partial and incomplete—such management of the national economy is depends on a variety of considerations, but of particular significance to us are two: how clearly the national objectives are held in view, and how systematic the exercise of the already given powers in the achievement of those objectives is.

The exercise of power by a central government inescapably raises questions of restraints on private freedoms, which we shall want to consider at a later stage. The line between the lateral independence of private organizations and their hierarchical responsiveness to government is shadowy—probably inescapably shadowy.[4] But while that is

---

[4] M. Jean-Paul Delcourt, president-director general of the Société Nationale des Pétroles d'Aquitaine, who has been involved in the French planning program, commented with respect to this shadowland: "I believe that this distinction between means of control and means of incentive is too fine. I would say that in a system where the public authorities have, in fact [as in France], power to deprive a firm of access to the means of credit, or to tax exemptions that are essential or very important to the firm, they dispose, in their relations with that firm, of means of pressure such that, in one way or another, they are in position to move the firm with, I repeat, the most powerful arguments, to undertake certain investment programs." From *French and Other National Economic Plans for Growth,*

reason for watchfulness that private discretion is not unnecessarily eroded, it cannot be reason for withholding the instruments of power from government. The power to tax, for example, is essential to any economic system, but, as the Supreme Court has warned, the power to tax is also the power to destroy. The danger cannot be escaped.

But if government—like any management—is a threat to the discretion of those who are part of its system, it can also expand their sphere of discretion. The system which it contrives may permit a degree of achievement by the subunits which they could not manage on their own. The goals of system and subsystem are certain to be competitive in some respects, but they are mutually reinforcing in others. The real problem is one of balance between the public and private sectors, or even more appropriately between the macro and micro sectors, since the latter include local public as well as private units. But balance cannot be achieved by relegating system objectives to a secondary role.

But let us waive further discussion of all such issues for the time being. The only point important to the present stage of the analysis is that given the instruments of governmental authority, however limited or extensive they may be, the national economic management which inescapably must take place may be good or bad, effective or ineffective, depending on the clarity with which the planning process is understood and appropriate planning procedures are followed. Planning does not require a whole new arsenal of central powers. It can be undertaken with whatever powers exist. In the process, it may develop that new legislative authorizations would be desirable, and these can be debated up and down and decided on the merits, but that is an issue for the future. For the present, we need only note that, just as in the case of the business firm, so too in governmental management of the economy the function of coordination can be performed ill or well, and that good performance calls for explicit consideration of techniques and the development of specialized skills.

In the realm of large-scale private business, the West has developed techniques and skills which are unsurpassed. It has drawn on the best which the scientific and academic communities have to offer in an

Report of an international conference sponsored by the European Committee for Economic and Social Progress (CEPES), Paris, June, 1962, and published by CEPES in 1963, p. 26.

effort to systematize its activities on behalf of objectives scattered over a time stretching ten to twenty years into the future. We recognize that business firms can be managed without such systematic effort, but we realize too that the performance will be less satisfactory as a consequence. In the area of public management of the nation's assets we have been more reluctant to arrive at similar judgments. We are willing to countenance opportunistic, pragmatic, and even casual management of our natural and human resources, sometimes in the fear that to do otherwise—to *plan*—would rob us of an even greater asset, our individual liberties.

To anticipate the results of the analysis which follows, it is suggested here that the old "forced choice" of plan or no plan did not present very meaningful alternatives. For unless one has reference to some very specific kind of plan, such as the Soviet system, that choice, if translated into the more general concepts employed here, would come down to a choice between systematic and pragmatic ("seat-of-the-pants") management. Would anyone really opt for the latter?

The issues with respect to appropriate planning procedures and philosophy are far from settled—even as concerns business planning. Nevertheless, there is general acceptance of the value of planning within such private units as corporations and even within public units —governments—as respects their own operations. It is at the point where one moves from the systematic management of these lesser systems, these private and public organizational units, to the notion of the economy as itself a system, and subject to management, that we move into terrain which is still relatively new and still largely unexplored. The notion of "managing" an economy sounds so imposing, so authoritative, so foreign, that we instinctively withdraw from the prospect.

But it is because of that withdrawal that we allow such national assets as cities to deteriorate into slums, countrysides to be eroded, recreational areas to be despoiled. transportation systems to wither, even such basic assets as our water supply to become defiled. What business management would tolerate such wastage of its company's assets? But what public management now exercises systematic supervision over the preservation of the value of our national wealth comparable to the solicitude which private management shows for the assets which are its responsibility?

At its simplest, then, we define planning at the level of the economy as the systematic management of the nation's assets to achieve such objectives as may be sufficiently accepted to provide a measure of executive authority in seeking them by means of such instruments and devices as similarly are permitted. In the chapters which follow we shall move to an examination of what this means with respect to the relation between public and private authorities, within the system which they jointly compose.

2...
planning
in the business firm

Planning starts with purpose. Until objectives are defined, there can be no sense of direction, no standard for measuring the adequacy of effort or acceptability of results, no basis for the management of assets. Purpose is difficult enough for an individual to identify in himself, let alone for an observer to describe for others. In the case of organizations it becomes an almost metaphysical problem to establish objectives. Nevertheless, they exist of necessity, as something which gives coherence to the component parts, without which an organized activity would not take place.

The majority of all business establishments in Western countries are small in size and closely controlled by a working proprietor. They are usually operated as a source of livelihood for a single household or several related households. They are in reality extensions of households. These are of no present interest to us.

In contrast there are business firms, varying from small to large, which are not proprietorships but organizations having a corporate life independent of the families of those who own or manage them. They have a time span of their own and objectives of their own. It is these which concern us here.

CORPORATE OBJECTIVES

Like individuals, business firms have a time dimension, and their objectives are spread along their time stream. Proximate objectives may include putting across an advertising campaign, the efficient expansion or contraction of production schedules, landing an important order, improving quality standards, securing or paying off a bank loan. Intermediate-term objectives could involve launching a new product, effecting a change in organization to accommodate growth, floating a new equity issue, establishing an overseas sales organization, carrying through a merger or a corporate acquisition.

Long-term objectives may relate to the position in an industry, or in the economy, to which the firm aspires, the creation of an unexcelled reputation for quality or integrity, continuity in growth, a leadership role in research and new product development, the establishment of a climate of operations congenial to the kind of people it wishes to build into its organization.

These objectives are subject to review and modification—almost necessarily so in view of the turnover of personnel, particularly in the managerial hierarchy. Nevertheless, whatever the changing specifics of the time stream of corporate objectives, two "portmanteau" goals tend to persist and embrace all the rest—growth and a rate of return on investment.

The objective of growth is more often left implicit, but it is an almost necessary complement to rate of return. A given *rate* of return could be accomplished on any investment base—a 10 percent rate is as feasible on assets of $1 million as $100 million, but few managements would regard the *absolute* size of net earnings as unimportant. Nor would corporations, except for those in the process of dissolution, normally be indifferent between retaining or selling earning assets even though the earnings *rate* of the remaining assets was unaffected.

Indeed, the effective management of assets almost necessarily implies growth. In part this may be due to the reason offered by one company president: "We recognized that if we didn't have a growth program we would not attract or hold capable key personnel," [1] and capable personnel are a prerequisite to maintaining the value of the company as a going concern. It is also almost certain to be the case for the reason which Mrs. Penrose has set out at length in her study, *The Theory of the Growth of the Firm*,[2] namely, that in any organization there is bound to be some slack simply because it is impossible to proportion the parts neatly, either people or physical assets. Indivisibilities thus virtually guarantee that there is time or capacity or potential partly unutilized. Efficient management seeks to improve the use of these existing assets, and to the extent it is effective, growth is the consequence. It is for these reasons that we can realistically include as part of our definition of economic planning, whether in the firm or in the economy as a whole, provision for some reinvestment of earnings in a meaningful growth pattern.

The growth process (in the cases where this corporate objective is achieved) is in turn certain to affect the specific short-run to long-run objectives in the firm's time stream. At some point in the course of its expansion, it must move from a single or limited product line to diversified and multiple product lines, and management's whole outlook is likely to be transformed in the process. Instead of identification with a particular product, perhaps a loyalty which would lead it to "stay with the product" even in the face of a declining rate of return and a shrinking value of the assets, the firm acquires interests which are more financially oriented. As it expands and becomes more conglomerate, it takes on more and more the nature of an investment trust, the manager of a bundle of assets, whose chief concern is to move those assets into and out of markets, products, and production facilities in ways which will preserve and enhance their value.

In this process its focus on rate of return becomes sharper. Instead of seeking to extract as high a return as possible out of some product to

[1] William C. Treuhaft, president of Tremco, quoted in Stewart Thompson, *How Companies Plan* (New York: American Management Association, 1962), p. 102.

[2] Edith Penrose, *The Theory of the Growth of the Firm* (New York: John Wiley & Sons, Inc., 1959).

which it feels committed, it regards its commitments as only temporary, subject to reexamination as assets become liquid again. Other
products may pay more; should assets be invested in them rather than
recommitted to the present product line? Over and over it must ask
itself, in the light of the changed philosophy attributable to its growth:
What rate of return is satisfactory? How much should it be able to
earn on its assets?

Thus rate of return tends to acquire a heightened importance in the
larger firm as its field of operations broadens. In much of the literature
of management it acquires almost single status, as the one most important objective of the company. This is perhaps because it is—despite all
the obvious difficulties and traps in its measurement [3]—the most convenient basis for comparing corporate performance, either one company's present performance with its own past, or its present performance with the present performance of other companies. In such comparisons of *rates*, the size base tends to drop out of the picture and
along with it measures or comparisons of growth.

The question of whether the appropriate measure of the rate of
return is relative to total assets or to net worth is of no interest to us
here.[4] The significant consideration is that comparisons of profit performance by a company provide the basis for setting its own "portmanteau" profit goal, enveloping all its more specific goals, for which
profits provide the wherewithal. On the strength of knowledge of
what other firms have been able to accomplish, a management can pose
a goal for its own organization which is reasonable in the sense that
other companies have been able to achieve it. In the light of its own
past accomplishments, the firm can set its sights for the future.

The arbitrary selection of a target because others have been able to
do that well would make little sense, however, unless based upon more
detailed analysis of why they have been able to do better, with accompanying efforts to improve the firm's own performance where it is
found to be inferior to that of the reference companies. The determination to rack up a result at least as good as and possibly a little better

---

[3] The lack of any real meaning to the accountant's balance-sheet figures is well
known, since they intermingle money amounts invested in years of varying real
unit values.

[4] In *The Firm: Micro-Economic Planning and Action* (New York: McGraw-
Hill Book Company, 1962), pp. 60-63, I have argued on behalf of net worth as the
base for measuring a return on investment. The next several paragraphs have been
drawn from the same source, pp. 410–412.

than the firm itself already has to its credit is meaningless without an examination of the respects in which both the organization and its environment may have changed. Since a long-run target allows time for correcting weaknesses and building on strengths, there is always a basis for justifying even an ambitious goal as "reasonable." There is no necessary expectation that it be gained in the current year, even if there is pressure to achieve it within the next three to five years. A long-run target is not unreasonable just because the company falls short of it during the present operating period due to general business conditions or factors more particular to it.

But to what extent should present conditions and circumstances be treated as excusing a below-average performance? To what degree should a shortfall be viewed as evidence of the organization's inability to cope with its problems? There is no objective basis, and little of an ex ante comparative basis, for determining how much of a profit (how much less than the "average" performance expected, how much more than the long-run target) should be viewed as acceptable in the short run. About all that a firm can do is to plan its forthcoming quarter or operating year as effectively as it can, in the light of the externally determining factors (market and competitive conditions expected) and its internal characteristics (product line, technology, and organization as given at the moment), with its long-run target serving as goad and whip.

Ex post it will be able to get some judgment of the effectiveness of its performance by comparison with what others have done. Ex post, analysis of the reasons for variances from its own budget or for a performance inferior to what it had expected or to what other firms have been able to do may suggest significant changes which should be made over time. But ex ante, in the planning of its upcoming year, the firm can only make and remake its plans until it is satisfied that it is making the most of its resources under the conditions given and expected.

The use of profit targets thus has its impact primarily in the long run, when it holds up some reasonable expectation of what profit a company ought to be able to earn if it operates as effectively as it itself or some other companies have in the past, perhaps adding a little more on by way of optimism and encouragement. Performance short of target encourages examination of the major determinants of profit performance over which the firm has control—its lines of activity, its production processes, its locations, the structure and quality of its organization—but about which it can do little so immediately as to affect short-run profits. In the short run, the principal adjustments a firm can make are often only in production and costs. Other actions are likely to be quite limited in their effect, except as they involve the acceleration of the end stages of some long-run adjustment such as the introduction of a new product. Measures to meet basic changes in the firm's external environment require time to be worked out and made effective. In the meantime, a below-target result may have to be accepted as the best performance possible, even though unacceptable as a long-run level of performance.

Over time the experience which molds expectations may itself change. With changes in the institutional environment it may be found that whatever actions are taken with respect to the variables under management's control, a profit target which once seemed reasonable and attainable is now out of reach and therefore out of date. The long-run target itself must be moved up or down. Its profit performance over the years, and that of other firms, will help to establish its own expectations, its own views on what achievement levels are to be considered feasible and satisfactory. In this sense the external factors over which it has no control will, over time, help to mold its goals. But both these external and internal determinants of profit expectations relate principally to the long run. The short run may be one of those plus or minus periods that go to make up the average or that fluctuate around a trend. But how much of a minus or plus can be considered satisfactory will not be revealed by any amount of comparative analysis, either with other companies or with the firm's own past.

The profit objective of a company is thus a rather specific figure, set in the light of its circumstances, its environment, and the particular objectives extending along its time stream. There is no point in pursuing here the stale controversy over whether or not firms can or do maximize, but there is one aspect of that issue which perhaps deserves a word, since it has found so large a place in recent literature, including the literature on planning. It has sometimes been argued that maximizing takes place within certain constraints or boundary conditions. But this only begs the question, assuming as it does some basis for setting magnitudes on the constraints or boundary conditions themselves. For reasons which are not apparent, certain objectives (boundary conditions) are treated differently from others (targets), allowing one to hold the first stable and to maximize the second. Why some goals are fixed and others flexible, or why some assume a priority relative to others, is not rationalized.

It seems more realistic to assume (in the case of the firm) that it is pursuing a number of simultaneously held objectives, many with different dates attaching to them but all more or less systematically related, the achievement of which is in turn dependent on attaining some given rate of return on assets of given or growing magnitude. It is the way in which profit envelops and makes possible a stream of objectives which has led to its characterization here as a "portmanteau" goal, along with growth. But it itself grows out of the more particular objectives of the firm, and is as specific as they. These "real" or "other" objectives do not set constraints on the profit goal but help to define it.

THE ASSETS OF THE FIRM

The assets which a firm commits to the achievement of its objectives are not the same as those which appear on its balance sheet. The latter are at best a conventional representation of the former. Cash, securities, and accounts receivable; property, plant, and equipment; patents, trademarks, and goodwill—these are only abstractions of the real assets which are subject to managerial manipulation and concerning which strategic decisions must continually be made.

The balance sheet provides only a rough measure of the value of the real assets, a money measure to which profit can be related to provide a rate of return. But the money measure and the functional assets are quite distinct.

The real assets which it is up to management to manipulate, and on the strength of which the representational figures emerge, are the firm's functional resources. To be sure, the process of obtaining liquid claims—money—and converting these into real assets is part of the managerial skill. But the assets which are the focus of its continuing attention are those that are frozen and illiquid, from which it must extract the most that it can. It unfreezes these only to freeze them again, usually in new shapes.

The real assets with which management must seek its objectives consist of a product line, a production organization, a marketing organization, and a financial structure.

1 In a moderately large corporation the product line often runs to several hundred major products—several thousand (or even several hundred thousand) if separately marketed replacement parts are included. Service-dispensing organizations seldom have so varied a line of activity although the spectrum of salable services offered by the modern bank, insurance company, or travel agency is often not much narrower than the range of products of a manufacturing firm.

These are products and services at various stages in their life cycle. Some have just been brought on the market and face an uncertain future. Others are enjoying a period of initial success and flush profit margins. Still others have won acceptance and have already fanned out into a number of quality-differentiated varieties. And some are fading from market favor and may even be marked for termination within a year or two.

With respect to each there is an associated price, which has probably been tested and confirmed and perhaps widely advertised. Some goods fit into well-established price classes (candy bars, books and phonograph records, men's clothing, automobiles) and have been carefully engineered and "costed" to provide a profit at a price which is more or less predetermined for the firm.

Patents, trademarks, copyrights, distinctive packaging and styling, public knowledge of and attitudes concerning the firm's offerings—these too are all aspects of the product line. Collectively they constitute one of the firm's principal assets despite the fact that this asset is carried on the balance sheet at a nominal sum chiefly reflecting what may have been paid to others for an occasional patent or trademark.

One set of strategic decisions which a firm must make relates to this asset. How diversified a product line should the firm promote? When should products be introduced, restyled, or dropped? How many quality classes should be included in a product family? How should they be differentiated from each other and from rival products? Are price adjustments called for? These and related decisions must be made over and over.

2 The production facilities which are "carried" on the company's balance sheet relate to physical property—land, buildings, and equipment. But these are at best the skeleton of the flesh-and-blood production organization which it is management's responsibility to put to best use.

If one contemplates the enormity of the task of creating an

organization from scratch, even an organization no larger than a hundred men, some appreciation of the real value of this asset is gained. First there is the matter of recruitment—winnowing out from a labor market the right assortment of skills, age distribution, and personality characteristics. Then comes training in particular assignments, and a shakedown with respect to developing appropriate individual-group, superior-subordinate, and workflow relationships. A communication system must be made effective for transmitting instructions, receiving information, and recording data.

A network of suppliers of materials or component parts and of various services must be organized, and they must become familiar with the company's quality and cost requirements. Not only must there be a choice of technologies, involving equipment and layout, but a development of the use of technologies, which necessarily means work rules and standards, safety procedures, formal and informal work routines, a sense of pace, group morale—and all of these appropriately related to productivity and quality standards. Systems must be devised for scheduling, coordinating, and inspecting production; for controlling costs; for servicing and maintaining equipment; for shutting down and starting up; for policing the premises. A schedule of hours and shifts must be determined.

There must also be a wage system geared to the requirements of the local labor market insofar as there is occupational mobility, broadly consistent with industry standards insofar as there is geographical mobility, internally consistent with the organization's status system, and bearing some relationship to the economic value of the work which is paid for. A schedule of holidays and vacations and an assortment of fringe benefits must be provided for. Presuming a union, a collective bargaining relationship must be established, including a written agreement and procedures for administering it.

The catalogue of requirements for a producing organization could be extended; these are only the obvious essentials. They are enough to underscore that the property and plant which are valued on the company's books are not the prime production asset to be managed but only one ingredient of a production *organization* which is the real asset. At the same time we should avoid giving currency to that mystical assertion sometimes encountered that "people are our real asset." Aside from the fact that a firm has no proprietary authority over its employees, the production organization is not just people, but people and technology in functional integration. The measure of its value is not its size in terms of numbers of people or payroll, but productive capacity in terms of goods and services. This is something in which it has an investment and which it can sell, if it chooses, as a functioning system rather than as pieces and parcels of equipment and plant.

The production organization is obviously related to the product line in the sense that the one turns out what the other specifies. But that relationship grows out of past decisions. In the ongoing time stream management must repeatedly inquire: for what can this production organization which it has at its disposal best be used? In what way can this production organization be adapted to the goods or services which it would like to produce?

This adaptive relationship between the product line and the production organization was perhaps most vividly demonstrated during World War II, when in all belligerent nations firms turned to producing goods quite different from their normal output but for which their production organization was suited or could be modified. The relationship has also been made manifest when companies formerly receiving substantial government contracts have had these withdrawn and, with no alternative customers, have had to face the conversion of their production organization to other purposes, as notably in recent years in the case of aircraft manufacturers. But these are only the dramatic instances of a continuing adaptive relationship in all companies between the product line and the production organization. Both are assets to be managed and manipulated as parts of a single system.

3   The marketing organization of a firm includes the network of sales channels which it has developed to dispose of the output of its production organization. In the case of most operations, this means a more or less continuous disposition of a flow of goods or services. Depending on the state of the market generally, due to levels of activity in the economy as a whole, or on the state of particular markets, depending on consumer tastes and competitive success, the flow of goods may have to be accelerated or retarded. Inventories are the buffer for all such shifts in the rate of disposition of products, permitting a temporary drawing down of stocks or accretion of stocks until the rate of production can itself be adjusted. Inventory management can thus be viewed as a link between the production and marketing organizations, even though for convenience it is here treated as part

of the latter. Inventories often represent a substantial financial commitment—almost one-third the total value of listed assets of U.S. firms, taken together. In the case of services, no such buffer is generally possible, and the production organization simply registers more or less slack until it can be adjusted to the size appropriate to the current market.

The stream of decisions which must be made with respect to use of the marketing asset relates to the kind of service which will be offered to customers (promptness of delivery, production to specifications, guarantee of satisfaction, willingness to accept returns, credit arrangements, price concessions, and other such elements connected with the sale of the product). All such decisions affect the nature and effectiveness of the distribution system on which the firm relies for the disposition of its goods.

Management of the marketing structure is thus directly linked with management of the product line (Does the product line give the marketing organization enough to work with? Is the marketing organization adequate to win acceptance for the product line against the offerings of rivals?). Management of the marketing organization is also linked directly with the production organization (Does the latter satisfy the needs of the former in terms of giving it goods of satisfactory quality in satisfactory quantities at satisfactory rates of flow? Does the marketing network keep goods moving at a steady enough pace to permit smoothing of the production process, with only a limited reliance on inventories as a balancing device?).

Similarly, determination of inventory policy involves a continuous stream of decisions integrating the uses of the firm's principal assets: With respect to the product line, how much of resources should be committed to existing products in the face of their possible obsolescence or deterioration? With respect to production organization, what is the cost of steadily maintaining output through impounding some fluctuating portion of it in inventories versus the cost of modifying the rate of flow of output? With respect to marketing organization, how worthwhile—both in the short run and the long run—is the prompt accommodation of customers relative to the higher current cost of inventories on which that accommodation is based? The systematic integration of these separate but related streams of strategic decisions, in the pursuit of designated objectives, are major aspects of the planning process.

4 The fourth principal asset of the firm, giving rise to another

stream of strategic decisions, is its financial organization. The real assets of the firm have their counterpart in its financial liabilities, and the manipulation of these affects its earnings and growth potential. The liabilities go back to a network of relations with individuals and institutions who are willing to commit their own liquid resources to the firm's management.

This network of financial relationships includes short-term and long-term lenders, from suppliers of materials on 30-days credit to major insurance companies holding 20-year bonds or 40-year mortgages. It includes stockholders with an equity, from the middle-income individual with 10 shares to the investment trust with 100,000 shares—or indeed a parent corporation which wholly owns the firm. The significant consideration with respect to asset management is not the structure of debt which has resulted from past relationships, but the nature of the continuing relationships on which present and future financing rests. If debt is falling due, will it be renewed and, if so, on what terms? If profits are slim, will stockholders be satisfied to go without a current return and still leave the present management in charge? Will maintenance of a steady dividend rate allow the firm to retain enough of its earnings to carry on its planned expansion?

In effect, each financial contributor has committed some of its own liquid assets to the firm for a period of time, and in that period its investment is frozen. But periodically the contribution becomes liquid again (in the case of debt) or a suitable opportunity to sell the frozen asset presents itself (in the case of equity shares), and at that moment the contributor must decide whether to recommit its resources to the firm. Over and over that decision must be made on the part of numerous financial contributors. To induce the desired decision, management may be driven to adjusting the rate of return, either interest or dividend; to making certain commitments as to use of the funds or granting certain guarantees as to priority of return; to modifying its management policies with respect to the real assets under its control as a means of winning increased confidence in the firm's earning power. Thus over and over again management must make its own decisions as to whether the terms which may be necessary to secure the financial contribution on which certain actions depend will be conducive to the achievement of the firm's stream of objectives over time.

But the financial relations which make possible the firm's continuity and growth are not really so *ad hoc* and tenuous as the above might suggest. Relationships tend to get formed and to persist. Ties develop between a firm and certain banks or investors or brokerage houses. If these are attenuated or broken, others take their place.

The management of a firm typically presides over a financial organization which has been put together and is preserved in the same way that its production and marketing organizations have been built and maintained. Through this financial organization it is able to gear itself into the leads and lags of the inflow and outflow of funds as far ahead as its investments take it.

This organization which makes possible the firm's ongoing streams of activity is an asset of enormous value, which the firm must manipulate with care if it is to preserve and enhance its worth. Just as in the case of the product line and productive and marketing organizations, the value of those assets must conceptually be measured not simply by their current rate of return but by the future earnings to which they may give rise—whether at the same or a better rate, but on a larger, growing, more valuable asset base.

THE INFLUENCE OF TIME ON THE STRATEGIC DECISIONS

Frequent reference has been made to the continuity of the firm, to its long-run as well as short-run objectives, to its ongoing streams of strategic decisions made in the effort to achieve those objectives. Obviously the time spectrum is of considerable importance in the management of the firm.

The firm which operates with a short time horizon is committed to limiting the amount of change in its present activity. It tends to keep on doing what it has been doing, without contemplating any major shift in its operations. The firm which quite self-consciously tries to project itself into a farther future, in an effort to achieve perspective on the significance of its present line of activities *at that future time* and to speculate about what other paths it might travel along if it wishes to play a larger role in the economy *then*, is more likely to think in terms of major changes which require advance preparation. The first approach involves building on one's present position by increments of activity. The second approach does not exclude, but neither is it confined to, such incremental activity. It is distinguished by a determination to reach a future plotted position having no necessary relation to one's present and which for that reason requires the forging of a relationship through a series of programmed intermediate steps.

Thus to some extent the time spectrum of a firm depends on both the farsightedness and vision of its managers and their ability to create the organizational instruments for translating vision into action. Obviously some firms enjoy more of these qualities than do others. But also to some degree vision and its implementation can be institutionalized, so that even if a turnover in the management hierarchy brings to the top a person of more limited imagination than his predecessor, the organization may itself compensate for his limitation. This is likely to be the case in those companies which invest heavily in research and development and which are therefore exposed to a continuing flow of new ideas from people whose function it is to come up with new ideas.

But what is there about long-run planning which makes it desirable? Unless it is treated as a value-laden word which, like "progress," is widely considered to be obviously good without requiring proof, there must be logical reasons why efforts to speculate about the future have some merit. There are at least two.

First, with the advances in science and technology, more products and processes require longer lead times to be brought to fruition. If a company seeks its growth in new fields of activity, it must often begin laying plans and making commitments now in order to be operative perhaps five years from now. Thus technological considerations induce a longer view.

Nor is it simply the fact that some—perhaps an increasing proportion—of investments require a longer lead time. The scale of many of the new developments is sufficiently great to require a detailed examination of their impact on total corporate operations over the time span during which they are being brought into being. Reciprocally, the extent of their requirements of money, manpower, specialized equipment and materials, governmental concessions or approvals, and so on, requires the coordinated contributions of a number of corporate departments, all meshing together systematically, in point of time. Even large corporations cannot afford repeated financial losses arising from failure to anticipate some need in connection with a new project, leading to costly delays, possible sacrifice of competitive position, or even the writing-off of the investment to date. Thus the relevance of specialized manpower was brought home to a Swedish firm when, after a major project in Argentina had been underway for almost three years, it found its investment jeopardized by an unanticipated shortage of certain professional skills.

A second importance of long-run planning arises from the fact that the accelerated rate of change in a number of variables affecting the value of the assets it is managing—including but not limited to technological change—obliges a firm to look ahead simply to preserve its asset value, let alone plow new ground for expansion purposes. As we have had occasion to note, a business firm assembles and nurtures assets which grow over the years, but the uses of these vary from year to year, and decade to decade, in response to changing tastes, population shifts, market structures, production processes, and inventions. The use of virtually any company's assets is quite different now from what it was ten years ago and from what it will be ten years from now. A company may almost be viewed as a bundle of assets which are molded in one form today and which it is management's job to metamorphose into a continually different form as time goes by. If it fails in this task, the bundle of assets which it is managing loses its value.

Management cannot wait until the form in which its assets are now molded becomes obsolete; it would be too late then to transform them into something else, since they would already have lost their value. The transformation of assets from the production of good A to the production of good B, from the serving of one region to the serving of numerous regions, from one production process to a more highly automated one—all these and a variety of other related activities must take place in advance of the time when current assets have lost their value.

In effect, what happens is that management freezes (that is, invests) funds in certain forms for specific purposes. These frozen funds are becoming liquid all the time, as inventories are liquidated, as credit is repaid, as depreciation reserves accumulate, as earnings are retained. And management must make decisions all the time as to whether the assets which have become liquid again shall be frozen into the same forms or into new forms. Sometimes the decision is relatively routine. If inventories become depleted of a product for which sales are brisk, it takes no soul-searching to decide whether to replenish them. But at other times the problem is more difficult. As an old piece of machinery has put in its time and has to be relegated to a standby role or scrapped, should the company buy another like it? Rival machinery producers or the company's own engineers may have other ideas as to how the job of the old machine can be done better. What form shall the replacement take?

Complicate the problem further. Should the machine even be replaced? Perhaps technological change has so outdated the whole production process of which it is a part that it is preferable to scrap not just that piece of equipment but the whole process, substituting a more efficient one. To carry that off effectively, it may be wiser to build a whole new plant. But if the company is to build a new plant, it does not have to place it in the same location; it might be more efficient to move it closer to a shifting source of materials or a shifting outlet for sales.

But the alternatives do not end there. If a firm is going to invest in a new plant and a new process, perhaps it should use these for a new product. How much longer will the present product remain profitable before being outmoded by something else? Perhaps the company had better consider substituting or adding a new product in its line.

We could multiply the questions which management must answer as it determines over and over again the form in which assets becoming liquid (through sales of goods and the return of once-invested capital, through loans repaid and refloated) shall be frozen. The answers to these questions relate to different points in the firm's future. The decision to invest in rebuilding inventories is one that affects operations in the next few weeks. Equipment replacement may be a matter of months. Process substitution may take two years or more. New product development at least as long or longer. The location of a new plant requires a time horizon of perhaps five years. And all these things are necessarily going on at the same time. These decisions relating to projected actions at various points in a firm's time stream must all be integrated in the company's short-run and long-run plans, and such integration means that they must be incorporated into its budget— given concreteness by having resources allocated to their phased accomplishment.

In the United States long-run planning was developed by business firms on their own initiative and has been spreading rapidly in recent years. In Europe too, although not as prevalent, its use has been increasing. There the stimulation has come from indirect government pressure as well as from inside the enterprises themselves. In countries which have been experimenting with national planning programs, business firms which in the past have tended toward short-run incremental planning have been induced to look farther ahead as part of the overall planning exercise. Particularly in France, where business has been drawn directly into the planning effort via the commissions on which many of its representatives sit, have managements been conditioned to peer farther into the future.

INTERNAL COORDINATION AND THE TIME STREAM

A good deal of writing and thinking about the firm still personifies it, thereby short-circuiting many of the problems of coordinating the decision making that goes on throughout the organization. Even to speak of the "decisions" of complex organizations such as a corporation, the army, a governmental body, a university, may be more of a literary analogy than an analytical concept. We are really concerned with the ways in which information is introduced into the organization, how it is made use of, and how it becomes transformed into action. This is less a decision-making process than a process of coordinating a number of decisions so that they tend to be sufficiently compatible with the objective which is the only basis for the organization's existence, while effectuating satisfactorily enough the personal objectives of all the decision makers (that is, the individual participants and subunits in the process).

The corporate objectives of profit and growth are focused on the product line, around which the activities of the production, marketing, and financial organizations of the firm are clustered. The theme or leitmotif which runs through all the relationships involved is the management of these four asset clusters to produce a functioning system geared to the effective pursuit of corporate goals. Each of the four families of assets loses most of its value except in association with the other three. The function of management is to integrate them into an operating system, or what the institutionalists of an earlier period used to call "a going concern."

Leaving the product line to one side for the moment, each of the three functioning organizations—production, marketing, financial—is specialized in certain kinds of activity. Each has its own role to play in the business. But as an actor, it must be prompted by cues given by its fellow actors. It does not act on its own, independently, since its own specialized role is not adequate by itself to carry the play through to a meaningful conclusion. That requires the whole cast of characters.

Thus each of the three participants (the production, marketing, and financial organizations) simultaneously has an acting role and a cueing role. Each sends signals—creates information—which trigger off the actions of the other two, and thus itself receives signals—information —from the other two which prompt or authorize certain actions on its own part. Collectively the cues and actions, the information and triggered responses, create a meaningful play or functioning system.

But they do not carry this off without direction. Exits and entrances have to be timed, the bits of staging which determine whether a performance scintillates or falls flat have to be contrived. Actors who feel slighted have to be mollified; some parts have to be built up to satisfy esthetic proportions or egos; clashes of temperament and differences of role conception have to be mediated. All this is the job of the director, whose overall supervision is felt by the participants but whose contribution is much less obvious to the outsider. Similarly in the corporation, the meshing of specialized functions, the smooth flow of information and elicited responses, cannot be expected to develop on its own but must be managed in the same way. Terms, rewards, titles, piques, cliques, and professional pride must all be manipulated to allow the performance to come through as management conceives it.

We shall content ourselves with a very sketchy abstraction of this process which should serve the purpose of identifying it just enough for us to make use of it later.

The production organization responds to data from the marketing organization (orders) and from the financial organization (the terms on which production may proceed—wages, material costs, etc.). It creates data for marketing (goods or services available, orders completed) and finance (expenses incurred and bills payable).

Marketing responds to data from production (availability of goods) and from finance (the terms which may be offered customers). It creates data for production (orders taken) and financial (revenues earned, bills to be collected).

Finance responds to data from production (bills to be paid) and marketing (bills to be collected) and creates data for production (costs permissible) and marketing (permissible terms of sale).

Thus the three sets of activity, each focused around the given product line, constitute a complete and integrated system. To be sure, there are additional related activities which must be fitted into the picture to give it completeness, but these are the basic elements. In its most finished state it is a self-adjusting system in which information flows and workflows are integrally related.

But obviously we have described, in this abstract fashion, only the current operations of the system, the short run. In this abbreviated time dimension the leading role falls to the marketing organization—not necessarily in the sense that it is the most important or the most contributory part of the organization, but in the sense that its cues, the data which it feeds into the system tend to speed up or slow down the rate of activity. If it increases the flow of orders, then the responses of production and finance must accommodate the changed pace. If the orders it processes dwindle, then production and finance must adjust accordingly.

But in the previous section we stressed the longer-run time dimension of corporate activity. Provision for that longer run requires foresight and vision as to what actions—not necessarily related to the present performance—should be initiated now, while the present performance continues. It requires fitting these new activities into the organization without disturbing the systematic functioning of the daily ongoing routine. It further requires decisions and plans as to how the present performance may be modified—a new product or a redesigned product introduced, perhaps, as a second act might be rewritten—without missing a day's production. It requires decisions and plans as to whether or when a whole new performance might have to be substituted for the present one, or added to the repertory, using either the same set of actors or expanding the company with congenial additions.

These longer-run activities must also be systematized, timed closely so that the stages of development are smoothly coordinated, timed closely so that the new performance is ready for introduction before the public has tired of the old one. As we have already noted, the large firm must incorporate within it a whole population of activities, representing several generations, to give it the ongoing nature, the constant regeneration, which we associate with basic social institutions. The day-to-day activities which can be so neatly portrayed as a controlled system of reciprocal information and workflows are simply one subset of activities within a larger system, with which they must be integrated and coordinated.

The longer-run planning and coordination, for the most part, require a different initiative. While the marketing organization acts as the pacesetter in the short run, it cannot play that role as effectively in long-range planning. Involved as it is with the current product line and with its current relationships to production and finance, the same performers are unlikely to be able to free themselves of those involvements to look ahead to new potentials of a wholly different nature. When a new script is being written, it calls for different skills than those of the present performers. In longer-run corporate planning, initiative is most likely to come from a different set of participants than those who are immersed in the current production. Most large corporations develop special long-run planning staffs. This almost necessary step complicates the coordinating process, since it relies on one group of people for the ideas which others must make effective.

TECHNICAL–ECONOMIC COORDINATION IN THE FIRM

In Chapter 1 we became acquainted with the fact that coordination takes place in two fundamentally different ways. One involves treating the system as an objective mechanism which can be analyzed and controlled. This has been labeled technical-economic coordination. It is concerned with the ideal efficiency of the system as a whole. The second involves viewing the system—or its parts—as something for control of which the participating individuals or groups exercise whatever bargaining power they can muster, with a view to achieving as much of their own objectives as is compatible with retaining their position in the system. The integrity of the system is preserved in some, but not whole, measure only through the manipulative skills of management. This has been called organizational-political coordination. It is concerned with the feasible efficiency of the system, after allowing for such compromises as may be necessitated by subunit goals backed up by bargaining power.

Let us consider technical-economic coordination first, as it applies to the firm. We can perhaps obtain a clearer conception of this approach if we think of it as planning on paper. Although it deals with technologies and plant layouts as well as with people, it treats these all as symbols which can be programmed on paper and integrated by assigning them responses which are functions of other symbols. Values can be identified and written into the relationships so that quantitative results are predictable.

The problems for which solutions are sought may be either technical or economic, but the basic nature of the approach is the same in both instances. In the case of technical problems, the most efficient method of achieving a given result—assembling a component, organizing a payroll system or a flow of data—is subjected to an engineering type of scrutiny. In the case of economic problems, a choice among alternative actions is guided by cost-minimizing or revenue-maximizing principles—which products shall be processed on limited facilities, what method of distribution yields the most profitable results, at what level inventories should be maintained.

This kind of coordination thus lends itself readily to—indeed, demands—symbolic manipulation. Since people cannot be eliminated from the analysis, they are treated as part of the process. In time-and-motion study, still widely used but perhaps on its way out, people are studied as though they are aspects—unfortunately a little erratic—of a mechanical process. Special techniques for obtaining the results are of course required, involving the choice of a "representative" worker; a prior programming of the routine ("mechanical") way in which he is supposed to perform his part, since this is not built into his responses in the way it is built into a true machine; an averaging of time intervals required by a number of representative operators; an allowance for human (usually referred to as "personal") needs which involves recognition of the fact that people are not really machines, and so on. The efforts of workers to manipulate the situation to their own advantage are recognized and treated as objective data—identified and allowed for wherever possible.

We shall make no effort to describe the engineering and economic techniques which are used to catalogue the applications to which they lend themselves.[5] It will be enough for our purposes to illustrate, in order to clarify, concentrating on economic rather than engineering analysis, although the two have great similarities.

"Operations research" is a vague term for a method of mathematical programming which has become widely used in business since World War II, when its practice was developed for military purposes. It requires a clear definition of a specific problem: What inventory policy will be most economical given the cost of holding goods, the loss of sales through unavailability of goods, and the savings permitted by production smoothing? This method identifies the limiting parame-

[5] The quarterly journal *Management Science* is an excellent source of such information.

ters and relevant variables, attaches values to them, and then incorporates these into mathematical models to produce the solution.

Operations research has been used in such problems as finding the most economical transportation routes for distributing a product, the least costly regional location of warehouses given the markets for a product, the appropriate scheduling of different products using the same production facilities, the most effective allocation of cash funds among the subsidiary units of a company, the most profitable mix in the blending of gasolines, and the scheduling of aircraft maintenance.

Simulation is a technique made practical by the computer. In its purest form it consists of a trial-and-error approach to building a model of the firm, or some aspect of its operations, the validity of which can be tested against known data from the past, or the desirability of which can be measured against hypothetical data from the future. The value of the computer lies in permitting the testing of a much larger number of more complex patterns to derive the one of best fit.

This device has been used by Northwest Airlines to forecast the financing requirements and feasibility of a new fleet of jet airliners. In order to carry through the analysis with sufficient accuracy, a schedule for the introduction of planes over a five-year period was devised. Flight schedules were plotted for both the old aircraft and the new; passenger traffic and revenues were forecast, as well as returns from freight and mail carrying; operating expenses on both types of planes were projected; capital charges were computed; and so on, down to the preparation of income statements, cash flow exhibits, and balance sheets for each of the years in question.

American Airlines provides another illustration of the technique, as related by their vice-president for corporate planning; "When our pilot contract was under negotiation recently, the union requested a new limitation on the number of flight hours each pilot would fly per month. We were able to feed this limitation into our computers and relate it to production levels we have planned over the next five years. We were able to determine exactly what our crew costs over the five-year period would be with new flight hours and to compare them with present costs." [6]

[6] C. N. Oursler, in George A. Steiner (ed.), *Management Long-range Planning* (New York: McGraw-Hill Book Company, 1963), p. 60.

Program Evaluation Review Technique (familiarly known as PERT) and its twin brother, the Critical Path Method, both lend themselves to the programming of single operations as well as routines. They are designed to anticipate bottlenecks in performance and to permit at each bottleneck a choice between accepting delay, and the cost it entails, or removing the cause of delay, with its attendant costs. Its procedures include (a) the identification of the network of the *events* (stages of accomplishment) and *activities* (time and resources neded to move from one event to another) which constitute the total task or program; (b) the arrangement of events and activities in sequence according to rules whose logic is grounded in the process, so that no event can be considered completed until all the events preceding it have been completed; (c) the attachment of time values to the activities; and (d) the calculation of the "critical path" through the network of events and activities to task accomplishment, using the computer if the project is sufficiently complicated.

These and other related technical-economic methods have one objective—to establish a standard of efficiency relative to system objectives, a technically preferred way of achieving a specified result, eliminating waste, diversions, and the competing objectives of subunits. They assume "automaticity," in the sense that each stimulus produces a predictable response—on paper, and may even seek to achieve such a result in practice by building organizational procedures which "assure" that an event is followed by a rational consequence.

This automaticity of impulse and response endows the computer with special importance, since it not only enormously facilitates technical-economic planning by making feasible analyses which were previously economically impractical, but it can be incorporated into the operations themselves, increasing in fact the automaticity that is assumed in theory. It can do this in at least three ways: (1) by greatly expanding the amount and availability of "cueing" data, thereby presumably increasing the probability of correct human responses; (2) by facilitating the collection and analysis of "action" data, so that actions can be more promptly compared with intentions (responses with impulses) and improved on if necessary; and (3) by functioning as a link between information and action, itself providing the desired response to cues which it has also provided or which have been fed into it.

The application of technical methods of coordinating activity in the business system is sometimes viewed as dehumanizing, and indeed, their exponents have sometimes come close to suggesting as much. They have sometimes spoken of decision making in the firm as "servomechanistic," except at or near the top of the management pyramid. It has been said that "the idea of individual operating managers throughout an organization having identifiable packages of responsibility for cost experience and even for general performance is, to the average systems analyst, ridiculous." [7] The role of all except a few at the top, who direct the show, and their systems designers, is reduced to that of calculators, conductors, or thermostats, filling limited functions which have been designed for them.

But few of those making use of these technical-economic methods of coordination would go so far, at least in their nonapocalyptic moments, and the argument that systems planning ignores the human element miscasts it. What it does is to provide a standard of efficiency or a measure of potential performance for the system with which actual performance can be compared, or a set of expectations based on rational calculation. If some degree of efficiency in the achievement of system objectives is wanted, it can be judged only with reference to some measure of what is possible. If expectations are to be held, intuition is the only alternative to rational calculation.

The standard of efficiency which is relevant is one applying to the system as a whole, with reference to system objectives, and abstracting from any competing objectives of the component parts. The same is true of expectations. (Standards and expectations may of course apply to subsystem objectives when that is the area of analysis, in that case abstracting from the subsystem's components.) As long as we grant that organizational objectives can be established, efficiency "models" can be devised of the behavior patterns which would most nearly attain those objectives, providing some measure of the costs of the compromises necessitated by the fact that a social system is not a machine but incorporates subunits with individual objectives and a degree of bargaining power to achieve them.

Standards have value as a measure even if they cannot be enforced, and forecasts deriving from mathematical formulas can be tempered with judgment and hunch. The standard of efficiency and the rational

[7] John A. Beckett, "Management Accounting in the Age of Systems," *N.A.A. Bulletin*, April, 1964, p. 9.

calculation can have their influence on organizational coordination without dictating or dominating it. Nevertheless, there is an element of validity in the fear or hope, depending on the quarter from which originating, that efficiency models have some controlling effects on behavior. If standards are more rigorously established, departures from them can be more readily identified. If standards are used to encourage a closer approach to organizational goals, they may lead to managerial manipulations which are more restrictive of personal or group objectives conflicting with those of the "system."

What can be said, however, and perhaps the most that can be said, is that any belief that technical-economic standards of coordination can be implemented without respect to the aspirations and bargaining power of those subunits composing the organization is doomed to frustration. And any notion that such technically elaborated systems of coordination themselves constitute the whole of planning mistakes the point of departure for the destination.

SYSTEM–SUBSYSTEM DIFFUSION

As just noted, individuals and organizational subunits of the system have objectives which diverge from the overall objectives of the system. There is no reason in the world why a line worker should believe that a particular rate of return on the firm's assets should command his devotion. Even if he recognized that an "adequate" return may be necessary to corporate continuity and that his performance must make, or appear to make, a satisfactory contribution to an overall result if he is to have job continuity, this still leaves him a good deal short of any incentive for an all-out effort to achieve the firm's specified goal. His own preference may be to enjoy the company of his associates and to savor a bit more the flavor of a relaxed performance and to give occasional extra but unneeded attention to a particular assignment he finds more interesting than other duties. Who can blame him? Why should he dismiss his own objectives to embrace those of an impersonal system? But these individual preferences on his part conflict with the overall standards of efficiency which the technicians have established.

But it is not simply a case of individuals or groups "fighting the system." They are just as likely—right on up to vice-presidents of functions or departments—to seek some measure of control over it, relative to other individuals or groups in the organization, in order to promote their own interests more effectively. If a promotion can be won, or a department can secure favored treatment, this contributes to the enjoyment of the job: it constitutes a victory over the competition, something which has the elements of a sporting encounter, and gives a little zest to the day's work which no amount of dedicated slogging in the pattern prescribed by some standard of efficient coordination could possibly convey. It may also be parlayed into a larger cut of the revenues accruing to the firm. Contests over departmental or company policy, while couched in terms of what is best for the system, almost invariably disguise an effort to improve position and authority, or to win preferment through some obviously meritorious performance—perhaps more obvious than the performance warrants.

The technical-economic standards of efficiency do not allow for such internecine contests. They are designed to give primacy to the objectives of the system as a whole and to assign roles to the sub-systems and component parts which further the overall performance. The standards of efficiency which guide their designs cannot take into account subsystem goals, at least to the degree that these motivate the subsystems, since if this were attempted, the standards of efficiency would collapse into muddled confusion, of value to no one. Thus the systems analysts and the subsystem participants have objectives which necessarily conflict. This conflict creates one of the major problems of economic planning. Its resolution—a political matter—is neither more nor less important than the technical-economic analyses which precipitate it. Both are ingredients of economic planning, in a sense foils to each other.

The political-organizational coordination which must treat with the bargaining maneuvers of the participants in order to produce some preferred result must take its point of departure from some standard of the efficient way to achieve the desired result. That the standards have increasingly become expressed in mathematical form does not lessen their relevance to the political process, as some "humanists" imply. The degree of rigor attaching to the technical-economic coordination is purely a function of the stage of analytic development—we may anticipate even greater rigor in the future. But however imprecise or however rigorous, *some* standard of efficient performance to achieve set goals constitutes a necessary point of departure for any systematic planning. Some standard which is relevant to the objectives of the organization as a whole serves as an initial "proposal" for agreement among those from whom agreement on (at least acceptance of) a decision is needed.

The standard may even derive from a primitive rule of thumb—a markup policy for pricing, ratio analysis for financial structure, a percent-of-profit basis for allocating research funds, a job evaluation procedure for setting wages, and so on. The value of such rules lies in providing some standard which has—or had at some time in the past—the arbitrary sanction of reason or logic. That standard can then be modified as political-organizational needs require.

Thus, just as those who believe that technical-economic coordination is the whole of economic planning are deluding themselves, so those who argue that such technical-economic coordination has no relationship to political organization for economic activity are likewise misled. Both types of coordination are necessary ingredients in the planning stew.

But let us return to the internal rivalry for bending the system to the special interests of particular groups or factions. Each unit or subunit in the system has a degree of bargaining power which it can use in seeking to modify the standards of efficient coordination to its own advantage. In some cases the power is weak, or fluctuates with the shifting composition of factions and cliques. In other cases it is strong and even overt, as in the case of labor unions.

Bargaining power can assert itself in a variety of ways, chiefly in terms of an authority which the functional role performed by a unit gives over others whose position is dependent on that role. If cues are not given promptly or fully (information is not complete or timely), then the expected actions are uncertain or delayed, so that proper cueing is a weapon which can be used against others in the system. Similarly, if responses to cues are intentionally withheld, the system, either in whole or in part, temporarily ceases to function, with resulting injury which may be directed specifically or generally toward others. Or an individual or group which has been marked for "treatment" may find that somehow the faulty responses of others get attributed to an alleged faulty cueing on its part. Special skills or esoteric knowledge which others are not able to duplicate or understand confer special power on their possessors.

In an interesting study of the tactics of purchasing agents seeking to expand their influence over the engineering and production scheduling departments, with respect to whom they stood in a lateral relationship,

Prof. George Strauss has itemized some of the bargaining behavior which can be brought to bear, including charging an "offensive" department which asks for expedited delivery the added costs of air transportation, while ignoring such extras in the case of cooperating departments; going through the motions of complying with requisitions but with no intent to see that delivery arrives on time; ignoring a requisition altogether; working through "allies" in other departments to persuade an "enemy" department to come to terms; using influence to reorganize a relationship into an "integrated" materials flow in which scheduling is subordinated to purchasing; and so on.[8]

Some sociologists have suggested that typical bureaucratic behavior involves the effort to establish rules which protect a unit or group from the authority of others, while attempting to prevent its own authority from being hemmed in by similar rules imposed by others. To the extent that any bargaining maneuver to expand the position or privileges of some component of the organization succeeds, it runs the danger of carrying the system farther away from the standards of efficiency. The cumulative effect of all these departures from efficient performance can be disastrous for the system as a whole, in terms of accomplishing its objectives, and the resulting inefficiency of system performance can even have its own adverse repercussion on the accomplishment by the subunits and components of their own divergent goals, but from the single viewpoint of each subunit this is not apparent. Any subunit is likely to gloat in the success of some competitive ploy which adds another barnacle to the excess weight which the system must carry.

ORGANIZATIONAL–POLITICAL COORDINATION IN THE FIRM

In all this internal bargaining, which is inevitable in any system, the function of top management is to use its authority to keep all the parts as much on target as possible, as close to the standards of efficiency as its own objectives require and its own bargaining power permits. The same managerial role must be played within each subsystem in the organization, but the divergence between system and subsystem objectives introduces the problem which we have recurringly encountered: each subsystem manager may bargain as hard with his people as other

[8] George Strauss, "Tactics of Lateral Relationship: The Purchasing Agent," *Administrative Science Quarterly*, September, 1962, pp. 161–186.

managers do, to keep them as close to the standards of efficiency as his own objectives require, but because each one's objectives diverge to a degree from those of the overall system—as well as from the objectives of those whose efforts he seeks to coordinate—there is inevitably a growing looseness of performance, measured in terms of overall standards, the farther one goes down the organizational ladder.

Such organizational diffuseness is a product of the necessity for delegation of authority. This dispersion of authority, as Prof. Herbert Simon has pointed out,[9] follows a general rule of behavior. The decisions which are made at each level in a hierarchy must be accepted as the *premises* on which decisions and actions are based on the level below. Management in each organizational level or frame may exercise its discretion as long as it conforms to the premises which have been transmitted to it. We may expect that the discretion will be exercised in ways which seek to achieve the objectives—to some degree divergent, as we know—of the subsystem management, and we may assume that any inventive subsystem management will be able to exercise its discretion, to that end, in ways which may not have occurred to those in the level above, who framed the guiding premises.

At some point the unanticipated divergence by subsystem from system objectives or standards obliges the "tightening up" of the premises from which the subsystem derives its discretion. There is a tendency toward centralization of authority, as top management seeks to protect the system's integrity. With the passage of time the tightness of the premises is likely to result in an unacceptable inefficiency, since in closing off discretion it closes off the capacity to deal with the unexpected. Once again in order to preserve the efficiency of the system, top management must act, but this time to enlarge subsystem discretion—decentralization becomes the order of the day.

It is hard to see how such cyclical alternation between the exercise of hierarchical power to delegate discretion and to withdraw (or redraw) it from time to time can be avoided. It is an almost integral part of top management's job. There are those who believe that the problem will be solved by the computer, which will enlarge the capacity of top management to cue the action which is wanted, with an automatic response assured since transmission is by tape (which is without divergent objectives) rather than by people. But at most one

[9] Herbert Simon, *Administrative Behavior*, 2d ed. (New York: The Macmillan Company, 1960), p. 125.

could say that this shortens the hierarchical lines. Unless we assume that top management at its computer console can control all the operations of its farflung corporate units, cueing automatic responses, some intermediaries exercising discretion must be present, and the problem of delegated discretion which we have just noted will intrude, affecting the achievement of the technical-economic standards of coordination.

This delegation of discretion, and its consequence of some degree of divergence from system objectives and standards, is what necessitates the overlay of political coordination. The divergence of subunit objectives cannot be avoided, so it must be provided for by a process of coordination which takes account of it, as the technical-economic processes cannot do. The latter can set out an ideal, which must be treated as a first approximation, but from which deviation must be permitted—even planned for—to the extent necessary to achieve the performance which is essential to the system's functioning. System optimum and suboptimum must be blended, and this can only be done through a bargaining process, not through a solution imposed by experts.

But if the result is to constitute a *plan* rather than a continuous sequence of *ad hoc* bargains, there must be some instrument for setting forth the agreed-upon departures from the ideal, some device which itself integrates the participants in the system in a way which is viewed as efficient and feasible even if not ideal. That device is supplied by the corporate budget.

The corporate budget sets forth the expected performance of all the cooperating parts over a period of time which varies with the vision of management and the technical requirements which it faces, as we have previously observed. The short-run or current budget is elaborated in greater detail and involves the contributions of most of those in the system—the players who are actually "on stage."

The expected performance which is written into the budget is, conceptually at least, not a standard which is imposed but one which is agreed to. In practice, superior authority frequently cannot resist forcing on a subordinate a budgeted performance which is unacceptable to the latter, but when this occurs the subordinate feels free to undercut the imposed standard by means of whatever bargaining power is available to him. If the political intent of the budget is effected, however, and it emerges as a product of bargains which take place *around* the ideal standards of efficiency, it constitutes a kind of contract or commitment on the part of all those who compose the system. In this respect it is quite analogous to the collective bargaining agreement negotiated between management and union, which likewise sets out mutually determined standards governing the relationship, which both expect to fulfill.

The bargains which are incorporated in the budget relate to levels of remuneration, promises of advancement, assurances that personal or departmental judgments on desirable practice or policy concerning the use of assets will be followed, and a congeries of other terms. Since the demands which are made by conflicting groups or subsystems cannot all be accommodated, this is where management must manipulate the demands in such a way as to make them apparently compatible with each other and reasonably approximating the initial efficiency standards of the system as a whole. Whatever additional costs are entailed in the meeting of these demands (that wages be raised, that stock options be granted, that research funds be increased, that advertising for a new product be doubled, that office space be expanded, that severance pay be awarded, that prices of a product group be reduced, and so on) must be embodied in the budget, and in such a way that they are adequately covered by revenues (even if this necessitates borrowing) and do not carry the system too far from its own efficient objectives.

The budget thus sets targets or goals for all individuals and subunits in the organization, goals which are considered to blend the divergent interests which are represented. The contribution to the overall objective which is expected from each subunit varies—the target rates of return set for the divisions of a company are not all identical with the rate of return which is set for the system. The budget bargain takes into account, to an agreed-upon extent, the varying difficulties confronting each unit in accomplishing its task. In the process, disgruntlement can be expected, as one unit charges that another was favored or that its legitimate interests or peculiar problems were not adequately recognized. But when the bargaining is all through, and top management has pulled and hauled and exercised its power to bring the parts into a reasonably consistent and workable whole, the result is a plan which carries authority for two reasons. Its internal logic is itself compelling—each part can see how its performance is necessary to the intended result and see the responsibility which thus weighs on it to give rationality to the system. But the same could be said for the product of technical-economic coordination, and by itself is not enough. The plan which emerges from the organizational-political co-ordination which is represented in the budget presumably is also a compact, carrying at least the implicit acceptance by all the component parts of the performance which is assigned to them.

That this second intent is sometimes poorly observed in practice does not negate its conceptual function, any more than a poor job of technical-economic coordination negates the role which it conceptually fills. If a budgeting procedure is not followed, than the internal bargaining which is inevitable and which establishes the terms of performance will simply take place piecemeal, making achievement of organizational objectives a more difficult and more tenuous affair: coordination will consist of improvisation. Or if a budget is followed but is imposed from above rather than emerging as the product of an internal bargaining process, then it takes on the character of technical-economic rather than political-organizational coordination, and, again, the latter—which is inescapable—proceeds on a more opportunistic and less systematic basis: the *planning* process is incomplete.

THE SIGNIFICANCE OF VARIANCES FROM THE BUDGET

As long as the assumptions and forecasts on which the budget rest remain approximately valid, it constitutes the basis for measuring and controlling behavior. Why plan if it is not expected that the plan will be followed? Thus control becomes an integral and essential aspect of the planning process—control in the sense of an organized and systematic effort to be currently informed on how closely action follows plan and to do whatever seems to be called for to bring performance into line with plan. Without control in this sense, planning is an exercise which has some intellectual usefulness but limited organizational significance.

For the purpose of control, it is variances from the plan which are the signals to those in authority that corrective action is called for. In some identified respect—whether labor costs, inventory, promotional expense, or sales volume—the organization is going off the track, and unless it is brought back to the track it will not reach its destination. Variances constitute the red lights signaling to management, the engineer, that danger lies ahead unless something is done to meet the situation.

But this is by no means the whole story. Sometimes the plan itself must be changed rather than held to. Circumstances which could not have been foreseen at the time the comprehensive budget was prepared make it infeasible or undesirable to attempt to enforce, or control for, all its constituent parts. The premises on which planning was based are altered, so that the plan ceases to be realistic or effective. Now it is no longer the case that management is concerned with the achievement of the specifics of its original plan and with controlling the variances which appear. New plans must be substituted, and again management is guided by its long-run overall objectives in their preparation. In some instances, these may require only a modification of the existing budget. At other times, the change in the underlying situation may be sufficiently far-reaching to warrant starting the tedious process of preparing a master budget from scratch.

Thus variances signal the necessity for either control or revision. Which is necessary cannot be ascertained until they have been analyzed. Increasingly, variances are highlighted by a procedure known as "reporting by exception," which reduces the amount of detail flowing to higher authority by singling out those respects in which the plan has not been realized. The decision whether to seek to bring performance back to the original budget or, alternatively, to revise it, is not made lightly. If revision is too readily accepted, the budget—bargained out as it has been—loses its incentive effect. Underachievement should prompt the unit or units involved to intensify their efforts. On the other hand, budgets which are missed by an ever-widening margin equally lose their motivating force and are regarded as "unrealistic." To provide a standard by which performance can meaningfully be measured requires the possibility of realization.

If the decision is made to revise, then a new budget must be substituted for the old one. Assuming that the variances were adverse, the new budget is less favorable than the one originally projected, but presumably more favorable than the balance which has actually emerged. This presumption is based on the probability that analysis in the course of revision has revealed certain respects in which performance can be improved, even if not by enough to achieve what had once been expected. Thus the new budget calls for a better showing than had in fact been emerging; we may call it a "preferred budget"— preferred over actual performance.

This preferred budget becomes in effect the new projected balance from which—as time goes on—the actual balance can again be expected to deviate, since it is rare that budgets are ever precisely realized. On the strength of the variances occurring, once again management will have to determine whether to seek to conform performance to the budget or whether to revise further. Over and over this decision must be repeated. Over and over the actual balance will deviate from the projected balance, occasioning the substitution of a preferred balance, which—even if only informally—becomes the new projected balance from which the actual balance will again deviate, and so on successively. The firm moves into the future by a series of planned steps. Sometimes the revisions are piecemeal rather than comprehensive, but at any time some budget exists by which performance can be judged, and deviations from which signal the need for explanations why, followed by decisions as to whether further control or further revision is called for.

Sometimes the pluses and minuses of variances in income and outgo, relative to budget, offset each other. A poor sales performance by one product may be offset by an above-expectation showing by another product, or a high-cost operation may be offset by one which shows unexpected efficiency. At other times not only is an income change in one unit not offset in some other unit, but the changes may be cumulative or additive. A rise in costs in one shop or department finds its parallel in others, or a number of the major products in a firm's line sell poorly.

Whether a variance is offset or nonoffset depends on the level from which one is surveying operations. A variance which is not offset within a shop may be offset at the level of the plant. From the viewpoint of the foreman of the shop within which it occurs, it constitutes (let us say) an above-standard cost which he must explain to his superior and which he must attempt to control; but from the viewpoint of the plant manager it appears as a budget lapse which, while unfortunate and subject to correction, is not serious, because it is counterbalanced by a cost saving elsewhere in the plant, so that the level of overall plant costs, on which the projected budget balance in part depends, is maintained. Similarly, the variances in a plant's operations, nonoffset there, may be offset at the level of a corporate subsidiary, while the variances in a subsidiary may be offset at the corporate (consolidated) level.

The offsetting of income variances does not stop here, however. From the standpoint of the economy as a whole, variances which emerge within one firm may be offset elsewhere in the economy. Variances may be offset *between* firms, just as within them. Firm A has a lower sales achievement than projected, but firms B and C are doing better than they had hoped. If profits are down at the Jones Co., they are up at the Smith Co. This offsetting of income flows between firms may occur between firms in the same industry (one automobile manufacturer sells fewer cars and another sells more), or it may go on between firms in different product lines (people spend less on clothing this year, but more on travel). The fund flows between firms are altered because consumers have shifted their preferences. Overall levels of spending, or of GNP, may show a stable growth pattern, but within the aggregate there is a good deal of churning of income flows to and from individual firms.

As in the firm, however, so in the economy it may be the case that the changes in flows in one firm or sector are not offset in other firms or sectors. All sell less. Reduced inflows in one industry are not offset by heavier selling in others. Or all sell more, and the increased income in one firm is not at the expense of income to rival firms. Similarly with costs: wage rates and materials prices may rise for all firms (outflows increase) or decline concomitantly. The phenomena of recession and inflation may be described in terms of nonoffsetting income flows.[10] This offsetting or nonoffsetting character of corporate variances at the level of the economy has significance for what the individual firm can do about its own budgetary problems.

If the variances within a company are favorable, management is likely to take a relaxed attitude toward them. If the favorable variance is short-run and accidental, it constitutes a windfall gain. If it is the result of longer-run factors which are likely to bring continuing benefits (an expanded market for some product, so that sales can be expected to grow faster than had been expected, or a change in workflow or materials handling that cuts costs), the improved experience will be built into next year's budget and the favorable variance, while not accidental, will disappear in the same manner as though it had been.

In the case of an unfavorable deviation, the whole nature of the budgeting process creates an expectation that something should be done about it. If the variance has been offset within the firm, however, so that underperformance in one respect has been counterbalanced by overperformance in another and the overall target is approximately

[10] As I have sought to do in *A General Theory of Economic Process*, chap. 16.

realized, the pressure for corrective action is relieved. An energetic and ambitious management might still move to improve the below-budget operation, so that the total profit showing would be better than planned, but in most instances the effort would not be so insistent. If adverse variances are not internally offset, however, so that the profit target is missed by more than a tolerable amount, then they constitute an incentive to top-management corrective action.

If the variance arises in the cost category, it typically is traceable to a rise in factor prices or a decline in productivity. Now, it is true that any variance will have its offset somewhere in the economy except in circumstances when total flows (GNP) are increasing or decreasing. Thus a cost variance emerging in one firm must be offset elsewhere, if we assume GNP temporarily stable, but the offsets are too diffused to be readily discernible. If costs are up at the A. O. Smith Company or the General Motors Corporation, this means a greater outflow of certain payments (to workers, to suppliers, to capital providers), but a lesser flow of certain other expenditures (profits or investments), leading to a shift in the composition of goods sold in the economy at large and hence in the receipts and disbursements of other firms. But these effects are far too widely distributed throughout the economy to give anyone a feeling of aggrievement if A. O. Smith or General Motors takes steps to improve its cost position. Thus they are relatively free to initiate such actions in their production, marketing, and financial organizations as may seem appropriate to bring performance into line with projected costs, based on technical-economic analysis and internal bargains. Even rival firms would see nothing amiss in such behavior.

But revenue variances are in a different class and present a more difficult problem. They may be offset within a firm and also identifiably between firms. A causal relationship may exist between a decline in revenues in company A and an increase in revenues in company B. Whenever adverse revenue variances are considered to be a consequence of such specific offsetting shifts in fund flows between firms, they invite a responsive reaction. The offsetting shift in sales revenues may be traceable to a price action by rivals, or to their promotional activity, or to some change in their product line—to some respect in which rivals have sought to manage their product line and marketing organization to better advantage. If a response is to be made, in the short run it must be made in one of these same areas—but if it is successful it will, for exactly the same reason, invite further reaction from its rivals. Even before the effectiveness of such maneuvers has been established, they may evoke retaliatory responses in anticipation of their possible success. To engage in a defensive action, a firm must be prepared to take the offensive, and vice versa.

In general, price as a means of reestablishing position is used only in instances where rivals have already undercut the firm's price. Only with reluctance does a firm openly initiate a reduction in the market price of some product line in an effort to rebuild shrunken sales, since it can realistically expect that its more profitable competitors will quickly move to match its actions, leaving all worse off than before and the firm itself worse off than its competitors. As long as it has reason to believe that its rivals have not clandestinely cut their listed prices, it has no reason for concluding that its declining revenues are traceable to competitive price relations, which remain as before. The firm is more likely to look to relative product designs and marketing patterns for the cause of its misfortune.

There is no necessary reason, however, why a firm experiencing a poor sales and profit performance need attempt to answer *directly* those firms which it regards as the cause of its troubles. Suppose a rival's promotion of a product coincides with the falling-off in sales, in this firm, of a product which is a substitute, so that a cause and effect relation may be imputed. It does not inescapably follow that the firm must meet this competition in any one of the three ways which are open to it. Its primary goal is some target rate of return on investment, an aggregate profit. A specific share of some particular market is at best a secondary objective. An alert management, watching its position in a given market deteriorate, might decide that the investment required to hold that position would bring less of a return than if put to use in building up its position in some new and developing market into which it had moved or was about to move. If a price-cut by a rival was diverting sales and reducing revenue and profit, management might conclude that a matching price-cut would lose more than could be gained through any recapture of sales, so that its best strategy would appear to be to leave price where it was, accepting the smaller revenue from that product, but to raise prices on another product line in which it occupied a superior position (particularly if the price increase could be timed to coincide with a product change which contributed nothing additional to cost).

The one thing that is inescapable is that whatever response is provoked by the revenue variance, survival of the firm dictates that it be in the product-sales arena. If a firm's sales revenues slide, its long-run future cannot be assured by any amount of cost-cutting, even though such an effort may win it its target profit in the short run. The challenge must sooner or later be met on the field of sales. In the long run this inevitably means product innovation and a particular concern with managing the product line.

Revenue variances may be nonoffset within an industry but offset between industries in cases where a whole industry is rising or falling. A change in consumer tastes or production technology is likely to be the underlying cause. Once again the only cure is long-range attention to the product line, the addition or substitution of wholly new goods or services.

But variances—whether cost or revenue—which are not offset anywhere in the economy, within other firms or within other industries, present quite a different problem. There is virtually nothing which a management can do about them. The cause of the variance runs deeper than any deterioration of cost position peculiar to the firm or than a product relationship to a rival or rivals. It is tied up with a downward or upward movement of GNP in money terms, that is, with recession or inflation. Any effective action must come from some force acting on the general circumstances affecting all firms, and such a force can only be supplied by some external agency, principally government.[11]

THE TIME PATTERN AGAIN

In the course of bargaining a budget, management must satisfy the interests of the participants sufficiently to maintain their adherence to the organization. As long as it keeps to its part of the bargain and provides the rewards and degree of discretion on which the plan is

[11] "Offsetting" and "nonoffsetting" occur with respect to actual flows of funds, while variances relate to deviations of projected from actual flows. The two are not the same thing, though they have been treated here as though they were. Analytically this seems to present no problem. If firms treat variances the same as actual changes in flows, this implies that they take their planning seriously, and their behavioral reactions would be as pictured here. If they do not treat them the same but respond only to changes in actual flows, this suggests that they do not really have faith in their planning. Their actions will therefore be delayed until variances from budget become variances from "normal" (seasonal) or recent flows. Their cue comes more tardily, if at all, but their action, when and if cued, would presumably be the same.

premised, it preserves for its own use, as long as that use can be rationalized as being in the company's interest, whatever discretion it has not allocated to others or forgone the use of itself and whatever revenues it has not had to use up in meeting the terms of others. Under these conditions management may, if it so chooses, indulge its own predilections for attractive modern office buildings, or for heavy emphasis on pure research, or for corporate contributions of a public affairs or eleemosynary nature, or for a risky experimental venture into some new product line. It can do these things, we have said, to the extent that its bargaining power has preserved it the necessary discretion and resources, and a rationalization has been provided.

But in some firms top management is a better bargainer than innovator or creator, and it winds up with discretion and resources which it does not know how to use. It is reluctant to forgo these, but uncertain what to do with them. The evidence is clear that at times some companies have more cash than they can invest, but at the same time are unhappy at the thought of dissipating this as dividends to stockholders—or worse yet, as price reductions or wage increases.

Economists have always stressed the need for economizing. In the face of limited resources and numerous competing ends, difficult choices must be made. There is reason to question, however, whether this conception applies to all firms, even all the large ones, or always applies to any given firm. A growing company is always in need of new investment outlets, and it cannot always find them. No amount of careful tailoring of current operations will solve that problem. The more efficient the production, marketing, and financial organizations, the more resources there will be seeking outlets, and the more urgent the long-run problem of finding them.

It is thus primarily in the area of management of the product line that a company's future lies. It is here that the new outlets will have to be created. It is this asset which must be nurtured with greatest care. There is greater likelihood of finding the technically and economically efficient ways of producing and marketing and financing "it" than there is of finding "it" to begin with. There is more room for manipulating the political bargains which are necessary to the creation of a functioning organization if there is always new growth in the system.

The research department—management's built-in imagination—is of some assistance in meeting this problem, but it cannot be relied on for all the answers. More and more, it seems, does fundamental and experimental research require larger-scale financing, more extensive coordination of resources, and greater authority than even a large corporation can provide, and the kinds of consumer wants on which new industries can be built are not elicited by redesigning familiar products or even improving their performance.

This constitutes a creative challenge to management to envision a future in which the company's assets will have grown in fruitful ways, contributing to a continuously expanding return on its investment, even if the *rate* of return is unchanged. It constitutes as well a creative challenge to governmental authorities to encourage corporate managements to find bolder and more imaginative ways by which they can put their growing assets in the service of the community. This latter almost necessarily calls for public planning, at least if it is to be done in a systematic way. It is to planning within this larger system that we now turn.

3...
the objectives
of governmental
economic planning

The concept of economy-wide planning as the systematic management of the nation's assets in the pursuit of more or less well-defined objectives has been set out in Chapter 1. The national government necessarily serves as management: what other agency could perform that function? Systematic management does not require any grant of enlarged powers to control the private sector, but only the use in calculated fashion of such powers as are granted. Of course, once the planning approach has been adopted and objectives have been defined and the government has systematically exercised whatever powers have been allocated to it to coordinate the parts of the economy in an effort to achieve those objectives, the gap between missions and means may suggest an enlargement of government authority. But that is a matter which can then be debated more intelligently and a question which any society should not be afraid to confront.

The process of economy-wide planning differs from planning in the firm in several important respects which it will be useful to note now even though we defer discussion of them. First, when we deal with the economy as a system, the offsetting of variances from expected performance takes place at a higher level of aggregation. One firm or one industry suffers a decline, but this is balanced off by a firm or an industry on the ascendancy, so that from the standpoint of *aggregate* performance the overall level of activity is unaffected. But where such offsetting does not occur, the consequences are more widely ramified. The larger system is in a better position to absorb departures from expected performance on the part of its components, because these may average out, but where they do not average out, the consequences have a larger spillover in the form of inflation or recession.

Second, the assets for which the national government has managerial responsibility are more fixed than they are for the individual firm. A firm may sell off a plant or dismantle a marketing organization, but the same physical plant which may be passed from one company to another, drawing down the assets of one and increasing the assets of the other, remains a constant national asset. In the same way, for an individual firm the labor force is contractible or expansible, but for the economy as a whole it is relatively fixed.[1]

Third, the streams of strategic decisions affecting the use of national assets are usually more compelling for individuals because of being backed by the power of public law and often permitting fewer alternative courses of action. The national government, as top management for the system, can make decisions which become the premises limiting the discretion of everyone in the system.

[1] To be sure, we speak of the labor force as a whole as contracting or expanding under such influences as wartime emergency or local job availability, but the people who permit such fluctuations in the present size of the labor force have longer-run permanence. The labor force including the labor *reserve*, to use Professor Reder's terminology, remains relatively fixed. Also, the labor force is constantly changing because of additions, changes in age and skill composition, and retirements, but this is why we speak of it as being *relatively* fixed, since such changes are minor compared to the possible fluctuations in the labor force of a firm.

THE DUAL NATURE OF GOVERNMENT MANAGEMENT

The national government must perform two separable but related managerial tasks: on the one hand, it must coordinate the functioning of the parts of the governmental machinery, considered as an organizational system, just the same as the management of a business firm coordinates the parts of its organizational system. On the other hand, it must coordinate the functioning of the parts of the economy as a whole, in this case treating governmental operations as simply one subsystem (although the most important one) of the larger system.

This dual function was concisely set out in the President's budget message to Congress for 1963: "The Federal budget has a double importance. It is an agenda of our purposes and priorities in the form of a plan for the conduct and financing of the public business. It is also the most powerful single tool the Nation possesses for linking the private and public sectors of our economy in a common effort to achieve and maintain national prosperity."

Neither of these managerial tasks requires planning. Both can be carried through on a pragmatic and opportunistic basis. Or the "conduct and financing of the public business" may be planned without planning the national economy. This has been at least partially the case in the United Kingdom which has organized its governmental activities not only over the short run, but looking five years into the future and inclusive not only of central governmental activities, but of important aspects of local governmental affairs as well. Government there has planned almost as a large corporation with many subsidiaries and plants might plan (even if loosely and with important ingredients of the process still unattended to), but there has been no national planning, at least until the National Economic Development Commission appeared on the scene in 1962 and initiated its first tentative ventures in that direction.

The objectives of government in the first, the public business, sense constitute the programs of its departments and agencies, as provided for in the government's own budget, on the expenditures side. What distinguishes government planning from simple government management in all such operations is the tying of specific outputs of services or "missions" or goods to specific inputs, so that choices may be more meaningfully made as to resource use—benefits received for costs incurred. This avoids parceling out government revenues among departments or agencies along organizational lines, the inevitable consequence of which is that "management decisions bearing on specific problem clusters are made piecemeal, lacking a consistent goal-oriented policy framework, lacking comprehensive study of supply requirements..., lacking, in short, the information-decision structure essential for rational, efficient, and flexible choice among alternative options." [2]

Such cost-benefit analysis is not likely—at least yet—to be carried through on a quantitative basis which gives specific values to competitive expenditures, but at least some systematic effort to appraise relative benefits is called for if the government's resources are to be allocated in ways which achieve whatever it conceives to be its objectives.

Perhaps the purest, although partial, example of governmental planning in the West today is to be found in the U.S. Department of Defense, where, under Secretary Robert McNamara, who came schooled in Ford Motor Co. budgetary practices, and Assistant Secretary Charles Hitch, a professional economist, operations were conceived in terms of long-range missions, forces, and weapons systems—the outputs of departmental activity—and not only in terms of the customary budgetary categories of personnel, construction, supplies, and equipment. "A decision to procure a given quantity of hardware carries with it requirements for facilities, acquisitions and training of personnel, personnel housing, support equipment and a host of other related items, all of which must be paid for. In addition, a procurement decision implies a decision to incur annual recurring costs so long as the system remains in the inventory. A clear identification of the tim-

[2] David Novick, head of Cost Analysis Department, The Rand Corporation, in *The Federal Budget as an Economic Document, Hearings before the Subcommittee on Economic Statistics of the Joint Economic Committee*, 88th Cong., 1st Sess., 1963, pp. 56–57. Novick comments with respect to the absence of such a planning approach in the U.S. government generally: "Many examples could be cited, but for dramatic object lessons one need go no further than (1) the multiple, interlaced, overlapped, often internally inconsistent foreign economic activities embedded in so many departmental budgets; (2) the unmeasured aggregate Federal funding of R. & D. [research and development] activities, with the resulting competitive, even inflationary pressures on the scarce supply of R. & D. talent; or (3) the numerous easy commitments to initial spending for incompletely analyzed programs (such as farm price supports, veterans' benefits, or HEW [Health, Education, and Welfare] activities) whose future costs are seldom brought into the decision focus in the appropriate time and magnitude perspectives."

ing and cost of these requirements is essential to a full understanding of the resource impact of a given decision. It is to provide the Secretary of Defense and his military advisers with this understanding that the new programming/budgeting system has been instituted." [3] Thus the cost of attaining given results can be more accurately computed, and limited defense appropriations can be allocated where they are likely to make the greatest contribution to the overall result sought.

The problem of choice is made more difficult when comparisons must be made not between competing programs within the defense system, but between defense programs and competing programs for education or transportation or agriculture or other lines of activity, where the "objectives" of government operations must be couched in more abstract conceptions of "welfare," against which alternative uses of resources must somehow be measured. Capital decisions must be made between such alternatives as a subway system in Brussels or improved and extended ports and highways—the kind of "social investment" choice which was hammered out in the Belgian Interministerial Committee on Public Investments in 1962 and recurringly in comparable bodies in other countries. But here, as well, the decision, while more complicated, is facilitated by the planning approach, with its attempt at a more systematic weighing of the advantages of alternative uses of public assets.

Obviously such public-sector planning must take into account, if only cursorily, the effects of governmental programs on the health of the economy as a whole, and governments have thereby been led into discharging their second function of "managing" the economy. The government's budget embodies its "fiscal policy," and governmental fiscal policy has too clear and intimate a relationship to overall economic performance for it to be judged solely with reference to its own programs, without reference to the needs of the national economy. As Prof. Arthur Okun has noted, "No amount of information, however comprehensive, about the Federal sector alone can ever tell us whether the budget is doing its job." [4]

But this clear relationship between government management of its own sector and government management of the economy does not require planning. The second function may be and frequently is performed by means of *ad hoc* stabilization or contracyclical policy, with

[3] The same, p. 56.
[4] The same, p. 7.

a bit of fiscal maneuvering here or a dose of monetary manipulation there in the hope that these will have beneficial effects. The second function may be and frequently is focused on short-run performance in the economy without much respect to its long-run potential.[5]

The planning part of government's second managerial role enters when more specific objectives and targets are posed for the economy as a whole, in the long run as well as the present, and when governmental actions and programs are designed to influence the decisions of the private sector in ways which interact with public-sector activity to achieve the objectives posed, with magnitudes and a timetable built into the projections. In this role government acts as the top coordinator of the economic system as a whole.

There is of course no dichotomous division of countries into those which plan and those which do not. There are varying degrees of inclination toward the planning philosophy and varying types of organization to carry off whatever inclination exists—just as there are varying degrees and kinds of planning in the business sector. In one country a draft plan is considered simply a "framework for discussions on the country's economic future" (as has been said of Sweden), while in another, "goals melt easily into predictions, and its predictions into hopes," as Prof. Ben Lewis remarked of British planning under the Labor government.[6] In Denmark the reluctance of a new Conservative government to adopt interventionist policies led in 1951 to the conversion of the "government programme" into an "official forecast."

[5] An economist for a Belgian trade association remarked in 1962, in explaining his government's venture into planning: "The tendency has been for the State's economic policy to follow lines of political influence, so that it would go in one direction now and a different direction another time, with its actions being of a piecemeal sort. About three years ago during a period of very heavy unemployment, under pressure from the trade unions for the government to do something about it, a sentiment began to take shape that it was time for the government to begin to coordinate its policies both within its own area [sector] and also with respect to the economy as a whole."

A Swedish economist, in criticizing his government's inattention to the unofficial long-range program in an earlier period, commented that it is not rational to "take steps from day to day to meet the situation of the moment. Government measures have far too widespread and long-range repercussions for such a method of procedure to have any justification." Jan Wallander, "Experiences of Long-term Planning in Sweden," *Quarterly Review of the Skandinaviska Banken*, April, 1956, p. 55.

[6] Ben W. Lewis, *British Planning and Nationalization* (New York: The Twentieth Century Fund, 1952), p. 11.

In part, as the Danish action suggests, the firmness with which targets are held depends on the degree of influence which the government exerts over their realization. Those plans or parts of plans which can be most effectively carried out by the powers allowed to government will be held with greater assurance than those where private response must be induced. Thus in Norway "the program character of the national budget is frequently vague, partly because the distinction between target variables and other private variables is not always made sufficiently clear, and partly because the Government is able to exert only a weak influence on some of the private variables which are considered to be targets." [7]

Whatever the orientation toward planning, the economic projections or national budgets which grow out of it differ from forecasts of GNP, such as those annually developed in the United States and Germany, in that they set forth overall levels of activity which it is believed can be achieved if the appropriate policies are adopted, and usually elaborate the policies on the strength of which the projections are expected to be made good.

In this study we shall not be concerned with describing the present commitment to planning procedures, or the procedures themselves, of particular countries, though we shall draw on their experience for illustrative material. We are concerned with conceptualizing the planning process in a private-enterprise economy, in an effort to understand its generic characteristics, just as we have done in the case of the business firm.

[7] P. J. Bjerve, *Planning in Norway, 1947–1956* (Amsterdam: North Holland Publishing Company, 1959), p. 31. On pp. 329–330 Bjerve adds: "Opponents of the Labor Party in power in Norway have asserted that the national budget represents only a prognosis of economic events and not a program of economic policy. Some even maintain that the national budget publications are primarily political propaganda and have little significance for policy.... Nevertheless, the facts remain that in Norway the Cabinet officially declares the annual and long-term national budgets as programs for its economic policy, and that the opposition feels justified in criticizing the Cabinet if stated goals are not achieved. Indeed it cannot be questioned that national budgeting has been used in post-war years—and is still being used—in the design and execution of economic policy by the Cabinet and its Economic Committee; by the National Budget Committee and the National Budget Secretariat and by the Ministries, in particular the Ministry of Finance [which Bjerve subsequently headed], the Ministry of Commerce, and the Ministry of Public Labor and Municipality Affairs (which is responsible for the building licensing budget and the manpower budget)."

SOME PLANNING OBJECTIVES

The most commonly espoused objective of public planning is an accelerated rate of growth in the national economy, usually expressed as a percentage increase in GNP. This has been the goal in France, for example, where a procedure has evolved for identifying a target growth rate after rounds of discussion between the Planning Commission and the Economic and Social Council and then presenting it to the legislature for approval. The Fourth Plan adopted a target growth rate of 5½ percent. We shall come back to the French case in more detail later.

Belgium followed the French experience rather closely. The Bureau of Programmation, which reports to the Ministerial Committee of Economic and Social Affairs, was initially directed to plan for an increase in the rate of growth, which had been disappointingly low. In its First Economic Expansion Program for the period 1962–1965 it proposed an increase in the national product of 17 percent over the four years, rising from an initial rate of 2.6 percent to a 4 percent level.

The United Kingdom provides an interesting example. Here the initiative appears to have derived from the impatient reaction of a segment of the Federation of British Industries to a speech by a government official at its 1960 conference. The purport of the latter's remarks was that it was essential for the British economy to hold the price line and to manage its trade balance, and *then* if it proved possible it should also seek to grow. Certain industrialists who expressed weariness with price stability as an end in itself organized a philosophical counterattack which took the line that economic growth was essential *in order* to prevent inflation and maintain a trade balance, and out of a working conference on economic growth there developed the thinking which led a year later to the establishment of the National Economic Development Council. Here too the French experience was not without its influence. The Council, meeting for the first time in March, 1962, against a background of annual increments of 2 to 3 percent in national income, chose a "trial" target rate in rather arbitrary fashion. It was felt that 3½ percent did not represent a sufficient increase to galvanize the economic community, while a 4½ percent rate seemed somewhat ambitious. Four percent sounded just about right. In April, 1963, during the budget debate, the government for the first time committed itself to planning for that rate of increase.

There are a number of reasons accounting for the preoccupation of governments with growth rates in the postwar period. Some of these relate to the cold war—the feeling that nations are engaged in an economic competition in which their ideological systems are at stake. Socialism cannot be allowed to best private enterprise in such a race, even if that requires acceptance of a larger role for government. The presence of substantial numbers of Communist Party members and sympathizers in certain Western countries provides a sense of special urgency, notably in France.

Two other considerations, perhaps of less transitory nature, seem also to be influential. In all countries, however firmly wedded to Western politics, there is a new impatience to improve standards of living. Perhaps because of the spectacular wartime production results, workers seem less willing now, in peacetime, to wait until the operations of the competitive market bring them benefits "in the long run." They are convinced that private enterprise, if assisted and guided by government, can produce more goods more cheaply more quickly. Recurring spells of unemployment, as in Belgium, have given further impetus to the notion that the parts of the economy are too dispersed considering their interdependence and that some coordination is needed to make them into an effective working whole. Where this impatience is widespread and influential, an accelerated rate of growth becomes a natural objective of government planning whenever it is instituted.

A second reason of a more speculative (and partly conflicting) nature seems also to have supported the objective of growth in the more advanced economies. It has been argued that with rising standards of living, and a higher proportion of discretionary income, the pressures for growth which previously were stimulated by a people's desire to satisfy basic consumption needs lose their effectiveness. At least this is the case in the upper-income brackets. If growth is to be sustained, it can only be by satisfying less obvious and less pressing needs, or by directing the attention of the community to collective needs which are still inadequately met. If growth is not sustained, then we run into monumental problems of unemployment in which the old, more basic needs reassert themselves in the cases of those who lose their jobs. If more fundamental social changes are attempted, such as a redistribution of work and leisure, not only are there major problems of adjustment, but the potential is lost for satisfying higher-level wants which have not yet been sufficiently aroused. "It becomes necessary somehow to show the existence of these needs so that they appear clear to all businesses, and induce them to pursue their development efforts." [8] Thus, to maintain a rate of growth adequate to keep the economy fully utilized requires a greater initiative on the part of government; and the rate of growth becomes the goal of planning.

A different objective has taken precedence in other countries, or has been subsumed as a goal subsidiary to growth in those mentioned above: full employment. The 1946 Employment Act of the United States sets this out as an almost overriding objective of government economic policy. The depression years of the thirties underscored how tenuous is the achievement of this desideratum, dependent as it is on the offsetting activities of numerous firms and industries. In any large economy there are always firms and industries which are in a declining phase, and there must be other firms and industries in an ascendant phase to provide adequate work opportunities offsetting that decline —and providing additional jobs for those newly coming into the labor force. Workers seeking jobs must somehow be circulated to employers seeking workers, taking account of the possible occupational and geographical discrepancies between supply and demand. When one stops to consider the amount of coordination which is supposed to take place through the impersonal processes of the market, one is amazed that the market does so well. But not well enough to have prevented recurring and sometimes prolonged spells of unemployment, sometimes of substantial volume.

Governmental programs to stimulate the economy and induce the hiring of more workers, as well as to increase the efficiency of worker circulation in the system, have been the answer to this problem. And in some countries these have been elevated to the status of chief economic objectives.[9]

[8] Statement of M. Claude Gruson, director general of the French National Institute of Statistics and Economic Studies, in CEPES, *French and Other National Economic Plans for Growth*, p. 38.

[9] Thus Alfred Neal, president of the Committee for Economic Development, has commented that "in the United States we put the stress upon the maintenance of a very high level of employment.... We put less stress on the growth rate, the expansion rate, than is done in other countries." From the same, p. 132.

CONSTRAINTS AND BALANCED OBJECTIVES

With prices rising in the United States through much of the decade of the fifties, there developed a strong agitation to make price stability an objective equal in importance to full employment. On the European scene, the sense of dependence on a proper balance in the foreign trade account stimulated an equal anxiety to restrain wages and prices from rising to shut off export markets. Postwar planners began to speak of productivity-related wage increases, price stability, and a foreign trade balance as "constraints" on the pursuit of other objectives, which set limits on the vigor with which such objectives could be pursued. Growth and full employment could remain as the objectives on the attainment of which economic policy might be focused—as long as price stability and a balance of payments could be preserved.

In this sense the constraints themselves become objectives, but limited objectives. Presumably more growth is better than less growth, other things being equal, but once price stability is achieved, one cannot seek more of it. Thus, despite the fact that they are the *object* of policy, the tendency has been to regard constraints less as objectives in their own right than as limitations on the pursuit of objectives, conditions that must first be met before the real targets can be sought. Price stability is at best a conservative goal, the preservation of an existing set of economic relations or the reestablishment of former relationships; it does not represent some new level of achievement (*vide* the reaction of the Federation of British Industries insurgents mentioned above).

But the distinction between constraints and objectives is a tenuous one. Full employment is generally regarded as a target, but it could equally be treated as a constraint. Like price stability, once it has been achieved one cannot have more of it. Like price stability, failure to realize it threatens the attainment of other goals. The fact is that constraints are really the same as objectives, though their relegation to a special category is designed to give them priority, to assert the proposition that they must first be achieved before other goals are allowable. But this is a matter of judgment and preference. Some might elevate objectives to the level of constraints—full employment first, and then price stability to the extent possible. It is more impartial to treat them all as joint objectives which require some balancing, some trading-off against each other.[10] The nature of this balancing is suggested by the fact that in the mid-sixties Western Europe seemed ready to accept a price progression of as much as 3 percent a year as long as this was accompanied by an unemployment rate of no more than 1 to 1½ percent, whereas the United States was more inclined to reverse these figures. (At the same time, in the less developed countries of Latin America, price increases of 15 to 20 percent were viewed as representing "stability.") The treatment of certain objectives as constraints is of value only in facilitating the application of technical-economic (maximizing) procedures, something which we will consider later.

Once we have accepted the notion of concomitant goals which must somehow be related to each other, we can easily move to the next stage, in which the objectives of planning are conceived not as *rates* of growth or employment but as substantive *states* of the economy. We can think of the objectives of planning as a conception, a picture, of the economy as we would like to see it at some future date, filled in more fully in certain important particulars such as the growth of basic industry and the expansion of the educational system or health services or housing accommodations, along with rather definite views as to what export-import or savings-investment or wage-price relations are implied by the kind of picture being drawn. In other, less vital respects, such as some forms of private consumption, the picture may be left blank.

This approach has value in that it encourages the kind of long-run orientation to specific problem areas of high social priority which is

[10] This point emerges from an exchange between Prof. Carl Shoup of Columbia University and Senator Jack Miller of Iowa, in *The Federal Budget as an Economic Document*, pp. 41–42:

SENATOR MILLER—If the monetization portion of this [financing of government budget deficit] would indeed result in an inflation would you then advocate it?

MR. SHOUP—Let me say that if it would result in inflation I would then have to rethink the entire policy program and ask myself how much inflation, how much rise in prices, and what would be the price we would have to pay to reduce unemployment, and we are back to our discussion of some time earlier, I think, where it became a question of balancing one against the other.

In other words, I am not willing to say that any amount of unemployment is preferable to even a 10th of a percent rise in price per year. I am not willing to be an extremist in price stability to that extent, but I do prize price stability highly, and would not want to incur the cost of rising prices to eliminate unemployment without first searching for all other possible methods of curing it.

essential if lead time is required for their solution. Growth rates and full employment can be sought by a series of short-term improvisations, which might even pass as planning, but an objective such as the development or transformation of a nation's transportation system requires more foresight and phasing. Education planning, for example, would call for projections of the school-age population at some future date: judgments as to the likely forms of economic activity in the years ahead, based on assumptions as to changing tastes, political requirements, and technology which would affect the desired composition of the labor force of the future and would in turn have their repercussions on the kind of education which might be suited to people coming into that kind of economic world. All these estimates and judgments would obviously be subject to error, but they must nevertheless be attempted if decisions are to be made as to how much of the national resources are to be put into school buildings and their equipment, into teacher development in a variety of subject areas, and into student subsidies. Questions about the sequence of the whole program and about geographical distribution would also have to be faced.

Objectives of this sort belong in the national-planning category, rather than simply public-sector planning, since the whole activity is based on an implicit assumption that industry will realize its technological potentials and that the labor force will find employment opportunities. These assumptions cannot be left wholly to "natural" evolution but must be treated as a kind of "cartoon" of the future which, if it is to be realized, must be filled in in its important details. The parts make the whole.

At least in Europe, an impressionistic survey would suggest that this substantive emphasis in planning is winning more converts. Even businessmen—in what proportion it would be impossible to say—are recognizing that only the government can provide adequate guidelines to national interest, and this carries as a corollary the establishing of priorities of economic activity. This shifting attitude is perhaps in part encouraged by the fact that few appreciate more than the planners the importance of private investment to growth.[11] Among the planners

[11] Thus *Business Week* (July 14, 1962, p. 72) commented of a country which many U.S. businessmen have mistakenly been inclined to regard as "socialistic": "Today, Sweden is more like a giant corporation whose employees pay for most of their national 'fringe benefits' out of wages—freeing management to provide for a growing economic pie."

themselves there is an even clearer tendency to move from construct-
ing simple ex ante national income estimates incorporating desired
growth rates to a more detailed examination of the real components
and the dynamics of their interaction.

GROWTH AS A "PORTMANTEAU" OBJECTIVE

As one reflects on these several approaches to the definition of planning objectives, one is driven to the conclusion that concern with
growth rates and full employment as targets in themselves represents
an early and rather unsophisticated stage of development. A percentage increase in GNP is necessarily an ex post measure—even if it is
projected; it is the resultant of a variety of activities which have taken
place on many fronts, and hence cannot be meaningfully used as an ex
ante target except perhaps in a hortatory way. It would be as though a
company set a target rate of return on its investment without attention
to whether its underlying programs made such an achievement
possible.

This objection is no less relevant to efforts to anchor a growth rate
in an economy's past performance. Comparisons with previous levels
of activity, or with the growth-rate achievements of other countries,
are useful as something to shoot at (just as comparisons help business
firms to formulate their profit goals), but they are at best clues to what
a nation should be satisfied with, and not a program of action. One can
start out with a GNP growth figure as a trial approach, to see if there
are the makings of that growth in the planned or expected activities of
all the parts of the economy, but it is the latter—the potential and the
plans for its realization—out of which the growth figure emerges, as a
consequence.

And yet a growth rate does have considerable value as the same kind
of portmanteau objective for the economy as a rate of return on investment is for the firm. A growth rate in fact is the equivalent for the
economy of the firm's joint objectives of growth and rate of return.
The difference between the micro and macro objectives lies primarily
in the fact that the economy as a whole cannot seek a profit, so that a
rate of return in the sense of profit has no relevance. The macro
objective is the economic welfare of the nation and a rate of growth of
assets and of income deriving from them become objectives logically

derivative from the premise that enhancement of national wealth increases national welfare.[12]

But unless we adopt the further assumption that we are basically indifferent to the forms in which assets and income accrue, we are inevitably concerned not only with a growth rate, but with the composition of assets and of the income to which they give rise. To treat either the growth rate or full employment as independent objectives, without respect to the way national income is consumed or the kinds of employments in which people are engaged, would reflect a rather shocking materialistic insouciance. The growth rate constitutes only a convenient envelope for all the substantive achievements which are really the objects of planning. If the growth rate is used to express national objectives, it can only be in this representative or portmanteau sense—as the expected increment in national income over a period of time, arising out of public programs which are wanted for their own sake and private economic activity which is facilitated by such governmental coordination as seems necessary and appropriate.

Presumably it would be possible to have a given magnitude of GNP taking a number of different forms, and the relative desirability of these alternatives may not be something which can be left entirely to consumer tastes of the moment—a composition of GNP reflecting present dispositions—but may involve as well questions of longer-run rates and directions of growth, major national interests, which will be influenced by whatever choice is made now. This is a case where governmental management of the nation's assets calls for its exercise of programmatic leadership and not an attitude of unconcern over what its GNP is made of as long as it hits a certain total.

We cannot even say that the *potential* rate of growth sets limits on what objectives *can* be pursued, since there is not just one potential rate of growth but a whole array of growth rates, from among which one may be chosen as long as the economy is willing to accept the pattern or program of growth which it represents. As Professor de Wolff, director of the Netherlands Central Plan Bureau, has pointed

---

[12] It is convenient to waive at this point the more philosophical issues surrounding the question of what constitutes wealth and income and welfare in any real sense.

The growth rate is a more useful portmanteau objective than full employment, since the latter is difficult to define, involving disputable questions of what rate of *unemployment* is consistent with full employment.

out, the long-run rate of growth depends largely on the investment category, and this in turn depends on the savings which the economy generates, and the government can, by appropriate policy, influence the savings rate.[13] Individuals and business firms may be given inducements to save, just as business firms may be given inducements to invest. Thus the rate of growth becomes an option. But even in this formulation what is being chosen is not (except symbolically) the rate of growth—which is an abstraction of very little content to the people making and living under the policy choice—but the associated programs with their relative costs and benefits.

THE FRENCH FOURTH PLAN

This portmanteau use of a growth rate as objective is rather nicely illustrated in the French Fourth Plan. To begin with, the Planning Commission, in collaboration with the National Institute of Statistics and Economic Studies, made preliminary surveys of the implications for the major sectors of the economy of rates of increase of 3, 4½, and 6 percent. On the strength of these it tentatively opted for a 4½ percent growth, which in the course of discussion with other official bodies it raised to 5 percent. Its apparent caution was attributable to the fear that a faster growth would bring back the same inflationary pressures which led to drastic reforms in 1958 (the so-called "Rueff reforms"), including devaluation of the franc.

The Commission's plan proposal, which spelled out the general directions along which the economy would be expected to move to achieve the overall growth envisaged, was then subjected to the scrutiny of the Economic and Social Council. This body, whose members come from many professional and functional interest groups, pressured the government for a higher growth target. Its members expressed a preference for a rate as close to 6 percent as possible, but not exceeding it. The higher rate was not chosen capriciously but was a consequence of economic and political considerations. There was concern that a slower growth would not provide job opportunities for the expected repatriation to metropolitan France of a number of French Algerians. (It was anticipated that some 400,000 people, including 100,

[13] P. de Wolff and Th. A. Stevers, "State Budget and Planning," in *Les Prévisions Budgétaires dans le Cadre des Prévisions Économiques et leur Adaptations,* Université de Gand, 1963, pp. 98–100.

000 workers, would enter France within the plan period; as it turned out, a larger number entered within a briefer space of time.) A second job pressure was envisaged in the increasing rate of migration from farm to city. These two streams of migration were also expected to increase the need for housing construction.

On the other hand, a higher growth rate seemed feasible. Manpower shortages were not contemplated in view of the influx of new workers. A favorable balance of trade by 1965 was projected, based largely on optimism with respect to a shift to franc-financed oil imports and higher farm exports. Preferential investment treatment for essential industries, perhaps further encouragement to private saving, and probable productivity increases would provide the remaining necessary ingredients. And if the projection proved overoptimistic, there was less fear in the Economic and Social Council about resulting inflationary pressures than there was in the Planning Commission.[14]

Under pressures from the Council, the Planning Commission accepted an annual target of 5½ percent, or 24 percent over the plan period. But perhaps more important than the rate which was decided on was the pattern of development which underlay it. Private, discretionary consumption, while slated for a substantial increase, was to rise somewhat more slowly than public consumption and investment. Social expenditures on education, town planning, regional development, and public health were stressed. There was an explicit intent to channel resources into such avenues rather than into what was openly labeled "American gadgetry." Private investment was marked for a more than proportional share in the increment, providing the base for future expansion. The inter-industry investment allocations, while guided by the projected pattern of final output, did not require assigning priorities to the same degree as under earlier plans.

[14] This last point was elaborated by an influential member of the Council in an interview in the summer of 1962, shortly after the Fourth Plan had been adopted. In answer to an inquiry whether there were not among the members of the Council those who were as sensitive to inflation as the government, he responded: "Who would they be? Not the businessmen, since most of them are heavily loaded with debts and would benefit from rising price levels. Nor the labor union officials, since they are only interested in higher rates of wage increases. Not even the exporting industries, which might be expected to be concerned that rising prices would shut them out of their markets, since they can and do look to the government for subsidies and subventions if that is needed to keep them competitive. And even more important—although the businessman will not admit this publicly he will admit it privately to someone like me—he really has little fear of devaluation, if it should come to that."

SPECIFIC, CATEGORICAL, AND HYPOTHETICAL OBJECTIVES

In a plan such as that in France it is by no means clear—perhaps even to the planning authorities—how much of it represents *specific objectives* which are considered important in their own right or because of their functional relationship to something else considered important, and to obtain which the government will exert such authority as it has; and how much represents what might be called *categorical objectives*, where it is inconsequential whether more of one thing and less of another is produced or consumed, as long as the total category (of private consumption, of private investment, of exports, of savings) adds to approximately the stated amount, and where, again, the government would use its powers to attain this quantitative result; and finally, how much represents what might be called *hypothetical objectives*, where the items and amounts which are included to fill out the plan constitute neutral expectations of probable results, but where the government would not use its always limited powers to attempt to influence the outcome either in kind or amount.

What may be a categorical objective at one level of aggregation (say private investment) may become a hypothetical objective at a different level of detail (say private investment in textiles), since some offsetting among items may be anticipated, or may alternatively be a specific objective (say a new steel facility) if no offsetting can be permitted.

In view of these major differences in the firmness with which substantive objectives—elements—of the plan are held, it is quite meaningless to treat the plan in its entirety (or even the growth rate which summarizes it) as a single objective, except as a convenient if loose manner of expression. The meaningful objectives are the major programs which the plan embodies, whatever these may be, and not all the parts or subtotals, however consequential or inconsequential, which are also included.

This is all the more the case if one introduces the time dimension, since annual deviations of items from the amounts projected may be relatively inconsequential as long as the broad national economic objectives are pushed forward in the intended direction year by year, not too badly out of phase.

Thus in the case of the French Fourth Plan, inflationary pressures mounting in 1963 gave temporary advantage to those who placed heavy emphasis on financial stability, in contrast to growth, with the consequence that the growth target for the plan's last year was scaled down from 5½ percent to something less. Some slackening in the pursuit of specific social investment objectives was accepted by the government. Nevertheless, one is not justified in treating this as a case where paper objectives fell before "hard" economic realities. In part it was a matter of phasing. The fourth-year growth objective was trimmed, but the four-year objective was more nearly attained due to greater growth in earlier years (not unrelated to the inflationary pressures which emerged). Perhaps more significant, however, is that while the rate of achievement of specified targets of social investment was scaled downward, in response to political pressures, the reduction was less than if they had not been set out as targets in the first place. The government simply could not cut as much as the financial equilibrium enthusiasts might have wished because it had committed itself to objectives in education, construction, highways, and so on, which could be trimmed (rephased, slowed now and perhaps made up later), but could not be slashed, since that would constitute abandonment of widely advertised long-run goals. The specific targets were not so firmly held as to override all other considerations, but neither were they so weakly held as to be meaningless.

As one influential financial administrator expressed it, when there is a collision between the plan and financial equilibrium, the plan must give way, both in overall growth rate and specific goals. But the important consideration is that the government gives ground on these objectives less than it would in the absence of a plan. If the plan calls for 400,000 housing units, the government might drop to 350,000, but it could hardly go lower, because it had committed itself. In the absence of a preset target there would be nothing against which to measure its performance. With a plan, it is more difficult for the government to be anti-inflationary! [15]

[15] Nevertheless, it seems probable that by 1964 the enthusiasm for *le Plan* had abated a good deal. Conservative quarters were suggesting that a 3 percent growth rate was enough to provide a steady increase in real income with price stability and were winning a more sympathetic hearing than they had had in years. Although some sentiment in support of expanded social investment still remained, particularly in labor quarters, the government was not proving notably effective in asserting a leadership role around this sentiment.

To what extent French preoccupation with its position on the world stage diverted attention from domestic objectives and undermined the social investment program, which had been announced with such great hope at the time

THE TIME DIMENSION IN PLANNING

Just as in the firm, it is only as a government or a nation looks beyond the immediate horizon to a somewhat more distant future that it can talk in terms of objectives which have more than temporary meaning. To paraphrase one official in the Norwegian Bureau for Planning, in most fields or sectors short-term planning is really equivalent to prognosis. It is only in the long-term or four-year planning that both government and industry move into policy matters.[16]

The specific long-term objectives may fall in the area of "public business" activities, which government in its role of manager of that area must plan in the same way a business firm plans its operations, or they may be privately sponsored activities which the government facilitates or induces. But their dimensions and rate of scheduled completion affect and are affected by the level and kinds of activity in the economy as a whole, and the two must be coordinated by government in its capacity as manager of the economic system, to the extent its powers permit.

In general, the objectives of short-run policy are the realization of the potential output for current use after longer-run programs have been provided for (a categorical objective) and the allocation of that output among competing interests, with special consideration to making effective any specific objectives of the economic plan. This formulation suggests that short-run (categorical) targets are subordinate to long-term (specific) goals, and in one sense, as we have just noted, that must be so. Once the latter have been chosen, the former must be made consistent with it. As the Netherlands planners de Wolff and Stevers have forcefully put it, "Deliberately, priority has been given to

the Fourth Plan was launched, is anybody's guess. French officials denied that the *force de frappe* policy, and all that went with it, was primarily responsible, but it remains an open question whether the French—so intent on escaping the bane of American consumer gadgetry—may not have embraced the more baleful U.S. nuclear gadgetry. At the same time, none of this suggests the inadequacy of the planning process itself, but simply raises a question as to the extent to which planning has been made an instrument of economic management by the government itself—a question to which we shall return later.

[16] At the time of this interview there was particular concern with the larger markets within which Norway would expect to operate (a) if it joined the Common Market or (b) if it remained only within the EFTA (European Free Trade Area) bloc.

structural policy. This is the primary one, cyclical policy being inconceivable without a well-defined structural policy." [17]

But on further reflection this becomes a matter of time perspective. It could equally be said that the long-run goals must be reformulated and modified, as possible and as necessary, in the light of short-run targets, as these are recurringly chosen. If time is viewed as a stream, the present and future merge and each is equally important in shaping the other. Long-run goals, however compellingly presented and however specific, cannot be firmly held unless the succession of short runs makes them possible. Underutilization of economic potential, uses of current income which are politically compromised or inconsistent, sacrifice the presumed long-run intent. It is politically infeasible to give to the future an inflexible grip on the present, just as it is politically infeasible to maintain the hold of the dead hand of the past. Some compromise between present and future goals is inescapable, since these are held in varying esteem by different groups of people, each with its own measure of political influence.

Here is the nub of the problem of planning. Planning is necessarily directed to the future, but a future of varying distance. For some specific purposes (education, for example), technical considerations require commitments of ten or twenty years if a desired result is to be realized. For other specific purposes the technical requirements are less, by varying amounts of time. Each specific purpose, with its own unique time requirement, must find its way into the current plan, and actions looking to its realization—at its own distant date—must begin running now; resources must be allocated to its fulfillment in a phased program, which can be modified only within limits if the event is to come off approximately when scheduled.

The initiation of actions and the allocation of resources looking to future specific goals are, however, only part of the current plan, which must also include provision for the satisfaction of the present wants of a society composed of competing interests and tastes. To effect some political compromise among these competing interests and still preserve the actions and allocations necessary to future objectives requires the achievement of short-run categorical objectives—general magnitudes sufficient to permit a politically satisfactory division among competing groups. But the categorical objectives—the magnitudes which embody the rates of growth in national income and which determine

[17] *Les Prévisions Budgétaires,* p. 111.

how much there is to allocate—*over time* themselves depend on long-run policies which can be made effective, such as those concerning rates of saving and investment, policies which have been chosen because they make possible not only a rate but a pattern of growth. The succession of short-run objectives—mostly of a categorical nature—themselves are determined by more distant goals.

Thus the time stream flows, inescapably mingling present and future, as each partially determines the other. The planner cannot afford to focus primarily on one without sufficient regard to the other. Each must be fitted into a pattern, a flow, which, pulled and hauled though it may be by the political process, still preserves some integrated meaning. It is the job of government in its economic planning function to manipulate the system of relations, within the limits of the powers granted it, to manage the assets of the economy in a way which satisfies as well as possible a time stream of objectives which are politically acceptable.

4...
national assets and influences over their use

The function of government in its role of managing the national economy is to make effective use of the nation's assets in achieving national objectives. Planning is simply the attempt to systematize the carrying out of this function. This assignment, as we have seen, differs from the other managerial role which government must simultaneously fill—that of managing its own assets in the effectuation of its own organizational objectives. The two roles are related, since each affects the other, but they are distinct, and the distinction is important conceptually. The justification for an action or an expenditure may depend on one role rather than the other. An example is provided by an exchange between a U.S. Senator and an economist who were discussing the advisability of a capital budget for the Federal government, in the course of which the Senator remarked:

> You said you would advocate a concept of public investment which includes outlays for education, scientific research, etc.
>
> It is a wonderful idea but where do you stop?
>
> You get into a situation where you put almost everything in the capital part of your budget. I think you are right that probably the best investment we can make is in training and education, but how can you really call it capital? ... Would you actually isolate educational expenditures and say the Youth Employment Act, the expenditures involved in this manpower training, and any aid for education, all as part of the capital investment?
>
> You certainly would not say there was an increase in the government's net-worth position? [1]

The Senator was of course right in respect to the government's own asset position, but not in respect to the nation's. He was applying to government in its economy-managing function, tests which were relevant to the managerial function of its public-business capacity. Failure to distinguish between these two functions can introduce gross distortions into cost-benefit comparisons by leaving out of the calculation costs and benefits arising elsewhere in the economy but attributable to government programs—in effect treating national assets as a nonexistent or at best philosophical category rather than an economic one.

NATIONAL ASSETS

National asset management must first start with an inventory of assets to be managed, since assets are not likely to be used effectively, or even used at all, unless they are first identified. There is no advantage in attempting to construct here a comprehensive checklist of national assets, as it would only divert our attention from the conceptual and analytical matters which are our chief interest. But we can readily identify four major types of assets which must occupy the attention of any government.

The most obvious is the natural resource structure of the economy, complete with provisions for continuing exploration and identification;

[1] *The Federal Budget as an Economic Document*, p. 26.

legal principles for encouraging private exploitation consistent with national interests; public regulation of private use of natural resources; public development of natural resources where private initiative is not feasible or cannot be relied on, including regional development; conservation measures in the light of long-term requirements; appropriate use of the domain to which public title is held.

An equally apparent asset is the population, from which the labor force derives, not in terms of numbers, or not only that, but even more importantly in terms of health and vigor, intellectual development, skills and training, moral and morale development, and geographical distribution. This is an asset of which we cannot simply say the more the better, in a purely quantitative sense of the larger the population, the greater the nation's wealth. There are circumstances when a larger population does represent a net gain, but other circumstances when it does not, and in most countries today there is greater economic gain from improving the quality and capabilities of the existing population than from adding to its numbers, and perhaps, too, more gain from a more diffused geographical distribution of people than from their continuing agglomeration in urban centers.

A third category of national asset is less obvious—an economy's private-proprietary productive facilities. We tend to think of the factories, department stores, shopping centers, insurance companies, and so on, as representing private wealth, and their inclusion as a national asset has an unpleasant connotation that socialism may be just around the corner. But of course that is not implied. It is only that we could not possibly describe the wealth of a nation and leave out of account its productive facilities. A country's GNP depends very largely on its business sector, and that is a fact without respect to ownership. General Motors, Renault, and Volkswagen each constitute the same national asset in the United States, France, and Germany, respectively, even though the first is wholly in private hands, the second is wholly publicly owned, and the third has both public and private proprietors. It is because privately owned business represents a national asset no less than publicly owned enterprise and has, as we think, certain added values of its own, that we foster the private-enterprise system. Moreover, it is an asset from which we can derive more or less, depending on the policies and programs which the government adopts affecting it.

The fourth national asset, and the last category which we shall list

here, is social-proprietary productive facilities. The distinction between private and public ownership is important less for any qualitative differences in the two classifications than to ensure that our
count of major productive facilities is complete. Schools, sanitation
services, telephone and telegraph networks, railways, and other operations may be either or both privately or publicly owned and operated,
even within the same country. Highways, fire and police protection,
military services, a passport division, a factory inspection system, and
so on, similarly supply goods and services important to the community. They represent producing assets no less than those in private
hands.

Classification always introduces its own problems of establishing dividing lines, but that is not vital here where we are concerned with the
general principle rather than specific totals. Whether an asset is private
or public is not always clear. Housing, for example, is usually private,
but collectively it helps to create a city which is more of a social asset.
An individual dwelling without the public facilities of roads, water,
sewage, protection, and so on, might still be a private asset, but it
would be quite a different one. From the standpoint of managing the
economy, the two types of ownership are important primarily in requiring different instruments for influencing their actions along lines
which comport with national objectives.

With respect to all national assets, whatever their classification, the
function of the government is clear—to preserve and enhance their
value. As in the case of the firm, this requires continual attention to the
effects of change on the form in which assets should be maintained;
over time there must be a continual metamorphosis of assets in order to
preserve their value. Changing tastes and technology affect the use to
be made of natural resources—even what resources must be viewed as
assets. Pure water and air, which in one stage of development might be
taken for granted as free gifts of nature, in a later, urbanized, stage
require special provision for their preservation. The body of knowledge held by the population is subject to continuing erosion due to
discoveries of new knowledge, and foresight is required to prevent a
diminishing value of this asset. The raising of standards with the
passage of time, as well as changes in the style of living, can lower the
economic usefulness of that part of the labor force which fails to
maintain the requisite standards of health or intellectual development
or adaptability; the rate of rejections of young men called up for mili-

tary service is statistical testimony to the pressing needs of human redevelopment if these resources are to be salvaged.

Similarly, the steady if not quickening pace of physical deterioration of our cities; the mounting problems of slum clearance and their replacement; the spectacular need for attention to the problems of public transportation before our highways are frozen with private cars and the airways and airport facilities become clogged to the limits of danger, while rail transport remains relatively backward and underutilized; the redevelopment of whole regions which have been allowed to become economically sicker over a period long enough to make their recovery the more intractable—these are examples of situations where the government, as coordinator of the economy, has failed or is in the act of failing to move promptly enough to metamorphose assets *before* they have lost much of their value.

SYSTEM AND SUBSYSTEMS

If we think of our economy as the system, composed of a number of subsystems, we are back with many of the same problems which we confronted in examining the business firm. In this case the organization is of course vastly more complicated: among the subsystems are governments at all levels, in their public-business functions, including the national government itself. Each business firm is a subsystem. If we chose to be comprehensive, we would have to add that each spending unit—each household—is a subunit of the overall system.

Without attempting such completeness of detail, it is enough if we recognize that the economy as the system is made up of numerous subsystems of varying importance. Each of these has its own objectives, which are consonant in some respects with, and divergent in other respects from, the overall objectives of the economy. As we earlier noted, some divergence is inescapable. The differences in function, in responsibilities, in interests, in foresight, all guarantee that the goals of each component diverge in some respect from what we recognize as the objective of all these treated as a functioning whole. There is no escape from it. Each individual, let alone each organization, takes his point of departure from a perspective which is inevitably different from the perspective of any other individual or organization. Each must be allowed to achieve as much of his own objective as may be necessary to preserve his functioning in the system, yet at the same time each must contribute enough to the overall objective to preserve his position in the system. We have been through this before and need not dwell on it again.

The national government, in its role as top management and co-ordinator of the parts of the sytsem, works through a network of hierarchical and lateral relationships to effect the synthesis or integration which achieves as nearly as possible the objectives of the system. Internally, within its own organizational structure, it can rely on its own hierarchical authority to elicit responses. On the strength of that authority it can establish at each organizational level the premises which not only define the discretion which is permitted to the level below but which also assign tasks to that subunit, within the overall plan. Whether those tasks relate to the production of goods and services (the operation of a TVA or a national park, for example), the regulation of private industry (through a railroad or waterways commission, for example), the definition of policies or the drafting of legislation (by a Bureau of the Budget or a Council of Economic Advisers, for example), the conduct of fiscal affairs (through tax collections and subsidy disbursements, for example)—in any of these actions or programs of the government the hierarchical authority both permits discretion, within the premises drawn for any unit by its higher authority, and requires responses.

Within the governmental establishment there are a multitude of lateral relationships as well, such as those between "autonomous" departments whose functions are related to each other or overlap. In these instances relationships are bargained out, but if there is disagreement or dissatisfaction, the question can be pursued to some higher level of authority where a decision can be imposed.

But externally, that is, outside the governmental organization, the situation is quite different. The government, within the limits of the authority which it is constitutionally or legislatively granted, can establish limits of discretion for all other units in the system. These are the premises within the bounds of which both private business firms and autonomous local governments can pursue their own objectives, divergent though these may be in some respects from the overall objectives of the system. But with respect to these external relations the national government cannot normally assign tasks which represent affirmative responses which must be performed within these discretionary limits, as it can do within its own hierarchical structure. The national government in a private-enterprise economy cannot instruct business firms what they shall produce, at what prices, at what times, nor can it require that cities establish fire departments and road networks and incinerators for rubbish disposal. Wartime is the notable exception which underscores the normal lack of such power: in time of war the national government comes into *extraordinary* power to exact responses from private and public subunits, to control their actions not only by limiting more tightly their discretion to pursue their own partially divergent objectives, but also by requiring the performance of tasks which are assigned to them.

But in normal times such affirmative actions may not be compelled. The Federal government, in its capacity as manager of the overall economy, seeking to integrate the numerous components of that system in ways which facilitate the achievement of its objectives, can use its hierarchical authority (which we call sovereignty) to limit private discretion, but it must induce the affirmative responses which it seeks.

What may at first appear as exceptions on second inspection usually turn out to be such. In the United States, for example, the Federal government can require a business firm to negotiate with a union chosen by a majority of employees and to pay taxes for special purposes such as social security and to meet certain standards if it is in the business of manufacturing drugs or processing foods, and so on, but none of these require a firm to stay in business or to perform any specific productive functions. They are more in the nature of true constraints—requirements which must be met as a condition of doing business, premises which limit the firm's discretion to pursue its objectives in its own way.

Thus the national government can limit the divergence between system and subsystem objectives by law and by administrative action, in a hierarchical relationship, but it can elicit the performance which it wants from the system's subunits only by inducements, in a lateral type of relationship. To be sure, what is presented here as a rather sharp dichotomy breaks down and becomes fuzzy at the edges: major business firms and autonomous local governments, once in being, seldom suspend operations, and once they are in being, the central government can sometimes use its powers in a regulatory way that has the effect of authoritative assignment of a task or imposition of a duty. In order to run a railroad or an airline at all, a firm may have to provide certain kinds of service at certain rates. In some countries, housing rentals may be fixed by law and "unreasonable" prices may be lowered. Government contracts with private business can be made the basis for exacting conditions of performance. But in a private-enterprise economy the national government simply does not have all the power which would be necessary to run the economy as though it were a single organization, like a gigantic business firm. Whatever the exceptions, the general rule prevails: in order to secure even an approximate version of effective integration of the component parts into a working system, the government must obtain the actions it wants by persuasion and inducement.

Under some circumstances, certain wanted actions may be difficult to induce, and part of the price which the government may have to pay to secure the desired performance may be a relaxation of the constraints or premises limiting private discretion, permitting the private unit or local government to pursue its own somewhat divergent objectives more actively, at the expense of the system objectives. To encourage private investment, a more tolerant depreciation policy may be allowed. To secure participation in retraining or area redevelopment programs, the national government may have to permit local jurisdictions to exercise certain veto powers in administration.

When actions are more easily induced, or where the government's compulsive powers are extended as in wartime, the constraints or premises can be more tightly drawn, and the leakage of national purpose through the divergent objectives of subunits can be lessened. Thus the national government, as manager and coordinator of the economy, must manipulate as it can the private and autonomous relationships of which the system is composed, using for this purpose such limited powers as it possesses.

From the viewpoint of the subunits the manipulative powers often loom large and ominous and compelling. From the viewpoint of the government, seeking the integrative result, the manipulative powers often seem puny and ineffective. Both perspectives have their validity. Circumstances change, and as they do, the relative bargaining advantage of the government as coordinator and the subunit being coordinated change too. In periods of distress and emergency—not only war, but large-scale unemployment—the government's coercive powers are likely to become greater without even the need for a formal redrafting of the premises. In periods of relative calm and prosperity, the efforts of a government to get on with programs looking to future needs may meet with resistance and apathy which it lacks the power to overcome.

What we can be sure of is that there will always be a political tug-of-war going on between the government in a private-enterprise economy, as it seeks to manage the national assets in ways which achieve its interpretation of the national objectives, and the subunits with their varying degrees of autonomy in the pursuit of their more specialized goals. National objectives will have to be compromised at times, to gain ground at all, and subunit objectives will have to be subordinated to the needs of the economy at other times if the subunits—private enterprise, local government—are to continue to play meaningful roles in the system. At times the constraints or premises which limit the discretion of subunits will be very loose, and the divergence between system and subsystem will widen; at other times the legal and administrative premises will be more tightly drawn, to secure greater convergence of objectives. This is the same process of alternating centralization and decentralization which we observed at work in the firm. The process continues when the firm itself becomes a subsystem within the larger system of the national economy.

GOVERNMENTAL INITIATIVE ON ITS OWN AUTHORITY

The function of government in its economic planning role is, we have said, to manage the nation's assets, consisting broadly of its natural resources, its manpower, its private and public enterprises, in such a way as to achieve the nation's objectives through time. This involves both the securing of an acceptable return on existing assets in the short run—acceptable in composition as well as level—and the growth and metamorphosis of the nation's assets in the long run. In accomplishing this managerial function, there are certain actions which the government can initiate within its own organizational structure. There are other supporting actions which it must induce from subunits which are more or less autonomous. It is the former which we shall now consider.

The government's budget is a financial statement of its intended initiative. As we noted in the previous chapter, it serves two purposes. In the first instance it spells out the public-business actions and programs with which the government is concerned. The financing of these constitutes its fiscal policy, and until relatively recently was viewed as the major if not the sole purpose of fiscal policy. But as the scale of governmental financial operations has expanded, their influence on the performance of the economy as a whole has become measurably greater, obligating the government to take this into account. The more explicitly and systematically it does so, the closer does it come to fitting its fiscal measures to the needs of the total economic perform-ance. Thus the shifting role of fiscal policy has been the major factor propelling governments into economic planning.[2]

The early stages of this reorientation of thinking with respect to the budget emphasized compensatory anticyclical policy, with deficits in depressions and surpluses in booms. This restricted the government's managerial role in the economy chiefly to categorical objectives—overall levels of output, the size of the GNP rather than its composi-tion. The original conception of the budget as the financial plan for the government's own business lingered on to the extent that a balancing of outgo against income was still considered essential over the course of a cycle. It is only in the last few years that the idea has gained ground that the first function of the government's budget is not to finance its own carefully delimited operations, even including counter-cyclical activities, but to serve as a national instrument for continu-ously promoting the growth of the whole economy. The need for any balance of governmental income and outgo—in the current year or over any time span—loses relevance. It is the pursuit of the nation's time stream of objectives which counts, the undertaking of programs important to national growth, either on governmental initiative or by private enterprise, financed either by current revenues or by debt. Fiscal policy is simply a means for dividing GNP between private and public expenditures, depending on which is more relevant to the meet-ing of identified needs, and depending on which sector possesses the

---

[2] Sir Herbert Brittain comments in *The British Budgetary System* (London: George Allen & Unwin, Ltd., 1959), p. 30: "In that Budget of 1853, Mr. Glad-stone had practically nothing to say about the general economic condition of the country or the state of its overseas balance. Compare this with the structure of the Chancellor of the Exchequer's Budget speech in 1957.... Successive sections of his speech dealt with the balance of payments, the internal economy generally, the Exchequer outturn for 1956-7 and prospects for 1957-8, the eco-nomic prospects for 1957-8, monetary policy and Budget objectives. He then con-sidered 'to what extent and in what directions he could properly reduce taxation, having regard to the state of the economy'.... This reorientation of the Budget into a wider economic setting may be said to date from 1941."

more appropriate instrumentalities and demonstrates the greater ebul-
liency in meeting those needs, including specific as well as categorical
objectives.

It is this newer conception of the government's managerial role in
the economy that has opened much wider the range of its activities in
the Western private-enterprise economies in the years following
World War II. The government's budget has expanded to include
numerous activities which formerly were left largely to local authorities or business firms. In such matters as education, housing, industrial
and pure research, the central government's role has grown enormously, even within an antiplanning atmosphere such as still prevails in
the United States. The enlarged sphere of activity is regarded as necessary to the nation's long-run survival and growth, supporting rather
than weakening local and private initiative. Although the thought may
not be made explicit, the underlying rationalization is that by these
programs the government is assisting in preserving and enhancing the
value of the nation's assets, including those within the jurisdiction of
local public authorities and private business firms.

Under this new fiscal approach, the government's share in national
income can be used for current consumption (either its own or—
through transfers of income—that of others) or for investment. These
can be made to serve the purposes of short-run stimulation or restraint
of economic activity, geared to the achievement of longer-run objectives, with much less emphasis on the financial and much more regard
to the programmatic aspects. To the extent that the net effect of its
programs is to preserve and expand the value of the nation's assets,
they are virtually self-justifying—virtually, but not entirely, since the
equity aspects of the distribution of income and power cannot be left
out of account and are not automatically provided for by economic
growth.

At any point in time, the degree of influence which a government
can exercise over the economy depends in part on the degree of its
involvement in the economy in its public-business capacity. This is
not because, or not only because, the larger the latter, the larger its
share of the national income. It is also, and perhaps mainly, because the
larger the public-business sector, the larger the sphere within which
the government can exercise initiative, can not only draw limits of
discretion for subunits, but can also elicit affirmative responses through
exercise of an hierarchical (organizational) authority. A government

whose activities account for 5 percent of GNP has less of a base from which to effect the economy as a whole, through its own initiative, than does one which is responsible for 25 percent of GNP. A government whose activities run in a great many directions has more avenues for influencing the private sector than one which must confine its operations to a few select paths. It should hardly require saying that this is simply an analytical proposition and not an argument for expanding the government's role.

The significant consideration is that over the years the share of the government sector in Western economies has been growing. To take only one, but an outstanding example, in the United Kingdom, "the total of public expenditure of all kinds, including that of the Government above and below the line, that of local authorities, of national insurance funds, and the capital expenditures of nationalized industries, represents about 42 percent of the gross national product." [3] Add to this the further fact that central governments have been increasing their already substantial control over the financial affairs of local governments, a tendency even more marked in Europe than in the United States, and the expanded possibilities for governmental actions in the pursuit of national objectives become even more evident.

This latter development has come about not so much through any conscious design on the part of the central administration as through the ineluctable requirements of a fiscal policy appropriate to the expanded role of the public sector. A national standard of health and education, for example, let alone of public highways, cannot be made good by throwing the financial burden on local authorities, with their grossly varying financial capacities. Only through the pooling and redistribution of funds on a national basis can such important services be made even approximately uniform throughout a country. In some instances the central administration may itself assume a greater authority over the function, but in other cases it provides only the financing, usually through grants-in-aid, leaving the function itself to local administration, perhaps subject to certain limitations of discretion with respect to standards (the drawing of the premises within which local autonomy may be exercised).

Several explanations for the accelerated growth of the public sector have been advanced. We have already encountered the view that with

[3] *Control of Public Expenditure*, Report of the Plowden Committee presented to Parliament by the Chancellor of the Exchequer, July, 1961, p. 6.

rising levels of national income, private consumer needs become relatively better met than collective needs, because of primary reliance on the market as the allocator of income, output, and investment. This leads to an imbalance in want satisfaction which can only be corrected by greater emphasis on public programs. In the words of the *Norwegian Long-term Programme 1962–1965*, "As incomes increase the relationship between private and public consumption will come more to the fore. In order to avoid the unfortunate distortions in consumption patterns, public consumption must continue to increase more rapidly than private consumption. At the same time higher incomes and structural changes in the economy will lead to greater demand for public investment.[4]

Two English economists have come up with a different explanation. In their view, crises such as wars lead to higher tax burdens than would otherwise be tolerated, to which people then become accustomed. After the emergency has passed there occurs a "displacement effect," in which the higher tax rate, or at least some portion of it, is retained but the proceeds are diverted to social welfare programs.[5] An example of this process currently—or potentially—at work is provided in the United States by official government and professional economic preoccupation with the question of "displacement" programs if military expenditures arising out of the cold war should be drastically reduced.

A third consideration relates more to the future. It has been suggested[6] that since the long-run tendency is for consumers to move from expenditures on durable ("hardware") goods to outlay for services such as travel and entertainment, and since the service sector

[4] Translation of extracts from the *Norwegian Long-term Programme 1962–1965*, Ministry of Finance, p. 4.

The same thought appears in the English-language *Summary of Prof. Saraceno's Report on the Italian Economic Development Plan*, University of Urbino, Ancona, Italy, December, 1963, pp. 6–7: "...certain institutions and activities which are of basic interest for the country's economic and social progress, are not sufficiently organized and do not receive the requisite funds to enable them to develop on a par with the country's present income level. The fact is that the striking development of private consumption over the past few years has been the decisive factor in deploying our society's available resources according to priorities which do not correspond to what—it is thought—are the real needs of that society."

[5] Alan Peacock and Jack Wiseman, "The Past and Future of Public Spending," *Lloyds Bank Review*, April, 1961, pp. 1–20.

[6] Among others, by M. Roger Nathan, in conversation in Paris in the summer of 1962. This argument contains elements of the Harrod-Domar growth model.

typically does not require the same rate of investment as the durable-goods sector, then private investment over time may become increasingly incapable of putting savings to work. Under these circumstances the more economically advanced a country, the more difficult would it be for it to maintain its growth rate—short of diversion of a growing proportion of GNP to public investment. A shift in the structure of private consumer wants, attributable to rising incomes, creates a disproportion between the rate of growth of national income and the rate of growth of investment necessary to sustain it, unless the structure of investment too is changed.

For these and perhaps other reasons, the proportion of national income subject to governmental disposition has been growing and will probably continue to grow. This enlarged public sector provides the government with greater power itself to initiate actions conducive to the achievement of national objectives. The sphere in which it may require responses as a matter of its own hierarchical authority expands relative to the sphere in which it must induce actions by others. The governmental budget becomes an ever more powerful instrument for manipulating the economy.

The country in which this power has been most evident in recent years is France, since among the Western nations it has moved most vigorously toward a planning approach. It has explicitly assumed the task of managing national assets to achieve national objectives, through systematic coordination of the components of the economic system. As we have seen, the Fourth Plan (1962–1965) moved quite openly toward an increase in social investment in such areas as education, health, and urban development, to avoid a "waste" of national resources on consumer "gadgets." But such a structuring of consumption could be attempted with relatively modest *proportionate* increases in governmental outlay because the public sector was already so large and varied. With appropriate shifts of emphasis and direction in the total array of public programs, each by itself quite modest, a major shift in the orientation of the economy toward the future could be initiated.

The influence of such government initiative on the economy need not be limited to its own expenditures. Its own budgeted programs can be made to exert a leverage effect on subunits in the system. We shall explore this influence more fully in the next section, in which we examine inducements to private actions. But it is worth noting at this point that programs in which the government holds the power of initiative may by themselves elicit affirmative responses, without further inducement. By initiating certain actions, the government may rationalize complementary moves by private business.[7]

Because of the importance of the public sector in the economy, wherever a plan exists the government cannot escape the responsibility for guiding its own initiative in the light of national objectives as expressed in the plan. In fact, it has been claimed—in Norway and Belgium, for example—that the principal value of a national plan lies in the guidance it offers to government, fragmented as it is into a number of ministries and agencies, whose efforts must be coordinated through the governmental budget. Since the government exercises hierarchical authority within its own organization, it can produce results there more surely than in the private sector, where it must rely on inducement. The existence of a plan ensures that it does not waste that opportunity by uncertainty of objective. The plan informs it of the results which it should seek in the exercise of its authority. In the absence of a plan, there is no firm standard to which the competing objectives of department and ministry heads can be referred for resolution, and the budget which emerges is likely to represent chiefly compromises induced by bargains among subunits with divergent goals.

In France, since 1963 the Ministry of Finance has required that annual budget proposals of the several ministries be prepared with explicit reference to their relationship to the four-year plan. In Nor-

[7] M. Pierre Massé, French Planning Commissioner, has described one such situation: "During the past year or two we have put stress on the development of our Western regions, especially Brittany and adjacent departments. Some years ago, a large automobile plant was established in Rennes. We thought for a while that a center of development at Rennes could save the situation in Brittany. After study, we realized that this was not sufficient and so we are placing another center of development in Brest. A large electronics factory is at present in the process of construction there—a pilot plant—and last Monday I laid the cornerstone of a factory that will begin operations next year at Saint-Brieuc.

"I think I can tell you that without the action of the Plan, without the agreement that has been established between the industries on the one hand, and the various governmental administrations on the other, all this could not have been translated into reality. It could only be done because technical and engineering schools are being founded in Brest, because the housing programs in Brest have taken this influx into account, finally because a domestic airline now connects Paris with Brest, which permits the managers of these concerns to make the trip from Paris to Brest and back in twenty-four hours." CEPES, *French and Other National Economic Plans for Growth*, pp. 11–12.

way, the figures for government operations incorporated in the national plan, also for four years, constitute "quantitative directives or instructions to the government agencies concerned." [8] In the Netherlands, departmental heads have been taught to look to the Central Planning Bureau for guidance. A procedure has been devised whereby the plan, in a tentative formulation, informally instructs the government budget, and the latter, when completed, formally provides the basis for the plan.

The practice in the United States stands in marked contrast to such efforts to relate the government budget to the overall economy, and both to national long-term objectives. In an article with the forthright title, "The Federal Budget—There Must be a Better Way," the *Morgan Guaranty Survey* recently commented:

> The piecemeal approach taken by Congress gives the annual budget exercise a haphazard character which, if fully realized, would shock most taxpayers. Surpluses or deficits are not planned. They just happen. Reasons and responsibility for the way the budget turns out are hard to pin down.[9]

The United States practice might well have provided the text for the financial sermon of the Plowden Committee's 1961 report:

> Decisions involving substantial future expenditure should always be taken in the light of surveys of public expenditure as a whole, over a period of years, and in relation to the prospective resources. Public expenditure decisions, whether they be in defence of education or overseas aid or agriculture or pensions or anything else, should never be taken without consideration of (a) what the country can afford over a period of years having regard to prospective resources and (b) the relative importance of one kind of expenditure against another. This may appear to be self-evident, but in administrative (and, we would hazard the opinion, in political) terms it is not easy to carry out.[10]

INDUCING AFFIRMATIVE ACTIONS

By far the largest proportion of economic activity in Western societies is private and local, in contrast to the centralized governmental initia-

[8] Bjerve, *Planning in Norway, 1947–1956*, p. 20.
[9] April, 1964, p. 4.
[10] *Control of Public Expenditure*, p. 5.

tives which we have just been considering. If the operations of numerous business firms and local authorities are to be "coordinated" in the pursuit of national objectives, this cannot be achieved by order or decree (the exercise of hierarchical authority) but by inducement and persuasion (the establishment of a network of lateral—literally co-ordinate—relations). The central government possesses a number of unique powers which it can use for this purpose, and at times the distinction between inducement and compulsion becomes rather hazy. Nevertheless, there are two genuine limitations on its capacity to gather control over the economy as a whole into its hands.

The first of these is political. In private-enterprise economies the sphere of governmental authority is delimited by constitution and legislation. The second is administrative. Centralization of control over the economy, pursued too far, leads to inefficiency and is self-defeating. The question of efficiency or inefficiency is of course always relative to objectives. In time of war we accept central controls which are inefficient by peacetime standards because they further an objective which, under the circumstances, transcends all other objectives. At such times we exclude all competing purposes and draw tighter the premises to which subunit decisions and actions "must" conform. But except in the event of such overriding emergency we weigh carefully the costs of inefficiency resulting from centralized administration.

Within the powers accorded it, the government, as manager of the nation's assets in the pursuit of national objectives, faces the problem of how to induce affirmative actions which may be needed to achieve national objectives, but which cannot be compelled. The objectives, the powers accorded the government, the institutional strength of the private and local authorities whose activities are affected, and the systematic nature of the government's effort (degree of planning) differ from one country to another, but the managerial role remains the same.

In performing that managerial function, a government must be concerned with the kind of activity which is wanted—with the direction in which the economy is headed. This is a qualitative matter and is concerned with what we have here labeled specific objectives. It must also be concerned with the level of economic activity, a quantitative result which is covered by the categorical objectives. What is specific and what categorical depends on the level of aggregation. If industrial research is viewed only as a contributor to some target investment total, it constitutes no separate target in its own right. It is only one of a number of components which go to make up the larger, more aggregative, categorical objective; whether there is more or less of it is inconsequential as long as the investment total is realized. But if some level of industrial research investment is identified as a target, this becomes a specific objective relative to the larger category of total investment. (Relative to the particular research projects which compose it and which can be substituted for each other in achieving it, it now constitutes a categorical objective.)

A government impinges on private and local operations most directly and most intensively in the case of specific objectives. By definition it will use its authority as necessary to elicit the action wanted from those who are in a position to provide it. Conversely, a government impinges indirectly, though extensively, in the case of categorical objectives: more firms and local authorities are affected, but precisely because of their number the government need not exert major influence on any one to secure the overall result which is sought. If some do not respond to inducements, others will.

As we have noted, in times of emergency, when national efforts must be coordinated to some central purpose, the emphasis is on specific objectives. In the period in which modern planning programs took shape, postwar reconstruction provided the most notable example. The Norwegian experience is illustrative:

> During the entire post-war period, government agencies have to a considerable degree determined the magnitude of aggregate investment and the structure of investment by means of controls. . . . For a large part of total investment, control agencies have made decisions as to *what kind* of demand and *whose* demand should be curtailed. This means that they have determined how much each industry could expand its various types of capital equipment and which firms within the industry should be permitted to invest. . . . Thus, the budgeting of investment represents an attempt of the government at controlling investment systematically instead of letting investment in each industry be determined more or less by a queuing up of applicants.[11]

[11] Bjerve, *Planning in Norway, 1947–1956*, pp. 204–205. On pp. 212–213 he adds: "...the national budget publication for 1947 advocated the following specific goals for the development of manufacturing industries:
  a) A great increase in the capacity of the electro-chemical and electro-metallurgic industries.

Normally, however, specific objectives represent a much smaller proportion of overall economic activity. Even in a country as planned as France the vast majority of business establishments are affected by the plan only indirectly. Nevertheless, the Commissioner of Planning, Pierre Massé, has commented that he believes "specific objectives are essential for the large basic sectors, as, for example, electricity and steel, and if electricity and steel failed to reach these figures, then the Fourth Plan could not succeed." [12]

The most categorical of objectives is a rate of growth in national income, and the instruments used to achieve that goal are suitably general. The more specific objectives are quite varied. Some relate to current operations—particular results which are wanted in the present period, such as imports or exports of a particular magnitude (a specific objective relative to total GNP) or to specific goods needed for military services or to satisfy foreign aid commitments. Others relate to identified projects which can be brought to completion in the longer run only if pushed along now—a new dam or roadway, modernization of the facilities of a major industry, the overhaul of a transportation system, regional rehabilitation, an improved educational system. The inducements offered to private enterprises and local governments to undertake activities leading to the realization of such assorted goals must be similarly varied.

SPECIFIC OBJECTIVES

One type of specific objective which is frequently encountered is a disproportionate rate of growth for some industry or cluster of industries which is considered strategic. Whether electric power or steel, housing construction or ship construction, oil refining or rail transportation, certain industries are selected for a concentrated expansion

---

b) Development of an effective food-freezing industry and expansion of the herring and cod liver oil industry.
c) Expansion of certain branches of the engineering industry, particularly the electrical machinery industry and the shipbuilding industry.
d) Expansion of the building industry, to meet the requirement of the extensive housing program.
e) Extensive modernization of the paper and pulp industry and its subsidiary industries."

[12] "Planning in France," in *Planning*, Papers read at the Business Economists' Conference, New College, Oxford, April 5–8, 1962, pp. 20–21.

effort. The intent may be to provide essential complementary facilities or to encourage diversification of national assets or to develop new centers of economic strength, and to carry through such an intent on a more accelerated schedule than the industries in question would be able or inclined to do on their own. Extra incentive is provided.

In some instances governments have extended special inducements not to industries generally but to individual (almost always large-scale) firms willing to expand in directions which appear especially promising for national development. Sometimes the initiative comes from a corporate management which is capable of projecting its future operations along lines which promise external benefits broadly supportive of long-run national objectives. At other times it is the governmental authorities who stimulate an interest in corporate managements by pointing out how a business's goal of a rate of return on an expanding asset base can be sought in directions which an unfolding national plan supports (and vice versa) and who dangle a few carrots of financial inducements to add to the attractiveness of the picture they paint.

Perhaps the most common device used to encourage desired investments is simply making available long-term loans at less than market rates of interest. Thus the Fonds de Développement Économique et Social in France was responsible for approximately 6 percent of total gross investment in 1961, with terms running to thirty-three years and rates at up to 3 percent below the market. The Planning Commissioner sits on the board which allocates the fund's resources. France's Caisse des Dépôts et Consignations, which is a kind of central repository for savings funds from around the country, specializes in loans to municipalities for public investments that fall in line with national programs and to a lesser extent does the same for private business ventures. As an example of the kind of influence these two funds are capable of exercising, they jointly took the initiative in putting together the financial arrangements which made possible the sweeping reorganization of the basic steel industry in the northeast region in the late fifties.

In Belgium the Société Nationale de Crédit à l'Industrie performs a somewhat similar lending function, but so far its use to effectuate specific plan objectives has been more talked about than acted on. Nevertheless, special credits at reduced rates of interest are available to firms and industries whose activities are considered of special importance to economic expansion or which are pioneering new products.

The use of special-purpose banks or lending agencies established and financed by governments, or the availability of government funds for special purposes through private banking institutions is also a common device. Norway has perhaps gone as far in this direction as any country. In addition to the Housing Bank, which has financed close to three-fourths of home construction in recent years, there is a Municipalities Bank (for power plants, schools, and other local investments), a Small Holding and Housing Bank which is geared to rural housing and farm investments, and an Industry Bank which handles hotel financing as well as industrial needs. These state banks are responsible for approximately one-third of all domestically supplied credit. Since the government establishes the total credit which each of these specialized banks can extend and can, if it wishes, prescribe priorities among loan requests within each of these banking sectors, it has a powerful instrument for influencing not only the total volume of investment credit, but also its composition. It is interesting to note that the United States, no less than the planning countries, has recognized specific objectives to the extent of creating specialized credit agencies for agriculture, small business, home construction, importing firms, fisheries, and other purposes.

Governments can encourage the extension of private credit to business and local authorities whose operations are considered to further specific national objectives by guaranteeing lending agencies against loss. This practice has been followed in France, the United Kingdom, and the United States, among others. In France, the Finance Act every year authorizes the Ministry to underwrite any credit extension, of any duration, considered important to plan realization. In effect, economic activity in areas considered important is encouraged by the social pooling of private risk.

The access of companies to the capital markets sometimes requires specific governmental authorization, at least for issues over a specified amount, as in France, Norway, and Italy. The primary purpose is to space such issues so that they do not bunch to create a disorderly market —"calendaring," as the process is called—but it can also be made to serve a secondary substantive interest by according priority to funding operations which are most closely in line with socioeconomic objectives. The procedure encourages preliminary conversations between governmental authorities and the issuing firm, sometimes leading to modification in investment programs in ways more closely effectuating specific goals.

Still other types of financial incentives may induce firms to undertake desired capital programs. Tax concessions are sometimes granted. In France, dividends up to 5 percent of new capital may be exempted from the profits tax for a period of seven years, providing the new capital investment has been approved by the Planning Commissioner. Depreciation allowances more favorable than standard provisions have been negotiated with individual firms or industries.

Subsidies for housing and construction have been employed quite generally throughout Europe and the United States. The United States has granted subsidies for construction and operation of commercial shipping and for the operation of private airlines. Explorations for minerals deemed important to national defense have also been generously supported from the public treasury.

Some governments have not hesitated to make direct investments in private companies for the purpose of promoting projects of special interest. Belgium participates in the financing of new enterprises and industries through its Société Nationale d'Investissements, as does France through its Fonds de Développement, and Italy through its Istitúto per la Ricostruzióne Industriàle. It has been proposed in Sweden that the very sizable national pension fund be put to similar use, and a comparable suggestion has been made in England with respect to the proposed National Superannuation Fund. In these cases government financing gives the state considerable leverage to shape investments in ways which further the overall interests of the economic system.

The influence of this assortment of credit and financial controls and benefits in the furtherance of specific objectives often operates quite subtly. In the first instance, it encourages more frequent consultation between major private investors and the public authorities, with the possibility that each may enlighten the other. In the second instance, the existence of a long-term national plan encourages business firms to guide their own asset development along lines whose value in part derives from the congruence of public and private objectives. Managements are led by normal business instincts to "zero in" on investment projects, the payoff on which is, in a loose sense, underwritten by the government program. This in turn allows the government to respond to a larger array of business plans and predilections which are broadly supportive of national goals, reducing the size of any special inducement which may be needed to bring private and public plans into closer alignment.

In addition to the more familiar credit and financial instruments we have noted, there are some less common which are worthy of attention if only because they raise more pointedly the issue of government influence on private actions. France has made use of a device which it calls the "quasi-contract." First employed in 1957 in an agreement between the government and the automobile industry, whereby in exchange for fiscal benefits the industry consented to export two-thirds of additional production, the quasi-contract became formalized in the Interim Plan of 1960: "The State may undertake to facilitate the carrying out in good time of the financial operations necessary for the execution of the Plan and may grant certain financial advantages in line with laws presently in force. In return, industrialists will undertake to carry out the investment, research, and production programs agreed on."

As the language implies, this amounts to governmental negotiation of a contract for specific business performance in exchange for a package of financial favors. Such negotiated agreements with individual firms, and sometimes with industries composed of a few large establishments, permit stronger governmental influence over corporate operations. Qualms have sometimes been expressed at the degree of government involvement in the affairs of a firm which this may encourage, but this worry has been countered with the argument that the arrangement is voluntary.

It can even be argued that the French quasi-contract is not remarkably different in effect from negotiated agreements between the U.S. Department of Defense and major U.S. corporations for the purchase of military systems; when the value of such contracts with individual companies runs as high as $1 billion for a single system, as it has, this cannot help but exercise a considerable influence over corporate "investment, research, and production programs."

The United States has made use of an instrument even more directive in the allocation of national resources to specific objectives. In setting up the Communication Satellite Corporation, it called into existence a private corporation organized to perform a specific function. It has, of course, made use of *government* corporations previously, the

Tennessee Valley Authority being the best known among a number, but a profit-making corporation, financed by public subscription of individuals and private companies, opens up avenues to the accomplishment of national objectives through the enlistment of private initiative, outside the government's own budget.

By virtue of the range of its operations and authorities, a government always possesses indirect means of bargaining with business firms to induce specific actions. These, however, must be used with caution and infrequency to remain effective. In Norway, for example, electric power—some 80 percent of which is governmentally supplied—has been a scarce resource for which businesses compete. The government has been able to bargain with industry for the carrying out of a specific program by raising the specter of possible power concessions to foreign firms for the purpose, if home firms remain reluctant. In France there is a shortage of good roads and relatively few kilometers of superhighways. A tax on gasoline adds substantially to its price. The automobile industry is interested in more of the first and less of the second, both of which are in the power of government to grant. There is no basis for believing that it has used this power explicitly to obtain industry action, but it lurks in the background to be displayed occasionally as an additional influence. All such indirect bargaining counters are insignificant, however, alongside the financial inducements which we have noted.

OTHER TYPES OF SPECIFIC OBJECTIVES

In addition to investment in basic, expanding, or innovating industries, there are other specific objectives which have been asserted as embodying national interest. They are worth brief attention because they suggest the recent programmatic emphases of Western economic systems, the more systematic attention to management of the nation's assets. Perhaps the most frequently encountered are modernization of industry, industrial dispersion and regional expansion, enlargement of the export sector, encouragement of industrial research, and improvement in social services, particularly education. We shall not do more than mention some of the ways in which these objectives have been sought, since they frequently repeat in a more specialized form the kinds of instruments which have already been mentioned.

The modernization of industry was an inescapable accompaniment of postwar reconstruction, and, as European governments could not fail to be involved actively in the latter (*vide* the case of Norway, referred to a few pages back), they could not escape becoming immersed in the former. The first Western planning efforts in fact grew out of reconstruction needs and in addition were virtually necessitated by the terms of Marshall Plan aid. The planning programs of France, Norway, and the Netherlands fall into this category.

But the need for technological updating is a constant one. The United Kingdom enacted the Cotton Industry Act in 1959 to assist in the reorganization of the Lancashire cotton industry over a five-year period. Some public subsidy was provided as compensation for the "orderly elimination of excess capacity" in the form of the more antiquated mills, but the greater portion of the amounts provided went for grants of as much as one-fourth the cost of new machinery and equipment.[13]

In France grants for re-equipping industry have been tied closely to regional development, up to 20 percent of the cost being allowed for identified regions, in a formula which also takes into account the number of workers benefited. In other countries investment in modernized equipment may receive preferential credit treatment of the kind we have already encountered.

One of the highest priorities among recent national objectives has been given to the development of regions which have failed to participate in overall economic growth. Perhaps the most systematic effort has been made in France, where twenty-one so-called *tranches opératoires* or regional slices of the economy have been identified, within each of which a program is to be developed and made consistent with the national plan, inclusive of private as well as public investment projects, provision for the financing and phased construction of which are to be spelled out. Equipment subsidies, loans at preferential rates of interest, loan guarantees, and tax concessions are other devices which have been brought to bear. In an effort to force the dispersion of industry, strict controls over the construction or expansion of industry in the Paris region have been imposed, with the consequence that only 15 percent of industrial building permits were issued for this area in 1961 as compared with approximately 35 percent a decade earlier.

The United Kingdom has had similar problems with respect to the

[13] J. W. Grove, *Government and Industry in Britain* (London: Longmans, Green & Co., Ltd., 1962), p. 257.

concentration of industry in the London region. The Board of Trade, from which industrial establishments must obtain authorization to locate in an area, has clamped down severely on new construction in the crowded London vicinity and has used its powers to push industry into some of the less developed areas, including Wales and Scotland. Affirmatively, the Board of Trade is empowered to recommend building grants and "initial assistance" grants. Capital loans to firms locating or expanding in the so-called "development districts" are interest-free for up to 2½ years.

Belgium too has made use of capital loans at preferential rates for firms locating in specified regions. Norway has done likewise and has also offered tax concessions to firms dispersing their operations. Sweden has made use of its special investment fund program, which we shall shortly examine, to ease regional unemployment by encouraging private investment. State-assisted financing, over the five-year period 1957–1962, accounted for approximately one-third of total investment in Italy's Mezzogiorno. In the United States an Area Redevelopment Program enacted in 1961 provided governmental financing to stimulate the economic recovery of distressed areas by such devices as loans to create new or expand existing private enterprises in those areas; financial aid for the improvement of public facilities needed for industrial expansion; technical assistance in the development of new products, markets, and resources; and support for training programs directed to unemployed workers.

With few exceptions, most Western countries have had to emphasize a lively export trade as a basis for their own economic expansion. With economic growth comes a higher level of imports of materials and equipment which are needed to sustain the expansion, coupled with rising levels of import consumption. To finance these, exports must be increased.[14]

Encouragement to exports has been provided by giving priority to investments in export fields, by giving preference on the new-issues

[14] It is not the case, as has sometimes been carelessly implied, that this drive to expand exports on the part of all countries and thereby to achieve a satisfactory balance of payments cannot be jointly achieved, so that the export objective of one country necessarily conflicts with that of the others. Normally it is not a proportionate increase in the world's export trade which they seek, but an absolute increase in their own volume of trade, sufficient to pay for the higher level of imports which their growth requires, and that is an objective which all can mutually entertain.

calendar to export firms, by insuring exporters against loss from a variety of contingencies, and by giving exporting firms especially favorable depreciation allowances. With respect to this last provision, some 4,000 firms in France at the beginning of 1961 had been awarded a *carte d'exportateur*, signifying that at least 20 percent of their output was entering into foreign trade and entitling them to accelerated depreciation for tax purposes.

Industrial research has received special attention because of its obvious relation to economic growth. This is a field in which the United States has been especially active, supporting by public grants research in nonprofit institutions such as universities and, through contract awards, research in private industry. In addition to the financing of university research, the United Kingdom has also made public grants supplementing business research funds when these have been organized on a cooperative industry basis. France has encouraged research through loans at preferential rates, tax concessions, and outright grants.

In the field of social investment, a central government possesses the means for inducing local authorities to undertake programs conforming to national objectives through the devices of grants-in-aid and preferential loans. In essence these are the same devices which it uses with respect to private business. The grant or loan made to a business firm to encourage it to conduct research, to locate in an underdeveloped area, to expand its export trade, or to modernize its equipment is paralleled by the grant or loan made to a local authority to upgrade its educational facilities or undertake public housing projects or cooperate in a national health or old-age program or a variety of other welfare activities.

Governments have been less successful in providing technical assistance to local authorities in carrying out such programs. Particularly in smaller communities is technical expertise often lacking even in such familiar matters as the design, construction, and financing of schools. The lag between central authorization and local implementation is often a lengthy one and is at least partially explainable by the difficulties which local authorities have in managing the operation. Without usurping local prerogatives, governments could profitably give more attention to providing consulting and administrative services to these subunits.

FISCAL POLICY FOR CATEGORICAL OBJECTIVES

The specific objectives give tone and direction to society. They put the nation's resources in the services of those goals which have been singled out for concerted effort, over a time stream stretching into a future far enough to permit their phased accomplishment. But quantitatively they constitute a relatively small part of total economic activity. Most of the nation's productive machinery is employed in turning out a vast congeries of goods and services demanded by individual consumers in accordance with their tastes, however those may be formed, and demanded by business firms as investment in the plant, equipment, and inventory which are needed to satisfy consumer wants.

But this larger and more amorphous side of the economy is not unrelated to national goals. It provides much of the employment and growth which are the portmanteau objectives of the economy. By satisfying immediate wants more or less well it permits the siphoning-off of more or less resources for future development. It constitutes the level of activity which is necessary if the economy is to travel in the direction which the specific objectives mark out. Thus these overall magnitudes—like GNP and gross investment and consumption—have been identified here as categorical objectives. We are not much concerned in what form they are achieved as long as the total is reached. If certain firms or industries sell more and others sell less, this is a matter of relative indifference. Their actions offset each other. If certain households save more and others buy more, again it is of no concern as long as there are no major shifts in the total magnitudes of private saving and consumption which are necessary to the meshing of the system's parts.

The setting of categorical objectives means that at times the government must seek to stimulate and at other times to restrain the major categories of private investment, savings, and consumption. How well it carries out this assignment is as vital to its management of the economy as how effectively it pursues the specific objectives.

The general rule is that consumption and savings should both be sufficient to call forth the use of existing assets and the investment in new assets on which the desired rate of growth (the portmanteau objective) depends. We are here concerned only with the magnitudes of these flows and not with the terms (prices) on which goods and services exchange for money.

There are two principal instruments available to the government to make this rule effective—fiscal and monetary policy. These are old familiar friends, and there would be no point in belaboring their operation. Nevertheless, there are differences in the ways in which countries put them to work, and there is some justification for pausing long enough to indicate some of the principal practices.

Without exaggerating differences, the United Kingdom and Sweden may be taken as examples of two quite different approaches to the manipulation of the government budget to achieve the rates of business investment and household consumption appropriate to the total level of GNP projected and to the rate of saving. In Britain the emphasis is on adjustments in consumption flows as the key to reaching the overall target, while Sweden is more inclined to vary the rate of government and business investment.

The British policy is based—implicitly if not explicitly—on the premise that both government budgetary expenditures and business investments are planned in advance and involve commitments not easily revised—upward or downward. Thus any slack in the economy cannot readily be absorbed by a sudden expansion of either government or business spending which would expand GNP, via a multiplier effect, to levels at which voluntary saving would support the additional investment. Neither government nor business can respond so impulsively to changed circumstance. Time is required for them to adjust. Similarly, an excess of total expenditures cannot be readily curbed by retrenching on government or business outlays, since these for the most part involve commitments not easily withdrawn.

But consumer expenditure is another matter. With more money in the pocket, consumers will quickly find outlets for it. With reduced income their spending falls off. If business investment has not fully utilized the savings in the economy, a change in income tax rates can elicit compensating consumption outlays on relatively short notice. Since the Chancellor of the Exchequer has the authority to initiate tax-rate changes, he can thus rather readily redistribute GNP in favor of or against households, thereby also changing the proportions of savings and investment in the income stream.[15]

[15] J. C. R. Dow comments in *Les Prévisions Budgétaires*, p. 153: "A British Chancellor of the Exchequer is in a position of unique strength among the Finance

Tax increases to curtail consumption at a time when government and business are absorbing a larger share of GNP are, it is true, politically difficult. Realistically, tax adjustments must be downward, except in times of emergency when people are prepared to make sacrifices. But as we have previously noted, with rising levels of per capita GNP, and with a shift from goods to services, periodic downward tax adjustments are more likely to be needed to stimulate an advanced economy than upward adjustments to restrain it. If restraint is needed from time to time, it can be better achieved through monetary policy. Thus a combination of tax reduction to stimulate consumption when that is needed (more frequently the case in Britain) and tighter credit controls, affecting both investment and consumption, when the economy becomes "overheated," appears to meet British needs best.[16]

Sweden has adopted a different route to securing its categorical objectives—that of adjusting government and business spending as needed, to balance gross saving at full-employment levels of GNP. A number of measures are available to the government to provide a stimulus when one is needed. For one thing, parliament customarily votes an emergency standby budget for public works, supplementary to the regular annual budget, available at the government's discretion in the event of slackness in the economy. In addition, the government provides subsidies to local authorities to plan investment projects which can be instituted on short notice. Supplementing these fiscal measures with control over credit for housing construction, some 95 percent of which is built with state loans, the government can use this industry as an offset to activity in the rest of the economy—the one up when the other is down, and vice versa. This latter device, it may

Ministers of the world. Though backed up by Cabinet solidarity he has barely to consult his colleagues, except the Prime Minister himself, about his budget. The cohesion of parties is such that what the Government proposes is rarely denied: tax changes take effect immediately, are debated later, and rarely reversed."

A policy of flexible tax rates, which the President could institute on his own initiative, was recommended for the United States by Alvin Hansen in *Economic Policy and Full Employment* (New York: McGraw-Hill Book Company, 1947), p. 142; and by the Commission on Money and Credit in *Money and Credit* (Englewood Cliffs, N.J.: Prentice-Hall, Inc., 1961), pp. 136–137. It was requested by President Kennedy in 1962, but Congress did not provide the necessary authorization.

[16] This case has been argued most persuasively by J. C. R. Dow, "Forecasting and Budgetary Policy in the United Kingdom since the War," in *Les Prévisions Budgétaires*, pp. 141–173. Dow suggests that British needs would be better served by a series of small adjustments, allowed to work themselves out, than by delayed major adjustments in tax rates.

be noted, is effective because the continuing shortage of dwelling units makes easy the expansion as well as contraction of construction as needed for economic policy—something not true in the United States, for example.

The most interesting Swedish innovation to control overall levels of activity (adopted also by Norway in 1962) is its investment fund program. Although dating back to 1938, it has become an important instrument of policy only in recent years.[17] In effect, this program extends to business the notion of an "investment reserve" which may be drawn on if needed to sustain a desired level of economic activity, comparable to a governmental reserve of public works.

During a period of high-level activity, companies are permitted to set aside up to 40 percent of profits in an investment fund, which is carried as a liability on the company's balance sheet and on which no tax is paid. A percentage of the segregated amount equal to what the profits tax would have been is deposited with the central bank, so that the overall liquidity effect is unchanged. Whenever the government determines that some stimulus is needed to achieve target levels of GNP, it (through its Labor Market Board) can authorize the use of the investment reserves for specified purposes, most frequently construction. In effect, business firms—some 2,000 of them by 1962—provide a pool of funds which the government can keep idle or can unloose as circumstances dictate. The government can even require business firms to use their investment reserves at particular times, though it has not yet used this power; failure to comply subjects the reserve to immediate taxation. Labor Market Board actions may involve a single firm, an industry, the whole economy or any part of it.

The advantages to a company are several. First, it is able to accumulate more rapidly liquid funds with which to finance its investment program. Second, it gains a direct financial benefit in being able to write off, for tax purposes, 100 percent of any asset acquired with the help of the investment fund, instead of depreciating it at the much slower normal rates. The value of this provision is equal to the discounted value of the annual depreciation to which the firm would have normally been entitled. One estimate suggests this would be

[17] Fuller explanation of the system is provided by Curt Canarp in "Investment Funds—and How They Can Be Used to Combat Recession and Unemployment," *Skandinaviska Banken Quarterly Review*, no. 2, 1963, pp. 33–40. Actually there are two different types of investment funds, one for forestry operations and one for industry.

roughly equivalent to a tax credit of about 7 percent of the value of investment in machinery with a normal five-year write-off, 17 percent of the value of buildings with a twenty-year depreciation, and 24 percent of the value of buildings with a thirty-three-year depreciation.[18]

Most authorized uses of investment funds carry an additional tax advantage of 10 percent in the year when used. Projects that cannot be wholly financed by accumulated investment reserves or completed within the prescribed time period may be given special permits, including the use of future investment allocations, for writing off up to 75 percent of the total value of such special projects.

A company which uses its investment funds for unauthorized purposes must pay a tax on 110 percent of the amount used, substituting normal depreciation schedules. But if the Labor Market Board has not authorized use of funds within a five-year period, a company is free to use up to 30 percent for investment purposes, at its own discretion.

By requiring that funds released be put to use within a specified period, the Board is able to concentrate the expenditure effect. Experience under the program is instructive in this respect. The first use of investment reserves came in a 1958–1959 downturn. Ordinary permits were granted to 600 firms to use reserves of 750 million kronor. Special permits brought the total to over 1,000 million kronor, or approximately one-fifth annual private industrial investment at the time. About 90 percent of this amount was in fact used. In the downturn of 1962–1963 investment funds were released for projects totaling about the same amount, but firms were alerted sooner, the release came earlier in the cycle, and the time period within which funds were required to be used was shortened. The maximum employment effect, which in the first case had required some fifteen months, in the second instance was secured in six months.[19]

The investment fund device has also been used as a restraint on a booming economy. Since normally the amount impounded in the cen-

[18] Krister Wickman, "The Swedish Investment Reserve System: An Instrument of Contracyclical Policy," Statement given before the U.S. President's Advisory Committee on Labor-Management Policy, March 25, 1963, appendix A. (Mimeographed.)

[19] The same, p. 7. Projects may extend beyond the time period specified, but to qualify under the investment fund program they must be begun within that period, and—except with special permission—only that portion of the project completed within the period may be financed out of the investment reserve.

tral bank is equal to what would have been paid to the government as a profits tax, the overall effect is neutral. We simply have another case of offsetting. But in 1960–1961, under conditions of high liquidity, investment gave indications of running ahead of real savings, and business firms were given an extra tax deduction (equivalent to a 10 percent return on their funds) for blocking the whole of their investment allocations and not simply that portion equal to what they would have paid in taxes. Moreover, firms were not required to block such added funds for the usual five years but only for a year and a half, on the average, nor were their allocations limited to 40 percent of profits. The net result was a sharp reduction in business liquidity, facilitating maintenance of a policy of monetary restraint and reducing total business investment from what it otherwise would have been.

The advantage of the Swedish system over the 7 percent tax credit on investment allocations which the United States initiated in 1962 is greater flexibility and more certain response. The investments in a year of depression are not limited to those which can be financed out of current profits but draw also on accumulated profits. The device is applicable to upturns as well as downturns. The financial incentive to accumulate and to use reserves is greater.

Although emphasizing variations in household expenditures through variations in the government's tax take as the primary instrument for achieving GNP objectives, Britain has by no means neglected the business expenditure side. It attempts to accelerate or check the flow of business funds into investment by means of variations in what are called initial allowances and new investment allowances. The former provide a stepped-up rate of depreciation in the first year, and thus constitute a form of accelerated depreciation; the latter is more in the nature of a special tax credit given in the first year of a new investment, on top of depreciation deductions. The two have been used singly and together, and rates have varied from 5 to 40 percent. One examination of the impact of these concludes that initial allowances have little discernible effect, while investment allowances do, but take about nine months to register it.[20] Dow judges that the "full effects" of such investment measures probably take as much as two years,[21] making them a rather blunt instrument. There has been no effort to

[20] R. M. Bird, "Countercyclical Variation of Depreciation Allowances in the United Kingdom," *National Tax Journal*, vol. 16, March, 1963, pp. 47–48.
[21] *Les Prévisions Budgétaires*, pp. 168–169.

pinpoint the timing of investment expenditures as the Swedes have done.

MONETARY POLICY

In addition to fiscal measures, the other chief weapon for achieving categorical objectives is monetary and credit control, affecting the availability of funds and the incentive to use them. In recent years there has been some leakage of central bank controls over monetary policy due to the increasing role of nonbanking financial intermediaries, especially insurance companies, whose activities are sometimes (as in the United States) outside the purview of bank authorities.[22]

Norway has adopted an interesting technique to overcome this weakness. A Joint Consultation Committee, chaired by the governor of the Bank of Norway and composed of representatives of the Finance Ministry, public and private banks, and insurance companies, is charged with drafting an annual "credit budget." This is an agreement, formal enough to be reduced to writing, which establishes general monetary and credit policy; determines the aggregate credit which shall be extended, in what form, by which institutions, in what amounts, on what terms; decides the portion of government bonds which will be taken up by private banks to provide loanable funds to public banks such as the specialized credit institutions we earlier noted, and the investment priorities by which their lending policies will be guided. Occasionally there have been violations of these agreements. When these have occurred, the government has exercised its authority to reconvene the Joint Consultation Committee and to dictate through it the policy which shall control. In a recent year ill will was engendered by what was construed as an actual if not literal violation of the terms of the agreement when certain private financial institutions raised funds abroad. In consequence, since 1963 the agreement has included provisions covering this practice. The willingness of the financial community to go along with this extraordinary assumption of power on the part of the government has been explained as rising from a realization that refusal to cooperate might subject them to even stricter legislative

[22] John Gurley and Edward Shaw have examined this matter in chap. 6 of *Money in a Theory of Finance* (Washington, D.C.: The Brookings Institution, 1960).

limitations by the Labor government, perhaps even nationalization.

In Belgium the de Voghel Commission (named after the vice governor of the national bank, its chairman) was established to survey present credit institutions and to suggest a program for their more effective coordination, in support of the new four-year program. Its 1962 report advocated, in more general terms, arrangements having some of the same purposes and effects as the Norwegian credit budget. A financial council which would be roughly comparable to the Joint Consultation Committee has also been suggested.

Without creating a formal structure for coordinating credit policy, France has informally achieved this result more than might appear on first inspection. The same people, or their representatives, often sit in direction of the Bank of France, on the Vertical Commission for Finance in the planning system, on the National Credit Council, on the Fund for Economic and Social Development, on the committee for housing credits, and so on. Thus, while the actual mechanisms frequently appear diffuse, even resembling the United States in this respect, they are more closely linked by overlapping personnel. Add to this the fact that the central credit institutions of France tend to take more selective measures than, say, the Federal Reserve Board, and these within the framework of the plan, and the system emerges as a much more consolidated and coordinated overall credit program than its dispersion among a number of separate institutions might suggest. As a staff member of the Planning Commission commented, the financial and credit measures may seem dispersed, but the government is in all of them, and a strong government will is all that is needed to coordinate them into a consistent policy.

Monetary and credit policy has quite generally been recognized as more effective in restraining than in stimulating expenditures, but this scarcely accords it the importance which it warrants in a planning program. In such a context its principal function can be seen not so much as "controlling" the level of GNP, as facilitating the credit arrangements which are necessary to the accomplishment of the whole bundle of specific and categorical objectives. In these terms its powers to devise credit policies appropriate to the spectrum of national objectives call for a closer integration of its decisions with those of the administration. Social priorities call for credit priorities, while general credit policy is relevant to the categorical objectives. Such a role would seem to call for more than the customary central banking functions, but would also involve some degree of influence over non-financial intermediaries and equities issues.

No prejudgment as to some "necessary" degree of coordination of policy among such institutions, or of governmental influence over their policies, need be made. How much credit coordination is desirable depends on the firmness with which national economic objectives are held and on the importance accorded individual discretion of private institutions over economic values in the social scheme. The only thing that is inescapable is the fact of the relation of credit controls, public and private, to the achievement of any economic objectives.

Nor is it only credit policies relating to business which are involved. Consumption too is credit-financed. Restraint or stimulation may be applied to consumer expenditures in line with overall decisions as to the division of the target GNP among business, governments, and households. In Norway, for example, this has been done through legislative provisions.[23] In France the National Credit Council not only sets the prime rate for business loans, but fixes the ratio of consumption loans to paid-in capital of the major credit institutions specialized in consumer financing (accounting for perhaps 90 percent of the latter). Decisions with respect to import priorities may also be involved if a balance-of-payments problem must be faced.

[23] Thus from the *National Budget of Norway 1962*, Ministry of Finance, p. 9: "At the end of the second quarter of 1961, lending by commercial banks and financial institutions in connection with hire purchase contracts for consumer goods was nearly 115 million kroner greater than a year earlier. To restrain hire purchase trade from rising too sharply, measures have been taken, pursuant to new legislation, to make the provisions for time payment sales more stringent. The guiding lines for the credit institutions also call for further stringency in the granting of hire purchase credit and personal loans for consumption purposes."

5...
financial terms
and institutional structure

In the last chapter we considered governmental instruments for achieving specific and categorical objectives in real terms. But the money-terms are important too. They are important for several reasons.

First, prices of goods and prices of factor services affect the distribution of the fruits of economic activity. An "appropriate" distribution or redistribution of GNP may itself be a national objective. (It usually is.)

Second, the distribution of income affects the balance between consumption and investment. Under changing circumstances this balance too may have to change if the economy is to make full use of its assets.

The balance may have to swing more toward savings and away from consumption when more private investment is needed to satisfy rising household demand; more toward private consumer expenditure when investment goods become more productive and less saving is required to keep pace with wants; more toward public expenditure with higher tax rates when private demand is still strong but needs balancing with more "infrastructure"; and more toward public expenditure with lower tax rates when private demand is weak and social investment can lay the basis for future expansion. An "incomes policy" becomes a significant element in economic planning by helping to steer GNP into the channels appropriate to the given circumstances.

Failing an appropriate price and incomes policy, inflationary pressures may be unleashed from either the demand or the supply (cost) side. Among the adverse consequences, one which is particularly important for Western European countries, with their greater dependence on foreign trade than is true for the United States, is the effect of inflation on competitive positions in world markets. Since production for export cannot be neatly isolated from production for domestic consumption, a nation's whole price structure is affected by this concern: "... We cannot expect our export target to be achieved unless, at the least, our export prices do not rise in relation to those of our competitors; and they may well have to fall relatively. Moreover, to encourage manufacturers to devote sufficient of their resources to exporting, the tendency for prices in the home market to rise relatively to export prices will have to be reversed." [1]

However reluctantly governments have been driven to the conclusion, a price and incomes policy is an essential ingredient in management of the economy. Private decisions in these matters affect achievement of national objectives, just as do investment and savings decisions, and the government must seek to induce, since it cannot normally command, the private actions which will achieve enough of both subunit and system goals to be satisfactory at both levels. The crucial element in our whole inquiry is this relationship between the parts and the whole and the facilitation of decisions which are effective in both spheres; decisions affecting prices and incomes constitute no exception to this necessity.

[1] National Economic Development Council, *Conditions Favourable to Faster Growth* (London, 1963), p. 50.

DIFFICULTIES OF AN INCOMES POLICY

One can readily sympathize with governments which have sought to evade this issue, since it is perhaps the knottiest economic problem of our day. The difficulties in dealing with it are numerous.

1 More than other kinds of economic actions, changes in prices and incomes are not likely to be offsetting but, rather, cumulative. We have noted, for example, that if some firms invest more, others may invest less, if some households consume more, others save more, and so on, so that the actions of some often offset the actions of others within a given category. Conceptually the same thing should be true of prices, and indeed the notion of a "stable price level" is based on an averaging of prices, some of which move up and others down. But there is a greater probability in the case of wages and prices that nonoffsetting, when it does occur, will be cumulative in the upward direction, since it does not depend solely on demand pressures, but may derive its impetus from pressures on the supply side as well.

Wage rates are related on a kind of escalator, so that if some move up—for any reason—the movement is likely to be transmitted to the rest. This transmission is importantly but not exclusively linked to the institutional practices of labor unions. Rising rates, in turn, have their effect on prices unless offset by compensatory cost-reducing changes. The cumulative effect upward is often aided, explicitly or implicitly, by the practice of "indexing"—the tying of a rate of remuneration to a price index. Thus in pursuing a price and incomes policy, a government has less assistance from the random effects of offsetting, but more commonly must cope with nonrandom cumulative effects.

2 This cumulative character often attaching to price and income changes also means that it is less feasible for a government to achieve its objectives by influencing the actions of just some subunits; instead it must influence the actions of all, or at least most. Major units—the U.S. steel industry or an automobile company like Volkswagen—may occupy the limelight when it comes to crackdowns on unwanted price actions, but while public attention fastens on them, the hundreds of thousands of decentralized units in, say, the construction industry, may be pushing up rates and prices without much restraint, and in doing

so initiating the cumulative effect which in time will sweep the big units along with it.

3   The question of income distribution involves a more direct and overt conflict of interest than is apparent in many other economic decisions. Labor unions are organized specifically for the purpose of influencing income distribution, in an adversary role. This functional characteristic of labor organizations makes them unwilling to engage in a commitment to a distributive "principle," [2] and this is all the more the case when such a commitment relates primarily to wage matters and ignores production, price, and profit considerations.

Under these institutional circumstances, the tendency is for labor unions to regard the pressure for financial planning as the opposition's flank attack:

It has not escaped our notice that the proposal for an incomes policy, which has come from several quarters, made its appearance at a time of full employment—some would call it over-full employment—that is to say, at a time favourable to labour claims. We could ask: what would they say in a period of unemployment? [3]

---

[2] Thus note this statement from the impressive paper of Nicola de Pamphilis, of the Research Department of the Italian Confederation of Workers' Unions (CISL), "Economic Programming and Union Policies," in *International Trade Union Seminar on Economic and Social Programming*, Supplement to the final report (Paris: Organization for Economic Cooperation and Development, 1963), p. 55: "The motive inspiring the behaviour of the unions has been, and to a large extent remains, that of obtaining ever higher monetary wage levels for their members. This motive is found in all practical aspects of union operation, whatever the bargaining unit levels at which wage agreements are negotiated. In such countries as the United States, where particular bargaining units are the practice, such as the factory or the firm, right through to those in which negotiation is centralized at national or regional levels, the objective is invariably to obtain higher pay in terms of money, which under existing conditions is within the contractual power of the various unions. To a certain extent, the unions are not particularly sensitive to either the particular effects which this conduct produces from the employment level standpoint, or to more general conditions, such as monetary stability and the rate of development. Their behaviour is immune to suggestions, requests, and admonishments from various sources, which would tend to produce a rational wage policy, either linked to such objective parameters as the growth of the average productivity of the economic system, or which invoke the necessity for a harmonious development of the income from labour in the various economic sectors."

[3] Gabriel Ventejol, Confederal Secretary, General Confederation of Labour—Force Ouvrière (CGT–FO), in the same, p. 17. The National Economic Develop-

4   The political position of labor makes difficult the enforcement of an unpopular policy. Labor's political role has been strong, more so in Europe than in the United States, and not wholly related to the strength of union organization. To the extent a public policy is unpopular because a legitimate alternative is preferred, there is no reason why a political position should not be used to oppose it. But to the extent it is unpopular because it is unpalatable, even though preferable to alternatives, most people would consider political opposition to be irresponsible. Nevertheless, the survival of a union as an institution may recommend to its leaders a policy of militancy simply to convince the members, or potential members, that the organization is looking out for their welfare.[4]

5   The responsibility for any adverse economic consequences of price and income decisions is diffused throughout society, between and within interest groups. The link between individual price and income movements within a firm or industry and the economic consequence for the economy as a whole is too obscure to suggest a genuine cause-and-effect relationship. Equity considerations give further sanction to a displacement of responsibility to others. The consequence is that no one assumes responsibility for, or even takes much interest in, price and income movements, except the government.[5]

6   The traditional fiscal and monetary instruments for dealing with the problems of price progression conflict with other social objectives which Western society is reluctant to abandon, notably full employment and growth. As the French Commissioner of

ment Council has taken note of this attitude in the United Kingdom: "A policy for prices and money incomes can succeed only if those concerned are convinced that it is a necessary part of a wider programme for growth of real incomes, and that restraint by one section of the community will not merely result in a gain by other sections." *Conditions Favourable to Faster Growth*, p. 51.

[4] In the absence of such militancy, workers might assume that the economic gains accruing to them stemmed more from the economic plan or the economic system than from their union's efforts. Lionel Murray, secretary of the Research and Economic Department of the British Trades Union Congress, in cautioning unions that they might have to reexamine their own policies, commented: "High and rising standards of some groups of workers may make them think that trade unionism is irrelevant to their immediate needs." *International Trade Union Seminar on Economic and Social Programming*, p. 32.

[5] The reader is referred to Chap. 3, footnote 13, for the comment of a member of the French Economic and Social Council on this point.

Planning, Pierre Massé, has pointed out,[6] short-run credit restriction as a countercyclical weapon ideally ought to make producers sharper bargainers in their relations with suppliers, workers, and stockholders, but in practice such policy cannot be sliced so neatly. In order to be effective, it is likely to be excessive. Its success is almost inevitably linked to a restraint on growth, so that traditionally a growth rate without inflation is almost always a growth rate less than resources make possible.

If the price paid for financial equilibrium were small—a modest sacrifice of perhaps a half percent of growth—it would be a good trade (continues Massé), but this is unlikely. The search for stability solely by restraining global demand is likely to lead to a considerably greater loss of growth and a not insignificant rate of unemployment. Not only would this be unacceptable by itself, but it would have the further consequence of reducing the amount going to social investment, on which long-term expansion rests. At the same time a lessened rate of growth, lessening also the availability of work, could provoke tensions in the labor market. Far from creating stability, general financial restraints are likely to create downward instability.

The same comment could be made to apply to restraint via taxation. The so-called "stop and go" policy of Britain in the fifties is evidence of the danger in using such global fiscal tranquilizers.

APPROACHES TO A PRICE AND INCOMES POLICY

That general fiscal and monetary measures have their limitations for controlling price movements does not imply that they are either unnecessary or unimportant. Without such general supporting actions any other measures would likewise prove inadequate. The difficulty is

[6] *Rapport sur la Politique des Revenus Établi à la Suite de la Conférence des Revenus* [hereafter referred to as the Massé report] (Paris: La Documentation Française, no. 47, 1964), p. 7. An OECD group made the same point in *Policies for Economic Growth* (Paris, 1962), p. 37: "... attempts to secure price stability which rely only on restraint of the general level of demand may involve lowering the pressure of demand to a level which reduces the incentive for growth.... Hence the importance of supplementing management of the general level of demand by other instruments of policy. These may include powers to influence specific types of demand, policies to increase the speed of adaptation of supply to demand in particular sectors, and policies which operate more directly on the determination of incomes and prices."

that they are relatively blunt instruments, and efforts to use them surgically can be expected to inflict unwanted damage on the body economic. More selective instruments with more predictable effects are needed to make the operation successful. The traditional instruments have not lost their potency; it is only that we have come to expect a quality of performance that they cannot provide by themselves. Over the last several decades a variety of supplementary approaches (some with more distant historical antecedents) have been attempted or suggested. Let us examine the most important of these briefly.

1 Part of the price problem, as we have seen, is its cumulative effect—the reinforcing nature of a stream of sequential bargains, accompanied by a diffusion between and within major interest groups of any sense of responsibility, with an institutional requirement of some sort of direct action by interest groups in the division of the national product, leading to a result which is ethically acceptable. Hence one obvious "solution" is a single national bargain among the parties principally in interest.

As one group of observers noted in an unpublished memorandum of 1963, this approach has been encouraged by "a growing conviction that greater success in stopping costs and prices from rising requires that the determination of incomes not be left wholly to decentralized market determination, but become more subject to conscious political choice and that it is unlikely that any such 'social contracts' about the distribution of the national income between the different categories of income can be secured without the different interests concerned being given a stronger and more explicit voice in the determination of policy about the distribution of the nation's expenditure."

When this approach has been tried, it has usually been on a partial basis. Perhaps the most frequently cited instance is that of Sweden, where the central labor and employer federations negotiate a national wage agreement which provides the basis for industry and local bargains. The national agreement usually emerges from a protracted and objective discussion of the nation's economic circumstances and their significance for wage determination, and customarily is linked to estimates of average productivity increases in the economy as a whole. The agreement concluded in 1964 provided for an average increase of $1\frac{1}{2}$ percent in that year and $3\frac{1}{2}$ percent the following year, which— coming at a time when the economy was generally characterized as "overheated" and the central bank had just initiated an extraordinary (9 percent) rediscount rate for banks whose loans exceeded a specified proportion of paid-in capital—appeared to embody a spirit of moderation and restraint.

But to some extent the appearance was deceptive. Sweden, like a number of other European countries, has been troubled with a "wage creep" which is not wholly related to the upgrading of workers into more productive assignments but reflects the state of labor demand. For example, following the 1964 national negotiations workers in textiles—not the most prosperous of industries—were presumably to receive an hourly increase of 8 öre, but the employers on their own initiative concluded separate local agreements for as much as 25 öre out of a feeling of need to satisfy and hold their labor forces in a relatively tight labor market. In other cases a reclassification of workers, without change of assignment, permits the payment of a higher rate even within the terms of the agreement, as, for example, when a painting assignment is reclassified from a category involving plain surfaces to one with broken surfaces.

This wage creep is estimated to have run as much as $3\frac{1}{2}$ percent in recent years and was certainly in the minds of negotiators when they concluded the 1964 national agreement on "modest" terms. In addition, by legislation workers were to receive an additional half-week of vacation that year and another half-week the following year, and employers were to pay full rather than partial pension and sickness contributions by 1966, adding perhaps another 1 percent to labor charges in 1964. When one adds up the total package from all these elements, the 1964 settlement jumps from $1\frac{1}{2}$ percent to closer to 7 percent—in the face of an average national increase in productivity of about half that amount. The resulting 3 to $3\frac{1}{2}$ percent of price progression is a figure that has come to be accepted as representing "reasonable stability," in the light of equal or greater inflationary pressures in many of the country's trading partners. The presumption is that in the absence of national negotiations the price increase would have been more.

Denmark too employs a national wage bargain. The Dutch case involves a more complicated mosaic of private and governmental participation and will be considered at a later point. National negotiations have also been suggested in other countries such as the United Kingdom and the United States.[7]

---

[7] In the United States, Sumner Slichter once commented that the greatest possibilities of collective bargaining are not likely to be realized "until representatives

One difficulty with the Swedish-type settlement is that it constitutes only a wage bargain. The question of prices and nonwage incomes is left aside. Negotiations with the association of professional workers and other organized groups often follow, using the national wage agreement as a base, with the cumulative effect we have already noted. An attempt to overcome this difficulty was undertaken in Norway in 1963. The preceding September, in anticipation of the reopening of private wage agreements and the public agreements on farm and fisheries' prices, an unofficial committee representing the relevant organizations and high-level government officials (including the Prime Minister and Minister of Finance) canvassed the general economic situation. While negotiations for the several agreements were kept separate, the parties kept each other mutually informed. Out of negotiations emerged a three-way overall price and incomes policy: wages were advanced an average of $2\frac{1}{2}$ percent. The price agreements in agriculture and fisheries were calculated to yield an approximately comparable increase in income. These income settlements were accepted on the premise that prices would remain relatively stable, and the government undertook to implement that condition by increasing consumers' subsidies by an agreed-upon sum for the remainder of the year. This Norwegian arrangement probably constitutes the most comprehensive effort at achieving a national agreement on a price and incomes policy that any Western government has yet undertaken in peacetime. Regardless of its initial effectiveness, it constitutes a significant experiment.[8]

---

of labor as a whole and of business as a whole are able to fix the broad outlines of a national wage policy." "Labor after the War," in Seymour Harris (ed.), *Postwar Economic Problems* (New York: McGraw-Hill Book Company, 1943), p. 254.

Arthur Meyer, former chairman of the New York State Mediation Board, commented in 1952: "Labor bargains are growing bigger and bigger, the public interest is growing greater and greater, the intrusion of government is becoming more and more frequent. Whether this evolution shall be encouraged or discouraged is an intensely practical problem. Those who see basic infirmities in the anarchy of formless bargaining will support an alternative which, though opposed by many, is clearly within the tenor of our way. The question is where are we going, and I discern in the national labor bargain a distant point towards which we are slowly moving, a destination already marked on the signposts of our journeying." Neil W. Chamberlain (ed.), *Sourcebook on Labor* (New York: McGraw-Hill Book Company, 1958), pp. 831–832.

[8] A word might be added about the French arrangement. Through the Fourth Plan, both specific and categorical objectives were stated in constant prices, and

Whatever one may think of the desirability of such national compacts, one institutional requirement is obvious if they are to be effective: the central federations which negotiate on behalf of their memberships must possess sufficient authority over them to make the national agreement stick. In some countries, notably the United States, this would require a considerable recasting of business and union governmental structures.

2　A second and more widely practiced approach to pricing decisions is "moral suasion." The government attempts to exert its influence on private organizations to make their money policies conform to the national interests. We can ignore those examples of this type of action which rely on official exhortation to "exercise restraint," without offering guidance as to what that implies. "Moral suasion" has meaning, as a committee of experts assembled by the OEEC (predecessor to the OECD) pointed out, only if the government itself has a "reasonably precise view, estimated by the best means they can devise, of the average increase in wages that is appropriate to the economic situation and consistent with stability of the price level," however that last condition may be defined. Additionally, if "suasion" is to be more than a pious wish, the government must actively attempt to mobilize support for its position.[9] The same approach can, of course, be extended to include other price influences than wages.

The problem with this policy is that it requires adoption of some general standard by which to judge individual price and income actions. The standard which has generally been employed is that of national average productivity. But this presents insuperable problems. Aside from the statistical difficulties of measuring productivity (within a given industry or sector, let alone for the nation as a whole), and the ethical difficulty that it implies some acceptance of the existing distribution as "right," despite denials of such an intention, there is an even more serious conceptual problem. There is literally no logical rela-

---

the income figures written into the Financial Commission's report were purely hypothetical projections. The Fifth Plan will incorporate target prices and incomes, so that objectives are couched in both real and money terms. Despite the extensive consultation characteristic of the French planning program, drawing in representatives of industry and labor, the indicative nature of the result puts this exercise in quite a different category from the national *agreements* discussed above, which—unlike the French targets—are binding on the parties.

[9] William J. Fellner and others, *The Problem of Rising Prices* (Paris: Organization for European Economic Cooperation, 1961), p. 57.

tionship between an average increase in national productivity and a firm's wage, profit, and price policies. The so-called "general standard" is understandably ambiguous if not silent on such critical questions as whether the level of activity in the economy (degree of utilization of its aggregate assets) as well as the level of activity in the individual firm or industry (profitability in the use of its specific assets) leave it with any meaning or applicability.

The basic problem boils down to whether the rule advocated is appropriate within the units where the relevant decisions are made. In the matter of an incomes policy, productivity may be a suitable variable to introduce into an efficiency (technical-economic) model of the total system at full employment. As such, it may serve as a measure of the degree of departure from equilibrium conditions which is likely to result from whatever wage-price actions the government succeeds in inducing. But the decisions which actually allocate income are made in the micro units, for which national productivity does not constitute, even technically, a satisfactory rule for the distribution of incremental revenues. Any efforts at "morally persuading" a business firm to apply a rule which has no relevance to its own standards of efficiency is doomed to failure. The ground is hostile to the seed.[10]

3   More authoritative and more flexible than moral suasion is the policy of requiring business firms to give notice and justification of proposed price increases and to establish a board of review for price and income actions considered "dubious" by some pragmatic standard. In most instances where an ex ante review procedure is now used it carries with it actual powers of approval or disapproval, but this is not essential. The authority of a review board may extend simply to consulting with the firm or publicizing its opinion of the proposed action, without power to enjoin it. This has been the procedure recommended for the United States by the United Automobile Workers, for example.

In some instances a review of price or income action (usually

---

[10] The manager who was generally held responsible for breaking the British government's "pay pause" of 1961 justified his action on the ground that the government had no basis for expecting employers to voluntarily adopt a policy inconsistent with the efficient management of their firms, which might call for wage changes more or less than those suggested by the general rule. Parenthetically he added that from the labor viewpoint he could see no reason why "pay" should be singled out for restraint. Some dividends which had been declared after the pay pause went into effect had been, he said, "unconscionable."

wage changes) may take place ex post, as is for the most part true of the British National Incomes Commission established in 1962. Particular settlements may be referred to it by a minister for opinion on its conformance to national interest. Those multiple standards particularly applied are:

a   the desirability of keeping the rate of increase of the aggregate of monetary incomes within the long-term rate of increase of national production

b   the desirability of paying a fair reward for the work concerned

c   the manpower needs of the service, industry, or employment concerned, consideration of any regional or local differences in such needs, and the importance of securing the most efficient deployment and use of national resources including manpower

d   the policies and practices in the service, industry, or employment concerned in such matters (where appropriate) as pricing, profit margins, dividends, efficient use of manpower and equipment, and organization

e   the repercussions which a particular settlement in the case concerned might have on other employments

The report prepared by the French Planning Commissioner following the Incomes Conference in that country in 1963–1964 recommended the establishment of a "college for the study of increases in incomes" which, like the British commission, would examine agreements and conventions after they had been concluded and comment on them in the light of overall criteria and particular circumstances of the sector or firm. The opinion would have no legal sanction but would be made public. The "college" would concern itself only with significant situations, to avoid jeopardizing its effectiveness by deluging it with too many requests for opinions.[11]

DIRECT CONTROLS

4   In some countries prices or wages are subject to formal governmental control. First, as to prices, Belgium requires producers and importers of specified commodities and services (some

[11] Massé report, p. 27. In the same conference a proposal was made for a continuing review of how major income categories were actually changing. The interest groups represented for the most part accepted this proposal with reservations.

eighty-two in 1963) to give twenty-one days' notice to the Minister of Economic Affairs before putting a price increase into effect. The notice must include a justification for the proposed advance. To assist him in deciding whether to authorize the increase, the Minister is advised by a representative Commission des Prix. The Commission also maintains a continuing surveillance of the general price level and is charged with making recommendations to the Minister when it believes action is called for.

Price supervision in Denmark is entrusted to the Monopolies Control Board, established under the Monopolies and Restrictive Practices Act of 1955, with its powers supplemented by the Price Supervision Act of 1963. As its name implies, the Board was originally not designed to stand guard over general price movements, but its functions in this respect were somewhat ambiguously tacked on by the later legislation. Any changes in prices in firms or industries designated by the Board must be reported within eight days. When the Board is of the opinion that a price increase is unjustified, it first attempts to secure agreement through negotiation, but failing in that it is empowered to enjoin the action. A private hearing is then held at which the firm or industry must produce any relevant data requested. The Board's opinion is not made public, in view of the confidential data on which it is based; it may be appealed to an appeals tribunal and beyond that to the courts. The 1963 act gave the Board authority to initiate inquiries as to pricing policies in industries generally, without respect to whether restrictive practices are involved. If prices are found to be unreasonably high, the Board may impose maximum prices or margins.

The Netherlands empowers its Economic Minister to impose price ceilings and to lay down accounting rules for the determination of prices, but in practice this authority is exercised more by negotiation than by decree, except for a few food items. The principal rule which the Minister has sought to establish has been that only cost increases caused by factors external to the firm, such as higher materials costs, should be reflected in higher prices. Since wages are an internal matter they cannot, in principle, be made the basis for a price increase, but are limited to changes in line with changes in productivity, though in this case productivity within the firm. (There are other limitations on wages which we shall examine in a moment.)

France has standby price controls, involving the continuing

classification of all goods and services into four principal categories: those which are entirely free of control; those which a firm is free to price at its own discretion, but changes in whose prices must be reported to the Direction du Prix; those on which a firm is free to set prices which the government may, however, disallow within fifteen days; and, finally, those whose prices are fixed by the government. The postwar period constituted a continuing movement toward greater price liberalization, until only a few basic products, chiefly steel, aluminum, and cement, remained in the controlled category. In April, 1963, however, the government reclassified approximately eighty products which had formerly been free, in a strenuous effort to curb rising prices.

The Italian government has full authority to control all prices under a 1944 law which established an Interministerial Price Committee. In 1963 this power was being used to establish maximum prices in half a dozen industrial lines (among them coal, petroleum, cement, and fertilizer), half a dozen foodstuffs, and the principal public services such as gas, water, electricity, telephone, and railroads.

Some countries specifically limit price controls to a few major items (Britain to steel, Germany to rents, medicinals, milk, and sugar). Again, such controls are designed not so much to influence the general price level as to set limits in a few industries which are deemed "key" either on social welfare grounds or because of their strategic role in the economy.

Wage controls are less common than price controls. The Netherlands provides the principal example, and a complicated one it is. After the war, a three-headed system of wage regulation was established which tended to diffuse power in such a way that it was sometimes difficult to tell where it resided, especially over time as the roles of the three supervising agencies shifted somewhat. In the early years, responsibility for advice on broad economic policies rested with the Social Economic Council, a tripartite body composed of employer, worker, and public representatives. The application of wage policy, in the form of negotiated agreements, remained with employers associations and trade unions, but such agreements required the prior approval of the Foundation of Labor, a bipartite body representing employer and worker organizations.

The sanction of the Board of State Mediators was required to make an agreement official, but such sanction was usually forthcoming on the recommendation of the Foundation (though the Foundation sometimes claimed it was simply responsive to the Board's views, which presumably in turn were in accord with the policies of the Social Economic Council). Once a wage scale was approved, deviations from it were subject to fine and even imprisonment: the wage creep was thus very substantially curbed even if not altogether eliminated.

The economic minuet between Board, Foundation, and Council has continued down to the present, but the steps have changed. Now the Board's approval of agreements accepted by the Foundation is no longer required, but the Board may take exception to agreements, in the light of Council policies. The latter are guided by analyses of the Central Planning Bureau. On opposition from the Board, the Minister of Social Affairs may interpose his authority, in effect to arbitrate between Foundation and Board.

The Dutch arrangement is thus a peculiar mixture of private and public control, since the Foundation of Labor is a labor-management body which is given official duties and powers. The system has had its difficulties, notably since 1959, when the whole question of wage control was reopened. "There were many differences of opinion, but it was clear that almost nobody wanted to return to a really free system of wage determination." [12]

One French proposal is worth a brief note. In the preceding chapter we encountered the quasi-contract as an instrument for inducing business actions in accord with the French plan. The government grants certain financial favors in exchange for a firm's agreement to carry out a given program. It has been suggested that one of the conditions which the government might include in such an agreement is that the firm should restrict any wage increases within a range bounded on the upper side by a weighted average of branch and national productivity improvements and on the lower side simply by the national average, thus giving some leeway to bargaining within a particular branch. [13] Regardless of the formula employed, the basic intent is to make use of governmental contracts with firms to establish maximum wage increases, just as the Walsh-Healey Act in the United States uses the government's purchasing power to impose minimum wage scales in supplier firms.

[12] J. Pen, "The Strange Adventures of Dutch Wage Policy," British Journal of Industrial Relations, vol. 1, October, 1963, p. 327.

[13] John Hackett and Anne-Marie Hackett, Economic Planning in France (Cambridge, Mass.: Harvard University Press, 1963), p. 323.

Direct controls serve two separable functions. They may be designed explictly as an instrument of general price-level control, in which case they are likely to involve standby powers extending to a wide range of goods and services. For this purpose they are useful only for short-run emergencies or brief periods during which other more effective steps may be taken to meet the problem of rising prices. They are certainly no long-run solution.

Alternatively direct controls may be used for curbing the effects of a monopoly market position of specific firms or unions. Here the objective is not the general price level but particular prices of a few major items, the production or distribution of which is concentrated in a few hands. The intention is to restrain not prevalent inflationary pressures, but specific exercises of market power. At the same time, a leash on the latter may contribute to a curb on the former. Price restrictions in the major highly organized sectors, notably steel, are likely to have some restraining effect beyond the sector in which imposed. But where upward pressures are experienced throughout the economy, selective restraints of this type will hardly keep a ceiling on prices in industries where power is more diffused, as in construction.

Whichever of these two distinctive purposes is served, direct controls hardly constitute a wage-price policy in a market economy. They may even be regarded as symptoms of the lack of such a policy.

FURTHER PROPOSALS

5 More unorthodox methods have been suggested for dealing with the price issue. One takes a different approach to the relation between productivity and prices. Instead of making an average rate of increase in national productivity a guide to income or price changes, it suggests leaving wages and prices to the free determination of the parties, but concentrating governmental attention on ways of increasing productivity, sufficient to justify the money movements. If more effective use can be made of resources, then output rather than prices is likely to rise with wages. On this approach, a government program designed to break production bottlenecks wherever these emerge is a protection against inflation. Government-supported research to improve industrial efficiency constitutes another device. In effect, the need

for a price and incomes policy is offset by a more active policy of inducing productivity gains.[14]

Another and somewhat more familiar line of thinking worries less about the allocation of incomes than their use. In situations where demand-pull rather than cost-push is primarily responsible for rising prices, as was generally true of Continental Europe in the early sixties, further inducements to savings may be more appropriate than attempts to clamp down on prices directly. Saving can be made more alluring through such devices as popularizing mutual investment funds (as has been notably true in the United States for some time but which France moved to encourage only as recently as 1963), granting tax credits for interest earned on bonds or for dividends earned on equities, and perhaps even a household equivalent of the Swedish investment funds for business. (Households which set aside a portion of their incomes in a blocked account could be allowed to deduct that amount from their incomes for tax purposes. An account would be released only when authorized by the government, and would then be tax free or would carry only a nominal tax.)

The counterpart of such savings measures would be a system of flexible excise taxes on certain major consumption items such as automobiles, which could be increased when demand was considered excessive (as was done in Italy in 1963–1964) and reduced or removed when demand was slack. The related device of flexible down-payment provisions is already familiar enough.

A much more radical proposal for curbing price increases emanating from corporations large enough to have a degree of

---

[14] The Massé report takes note of this possibility, but concludes (p. 7) that the most such an approach can do is provide more room for maneuver in meeting the still-remaining problem of appropriate distribution of national income. People would become accustomed to the greater increases in productivity and would scale their own income expectations upward. The augmented rate of growth would thus create its own instabilities.

There is probably some merit to this criticism, but it dismisses the matter a bit too lightly. The same argument has been made with respect to people's adjustment to a continuing rate of inflation (they anticipate it and base their actions on such anticipations), but it now appears that this is true only for higher rates of price progression than have customarily appeared in Western Europe and North America. Similarly, it seems unlikely that people would readjust their income expectations in the face of a continuing increase in productivity which, while enough to offset at least part of any inflationary pressures, would not constitute any radical increase over rates which have been achieved from time to time in the past.

control over their markets has been made by Gardiner Means.[15] His objective is to secure a performance by private business which would conduce to the public interest, while avoiding excessive governmental intervention. Briefly, he would provide managements a strong incentive to act in their own (not their stockholders') interests and at the same time establish performance incentives which would consciously formalize that harmony between private managerial interests and public good which in an earlier day was assumed to be provided by Adam Smith's magnificent conception of the "invisible hand" of the market.

Means would accomplish this by having the legislature establish a new tax category for corporations possessing discretionary pricing powers. The managements of these companies would (1) be required to set a long-term target rate of return on total investment equal to the market cost of capital; (2) prepare a detailed plan (budget) for achieving the target rate of return, both over time (using a standard volume concept) and for the operating year (when current profits would be measured alongside precalculated returns for varying degrees of operation above or below standard volume); and (3) be given substantial bonuses for achieving the performance spelled out by target and plan.

Since performance standards could readily be devised in terms of criteria corresponding to the public interest, the result would be to allow managements to conduct their corporate affairs just as they now do, without worrying about some vague standard of "social responsibility." They could follow the more realistic objective of earning good bonuses for themselves within a system which itself related bonus to public welfare. Prices would be kept lower by the reduced target rate; the objective of high profit levels would be replaced by a "fair" profit level; the limitation on profits would tend to curb organized labor's greediness for high wage increases which is now stimulated by the spectacle of high profits; the lower return required to justify investment would lead to an expansion of investment; and managements would themselves gain greater satisfaction in the knowledge that their performance added up to a result of larger social significance, giving greater justification for their handsome earnings.

Stockholders could of course be expected to object, since the inevitable result would be to lower the value of their present

---

[15] Gardiner Means, *Pricing Power and the Public Interest* (New York: Harper & Row, Publishers, Incorporated, 1962).

holdings, but their pain could be relieved by introducing the system gradually and by offering them appropriate inducements. Other objections are more serious. Perhaps the most damaging is that as long as prices are restrained not by the market but by intention (in line with the target profit rate), operating costs including wages can be increased as "circumstances" dictate and passed along in the form of higher prices. Profits could still be held to the target rate, so that management's bonuses would be unaffected. The formulation thus does not escape the need for defining an appropriate wage policy, and in the absence of a wage policy ceases to serve even as a price policy, and is reduced to being only a profits-control policy. In conjunction with some wage policy, however, the scheme does have an appealing quality of attempting to relate private institutions to public interest by means of procedures familiar to both sectors and making use of efficiency rules relevant to both.

PROFIT OR INVESTMENT SHARING

One device which has been around for a good many years deserves special consideration—profit sharing. In its earlier and even present manifestations, it has been chiefly regarded as an equitable means of dividing a firm's revenues. With some modifications it holds out interesting possibilities of serving as a vehicle for a public incomes policy and has been drawing attention from people concerned with that problem.

Profit performs three different functions, as the Massé report points out. It is used (1) to replace capital through repayment of borrowed funds or depreciation; (2) to pay dividends to stockholders; and (3) to provide funds for reinvestment.[16] Reinvestment, in turn has two separable aspects: the form which it takes, which is a technical-economic matter related to the objectives of the firm as a system, and its appropriation, which is a political-organizational matter and involves bargains among the subunits composing the system.

Insofar as worker compensation is equated with consumption, and profits (in any of the three forms noted above) tend to be associated with investment, even though with some leakage, straight profit sharing would tend to reduce investment and growth or to contribute to inflationary pressure. Corporate earnings which would have found their

[16] Massé report, p. 9.

way into capital would be distributed in part to workers who would consume them. There would be less financing for plant and equipment and increased demand in consumer-goods markets. As the economy adjusted to the new distribution, the inflationary pressure would be reduced, but growth would be increasingly inhibited.

If new forms of profit sharing could be devised in which the profit which is allocated still performs its investment function, then the division between investment and consumption would remain as before, growth would be stimulated and inflationary consumer pressure avoided, but title to the net new investment would be shared by workers as well as stockholders. In effect, reinvested earnings would be divided between them according to some bargained formula. The allocation of undistributed profits would have been altered without disturbing their growth function.

There is no necessary reason why profits need to be retained within a particular firm in order for this relationship to obtain. The workers' share could be deposited in an investment trust, in which they would hold shares, as in a mutual fund, though this would perhaps lessen employer interest in the scheme. A more critical consideration is whether workers would be willing to take part of their compensation in this form. On this there is mixed evidence.[17] Nevertheless, some potential receptivity is suggested by the fact that workers have been willing to forego present consumption (wage increases) in favor of pension rights. The investment share, which similarly constitutes savings for future consumption, could be associated with desirable objectives for which cumulated savings would be necessary, such as higher

[17] Massé reported at the French Incomes Policy Conference in 1963 that unions showed a lively interest in a division of the profits, either between shareholders and workers, or in some undefined way as payments into a national fund which could be used for transfer purposes (p. 15). This would not necessarily reflect an interest in participation in an investment fund, however. The Italian Confederation of Workers' Unions (CISL) has been an active proponent of the investment fund approach. Nicola de Pamphilis of its Research Department prepared an excellent statement of the rationale, included in his paper, "Economic Programming and Union Policies," in the OECD *International Trade Union Seminar on Economic and Social Programming* (Supplement), pp. 61–62. Neutral observers report that the other Italian labor federations and most workers who have expressed themselves are unenthusiastic, fearing that the proposal contains some hidden trap. A somewhat similar proposal has been discussed by German unions.

education for children, home ownership, or travel. Provision for liqui-
dating shares could be made, either freely as with mutual funds or
under specified circumstances as with pension trusts.

On this approach, the average annual increase in national productivity might be used as an enforceable limit to wage increases, with
wide-open bargaining permitted on the "investment share," that is, the
percent of profit accruing in the form of a partial title to a capital sum.
Such an arrangement could meet present objections to using the productivity estimate as a basis for an incomes policy, since it would leave
the total size of the earnings package to private bargains dictated by
the circumstances of the bargainers, while regulating the composition
of the earnings package in such a way as to serve the public interest in
growth and financial stability. Private and public ends would thus be
joined in a decision conforming to efficiency rules which were relevant
to both the micro and macro units.

There is an equitable basis for this approach, aside from the economic objective it serves. It avoids the dubious effort to urge wage
restraint as a stabilizing measure while doing nothing about prices except, at best "freezing" them. Whenever such a policy is followed and a
firm's specific productivity exceeds the restrained wage increase, the
consequence is to increase retained earnings and the value of the firm's
assets. Labor's restraint becomes the basis for an expanded capital
share.

By breaking the connection between the allocation and the use of
income, labor too secures benefits in the form of assets in return for
exercising restraint in the matter of present consumption. A "go easy"
policy with respect to spendable income can be accompanied by hard
bargaining for a larger investment share of the firm's revenues.

The potential unplugged loophole in such an arrangement would be
product prices. Workers would perhaps have less incentive to strike
bargains which required price increases, since they would gain no
present advantage—no additional money in the pocket; but if they
developed a sufficient regard for the future to collaborate with management in pushing prices up, in order to increase their capital stake,
some external price limitation would presumably have to be imposed.
But this possible threat to price stability might never materialize and by
itself seems hardly a sufficient reason to rule out consideration of this
device.

LABOR MARKET POLICY

One aspect of an incomes policy has won universal agreement—if the factors can be made more productive, they are more likely to contribute to financial stability by contributing to the pool of available goods in the same measure that they take goods from the pool. This result is encouraged to the extent that three conditions are met: (a) information as to alternative employments is generally available and generally accurate; (b) mobility of factors is good; and (c) factors may be retooled to their most effective use. In general, these requirements concern labor more than capital, though they are not without application to the latter. There is no need to elaborate here the variety of devices which have been employed to attempt to meet these three conditions more satisfactorily. By and large they concern the operations of a governmental employment service and involve such elements as advance notification to the service by employers of scheduled lay-offs, subsidies for moving to new locations and for enrolling in training programs, projections of skill needs for use in education and vocational counseling.

Perhaps the most significant development in this respect has been the growing realization that, even confining one's attention to the labor factor, these conditions are relevant not only to unemployed workers. If those with jobs can move to other jobs where they are more productive, the effect is economically the same as if a jobless worker had been put to work. This is particularly true in the matter of training and education, where a man's skill can be upgraded before it has been made obsolete by technological developments and before he is put under the compulsion of unemployment to do so.

Programs of this nature fall in the classification of seeking to increase productivity to match income distribution, as discussed in section (5) above. By themselves they probably are inadequate as an "incomes policy," but even by themselves, if undertaken with vigor and imagination, they can go a long way toward substituting for one.

STRUCTURE OF THE ECONOMY

The government's role of managing the economy is made either easier or more difficult by the institutional structure of the private sector.

The extent to which the market does and has done its job is of major importance in determining how effectively planning can be made to work. In Western societies, decentralization of most of the economic decision making to private subunits is essential if the values of individualism are to be preserved, even though that decision making takes place within the outlines of an overall plan and the actions of the subunit are rationalized only by the concomitant actions of the other subunits in the system.

The market economy is thus not antithetical to planning, or vice versa, as is often alleged to be the case. Western-style planning could not take place in the absence of an efficiently functioning market. Western planning operates *through* the market at the same time that it recognizes the limitations of the market in performing certain functions.

The market does not set social objectives, such as education and health, nor does it allocate resources between the achievement of such social objectives and the objectives of individuals and households. That must be done by political decision. The market economy, because it operates piecemeal, takes longer to adapt itself to major changes in environment which require a reorientation of economic activity generally, as notably in war. It is less effective in looking to the future where the future requires some concurrence in the design of economic activity, some agreement on the strategy which will give coherence to the parts.[18] The diffusion of decision-making authority also permits

[18] Prof. Phelps Brown has put the matter nicely in his article, "The National Economic Development Organization," in *Public Administration,* Autumn, 1963, p. 242: "The market seems to be better at tactics than strategy. Where a new product is to be diffused and serviced—the television set, for instance—there the incentives of the market economy, and its decentralized decision-taking, visibly operate quickly and pervasively. But adaptation is not so quick nor provision so pervasive when changes are called for in the whole structure of the economy. After the First World War the United Kingdom felt the impact of deepgoing changes in foreign markets and in the types of raw materials and fuel provided or called for by current developments. It met that impact with a structure of industrial equipment and expertise, and an infrastructure of location and transport, habits of thought and traditional channels of training and career, that had been shaped to meet the needs and seize the opportunities of an age now bygone. Experience showed the limits to individual adaptation within that framework: much was achieved, but much remained that required decision-taking of further reach. There has been no pause in technical development in the world, nor in changes of the channels of trade. The need for a strategy of adaptation remains. History goes on, and imposes tasks of redeployment hardly to be performed by the decentralized decision-taking of the market economy alone."

stalemates to develop in which resources are unutilized, when some central mobilization of effort is required if the nation's assets are to be effectively managed. For these and other reasons Western societies now all recognize that the market, by itself, is not an adequate organizer of its economic activities. The United States, no differently from United States Steel, cannot rely on the market, without direction, to integrate its widely dispersed and complex operations in such a manner as more nearly to achieve its objectives.

But if the market by itself is an inadequate organizer of economic activity, it is a supremely efficient organizer of activity in combination with a planning mechanism. Plans need be carried only to the point where the market can take over. Inducements and incentives can be built into the market system by plan, so that the market in effect becomes the executor of the plan, at least in major areas of operation.

The essence of a market is competition. In view of the importance of the market to effective management of the economy, virtually all Western governments have taken measures to strengthen competitive forces. These have tended to follow two lines of action. The first enjoins monopolistic and collusive practices. Indicative of the types of anticompetitive behavior which are frowned on are those listed in Article 85 of the Rome Treaty of the Common Market:

(a)   the direct or indirect fixing of purchase or selling prices or of any other trading conditions

(b)   the limitation or control of production, markets, technical development or investment

(c)   market-sharing or the sharing of sources of supply

(d)   the application to parties to transactions of unequal terms in respect of equivalent supplies, thereby placing them at a competitive disadvantage

(e)   the subjecting of the conclusion of a contract to the acceptance by a party of additional supplies which, either by their nature or according to commercial usage, have no connection with the subject of such contract

The second line of support for competition is through the removal or reduction of tariff or quota barriers to foreign goods. Through exposure to the rivalry of foreign firms, domestic producers are driven to more efficient performance. The EEC and EFTA enclaves have both had this effect on their constituent economies.

But if Western governments have moved to strengthen competitive influences, none has done so without reservation. Competition too has its drawbacks, as any businessman knows. Carried to an extreme it can be wasteful and destructive—a gas station at every corner of an intersection with none of them making much of a profit is perhaps the most familiar example. Excessive competition drags a whole industry down by forcing it to operate according to present market exigencies rather than by longer-run design. It impedes technological development by making it less rewarding.

In the light of these considerations, the same governments which have detailed anticompetitive practices which are to be outlawed, as in the Common Market list above, often—indeed usually—enter the proviso that this injunction shall apply only when the practice is "unreasonable" or "harmful." The United States is virtually alone in recognizing most of such practices as illegal per se, that is, regardless of their effect, and even the United States has wavered on that line.

Thus the same article of the Rome Treaty which spells out the five prohibited practices goes on to specify that this provision shall not apply in the case of any agreements or classes of agreements between enterprises, any decisions or classes of decisions by associations of enterprises, and any concerted practices or classes of concerted practices which contribute to the improvement of the production or distribution of goods or to the promotion of technical or economic progress while reserving to users an equitable share in the profit resulting therefrom, and which

(a)   neither impose on the enterprises concerned any restrictions not indispensable to the attainment of the above objectives

(b)   nor enable such enterprises to eliminate competition in respect to a substantial proportion of the goods concerned

Examples of legally permissible cooperation among rival firms are not hard to come by. They extend to joint financing (jointly floated bond issues in France, with the group guaranteeing the whole amount), joint research programs, joint labor policies, joint marketing facilities, market-sharing agreements, even group decisions on pricing.

Most indicative of the Western European belief that competition is not to be viewed as an end in itself is the widespread support for the "rationalization" of industry. It is quite generally believed—in government, industry, and labor circles—that the induced elimination of the weaker firms and the consolidation of many small firms into a few large ones would conduce to greater efficiency, with benefits to producers, workers, and consumers alike. The comment of the *Norwegian Long-term Programme 1962–1965* is one to which most Western European governments would subscribe:

> Many branches of Norwegian industry today are composed of a large number of small working units. In a number of these cases a concentration into larger working units or effective forms of cooperation will be essential if there is to be a rapid improvement in productivity. This process of adjustment will in many cases only be possible as part of a further rationalization of the structure of the economy.[19]

In France J. M. Jeanneney a decade ago criticized the French government for having slowed economic growth by giving unwarranted protection to small business units:

> The small firms have too often lagged behind possible technical progress. The reasons are intellectual and financial. New techniques are hard to find out about, to choose, and to put into operation. The head of a small firm, who has to keep track of everything, often lacks the time and qualifications necessary.... The direction of family firms being hereditary, they risk falling into incapable hands. When they need to carry out investment, they cannot tap public savings through bonds or stocks. Their owners, fearing the loss of full control of their business, often hesitate to use the financial help that they could obtain from banks or individuals.[20]

The techniques of rationalization have been varied. They have included consolidation under government ownership, as in the British coal industry, which is now managed by the National Coal Board. The reorganization of British textiles, a more recent development, was induced by governmental subsidies and compulsory industry levies—the former as partial compensation for the elimination of excess capacity and the installation of more modern equipment, the latter to compensate workers made redundant in the process.

In France, new steel investment has been planned in terms of most profitable scale and location, without respect to the financial or organizational possibilities of existing firms. The operations in whole regions

---

[19] English summary, p. 7.

[20] From *Forces et Faiblesses de l'Économie Française* (Paris, 1956), pp. 258–259, as translated by John Sheahan in *Promotion and Control of Industry in Postwar France* (Cambridge, Mass.: Harvard University Press, 1963), p. 241.

have been regrouped. In the north of France, for example, two major firms joined in establishing a holding company for all the facilities in that region. Their new operating subsidiary, Usinor, was largely financed through a combination of loans from several governmental financial sources put together under the overall supervision of, among others, the Planning Commission.[21]

There is obviously an uneasy relationship between these two aspects of structural policy—the encouragement of active competition, on the one hand, and the acceptance of interfirm cooperation and promotion of consolidation, on the other. There is no clear-cut basis for saying that one is right and the other wrong. Too many relevant considerations condition the results.

Among these considerations are whether a basis for competitive vitality exists within an industry, which can be supported and strengthened. This is a matter of technology, of administrative organization, of tradition, among other things. In the absence of a sound competitive foundation, integration and rationalization under government inspection may produce more benefits.

The degree of foreign competition is of special importance. Consolidation of a domestic industry may be necessary to achieve technological gains without which the industry could not survive competition from abroad. Rationalization within an economy is pursuant to competitive pressures from outside it. (The only danger on this front is that the habit of coordination and integration may be extended across national boundary lines.) In contrast, consolidation of an industry which is relatively immune to foreign competition leaves no external reins upon it except direct government control, or innovations which provide new product competition.

Conclusions as to the structural needs of an economy are something about which one cannot afford to be dogmatic. It is clear that competition is indispensable in a private-enterprise economy. It is likewise clear that at times competition can be carried to extremes and undermine the efficient organization of an industry, or that it can be made more effective in larger units. Balance between competition and organization is needed. Securing the appropriate balance is itself a matter for planning.

[21] Sheahan, the same, p. 69.

6...
techniques
of coordination

Coordination of the parts of any economic system to achieve some overall objective involves two distinct processes, each indispensable, as we have already observed. In the first instance technical-economic coordination is necessary to establish standards by which the quality of actual performance may be gauged. Whatever the objective or objectives of the system may be, their identification implies preferences in the use of resources. Certain results are to be sought rather than, or more than, other results. The introduction of this preference scale—one thing "more than" something else—has two immediate and inevitable consequences: first, it requires quantification, even if only of a very rough ordinal nature, so that the objective can be specified, and second, it requires economy in the technical sense of the use of resources for one purpose rather than some, or any, other.

The need for technical norms thus does not arise from any preference for one type of economic technique over another. It is rooted in the very act of goal seeking. As soon as one (or a group) establishes an objective, requiring the use of resources, then answers must be found to questions involving how much of one's resources may be used in one way rather than another. Nor is this the same thing as maximizing. Even if one adopts a satisfactory objective, measurement is still required to determine whether the objective has been achieved, and economizing is required to the point of achievement. If one adds the further consideration that objectives are seldom absolute but usually relative—what is "satisfactory" varies with the availability of resources, for example—then the need for quantifying and economizing becomes even more ineluctable.

The inescapability of some technical norm in the presence of goal-seeking behavior does not carry with it any connotation as to the preferability of one sort of norm over another. A technical norm—or a "model" of behavior—can be provided, as we earlier noted, by a rule of thumb no less than by some beautifully elaborated mathematical formulation. Intricacy and refinement are not necessarily qualities of excellence in this case. For the purpose of establishing standards of performance, in some instances rough measures may be superior to fine ones. There is a danger in pressing quantification to the point of giving specific numerical values to relationships the conceptual nature of which has been inadequately explored. Dubious assumptions are introduced into a model in order to permit the computation of "precise" results, without sufficient understanding that the precision obtained is purely mathematical and that its practical value as a standard for the system may have been reduced in the process. A mathematically "precise" answer may be farther off than a gross ordinal and verbal result if the functions represented by the system of equations from which it derives are invalid. Nevertheless, it is reasonable to expect that the direction of development of economic techniques will be toward more elaborate models, which take into consideration a wider range of relevant variables, clarifying relationships among the numerous parts of complex economic systems. This can only be to the good, as long as

functional relevance rather than formal elegance remains the touchstone.
The specific uses of technical-economic models in planning operations are several:

1 They provide an initial test of the feasibility of objectives in the
   light of the availability of resources and competing objectives.
   To take a simple illustration: How much of a program of social
   investment is compatible with the increase in GNP which is
   expected, given the estimated accompanying levels of industrial
   investment, technological coefficients, aggregate consumption
   propensities, increase in governmental "public business" activities
   following from the rising level of economic activity, and a few
   other relevant variables? The model from which one draws conclusions need not be perfect to obtain useful clues as to the
   workability of a proposed plan.

   The Netherlands Central Planning Bureau has, for example,
   contributed to the rationality of its government's planning by
   calculating the economic effects of a reduction in the length of
   the work week, or of providing improved pensions, to ascertain
   the cost of these in terms of alternative objectives; the cost may
   turn out to be unacceptably high or surprisingly low, in contrast
   to less well-based preconceptions. The estimates admittedly con-
   tain a margin of error which, ex ante, is unknowable, but the
   analyzed and quantified result, subject to whatever qualifications
   it may be wise to put on it, is a better basis for further government investigation and action than someone's leap of intuition
   or the pooled guesses of a committee.

2 Economic models help to establish the necessary relationship of
   the parts of the system to the overall performance. They thereby
   demonstrate the consistency of the plans of the subunits with the
   plans of the system. The functioning of any part is dependent on
   the performance of the other parts—not only those to which it
   is directly related, as in a consumer-producer relationship, but
   also those to which it may be linked at two or three or many
   removes. The level of activity in Industry A depends on Industry B, which in turn is affected by how well Industries C
   and D are doing, and so on in an almost infinite regression. The
   performance of Industry A which is "consistent" with the needs
   of the system thus depends on the performance in a number of
   other industries which in turn are dependent on Industry A and
   on each other. "No sector, it seems, can be forecast until the

other sectors have been forecast first." [1] This requirement can be met only by models which make simultaneous forecasts for all sectors, taking into account the technical relationships existing between them, or by less elegant models which seek the same result by successive approximation. But whatever the technique used, the purpose remains clear: to review the plans of any one part of the system by reference to the plans of all other parts. Alternatively, we might say that the purpose is to validate the potential performance of the system by reference to the feasibility of each of the key parts making its required contribution. If electric power cannot be provided to other sectors in amounts sufficient to meet their needs, for example, then the economy's overall growth-rate target will have to be shaved.

3　Normative models are helpful in achieving economy in the use of resources. They assist in seeing to it that resources are directed into channels which, over time, are most likely to yield the system's objectives. They do this by identifying the stream of resource requirements of goals and thus aid in anticipating and mobilizing the financial means necessary to their phased accomplishment.

They also help to ensure that assets are not wasted through disuse. By identifying the potential output of a system, they make possible its organization to achieve that potential. In line with the previous analysis, we can say that by assisting in determining the categorical objectives of a society they also assist in realizing its specific goals, thus achieving a double efficiency in the use of assets.

4　In the absence of some systematic organization of expectations concerning the future, we would be reduced to relying on hunches, guesses, and instruments of chance. For these a model substitutes sets of rational expectations, rational because based on a predetermined set of functional relationships which can be given contemporary significance by the infusion of current data—a set of relationships which have been tested by their explanatory value with respect to the past, and which abstract from any temporary sense of optimism or pessimism which may influence judgment. Thus on a day-to-day and week-to-week basis, as actual performance materializes, we are provided with clues to what we can

[1] Everett Hagen, "The Role of Economic Forecasting in Income Stabilization," in Max F. Millikan (ed.), *Income Stabilization for a Developing Democracy* (New Haven, Conn.: Yale University Press, 1953), p. 190.

expect in the future, on the strength of which we can take more informed action. A model is an instrument for organizing data in an intelligence system.

THE TOOLS OF TECHNICAL–ECONOMIC COORDINATION

It would be possible to itemize quite an assortment of analytic tools for the kind of technical-economic coordination whose uses we have just noted. Our purposes will be served, however, by recognizing two principal types: (1) approximation procedures and (2) mathematical formulations.

The first is exemplified by the French and Swedish planning systems. In the French plan, the point of departure is actually a very simplified econometric model. On the strength of several "trial" growth rates, estimates of GNP for the terminal plan year are broken down into household consumption, public consumption, housing, gross capital formation, and net balance of trade. Input-output analysis assists in determining intermediate demand (in the Fourth Plan, on a twenty-eight-sector basis). From the intermediate levels of production are derived estimates for the allocation of investment and employment among the sectors. All this is preliminary to the principal effort, which consists of referring the results of these computations to committees representing the principal industry sectors (*commissions de modernisation*) for their evaluation of the reasonableness of the estimates. The Commissions are staffed predominantly by members of the industry supplemented by government and labor union officials. The estimates by sector are further disaggregated by referral to subcommittees— sometimes as many as seventy for a given sector.

These assessments by the "working" members of the economy are then reassembled for review by the Planning Commission. Discrepancies between committee estimates and original estimates are noted and attempts made to reconcile them, often by direct discussion. Similarly, discrepancies between the estimates of any two branches or sectors must be reconciled, as when the steel industry's proposed output fails to provide for all the demand estimated by the steel-using industries. Reconciliation may require a number of "rounds" of estimates and revisions, a process of "iteration" or successive approximation. Eventually the plans for each of the major subcommittees and its branches are made mutually consistent, and the whole made consistent with the overall target growth rate.

The Swedish practice is far simpler. Formerly an *ad hoc* commission, now a planning staff, receives estimates from firms and trade associations as to production and investment plans over a specified period, assuming overall growth of the economy to continue approximately as in the past. Sometimes round table discussions with an industry group provide insight into the basis for the estimates. The commission or staff then organizes the acquired data, without attempting to force it into an internally consistent mold. It does, however, note major inconsistencies, primarily between aggregates such as planned production, planned investment, expected labor force, and expected consumption. The existence of discrepancies is the basis for policy recommendations with respect to governmental actions (less frequently private actions) designed to forestall unfavorable effects. It is only with the inclusion of these policy recommendations that the Swedish exercise can even be viewed as an effort at technical-economic coordination, something which aims at pulling the pieces of the economy together in a way that accomplishes—on paper—an overall objective (in this instance, simply the categorical objective of a growth rate).

The mathematical or econometric approach is typified by the Dutch planning program. It consists of a system of thirty-six equations which, in contrast to the French preoccupation with intersectoral "coherence," compose a macro model which is geared only to the categorical objective of a growth rate, bounded by a number of "constraints." [2] The target—a percentage increase in GNP—is taken as given. From this can be derived the accompanying increase in consumption. Private investment needs are given by the incremental GNP, as a function of capacity utilization, liquid assets, profits, and so on, and appropriate governmental policies can be recommended to ensure its reaching and holding at this level. Housing investment is given by population growth and family formation. This leaves government consumption and government investment, the "budget margin," which the government can itself control. Thus all the pieces fit together to realize the target—that is, the given GNP with which the process began.[3]

[2] There is no need to repeat here the previously expressed view that there is no value in treating joint objectives as "constraints" except to facilitate mathematical solution.

[3] de Wolff and Stevers, "State Budget and Planning," in *Les Prévisions Budgétaires*, pp. 96–124. Prof. Henri Theil, director of the International Center for Management Sciences at Rotterdam, who has himself been involved in the refine-

Although the Dutch plan is expressed in aggregative terms, the Central Planning Bureau also prepares sectoral estimates which are checked with industry representatives, not only to validate the macro results reached mathematically, but also to improve the technical coefficients which are part of the model. As the Central Planning Bureau has pointed out, the volume of statistical data, on the basis of which the coefficients of the equation system are estimated, grows annually, permitting a reestimation of coefficients and an improvement in the quality of the results.[4]

POLITICAL–ORGANIZATIONAL COORDINATION

The analysis which emerges from technical-economic coordination is an ex ante view of desired ex post results and the conditions which presumably must obtain if they are to be realized. It is thus a normative exercise.[5] It says to the policy makers, If this, this, and this are what

---

ment of Dutch planning techniques, comments: "...There are about a dozen equations, which deal with such variables as employment, imports and prices. There are also numerous definitional equations, partly derived from national accounts relationships. Now this system is built in such a way that it contains both the important decision variables and the most important variables which are not government controlled. Among the latter I should mention the level of employment, the surplus on the balance of payments, the price level of consumer goods, the level of investment, and the share of wages in national income. The most obvious decision variables are government expenditure and various tax rates. By solving the equation system one can estimate the effect of alternative measures of economic policy on the noncontrolled variables. For example, when it is decided to raise government expenditure by 1 billion the result is that the surplus on the balance of payments changes by so-and-so, possibly after a certain lag, that the price level goes up by a certain percentage, and so on. Needless to say, such effects cannot be given with complete precision; they are only estimated. But it is, I think, an interesting example of a mathematical technique which is used as a guide to policy." *Institute of Management Sciences Bulletin*, May 15, 1964, p. 2.

[4] Central Planning Bureau, *Central Economic Plan, 1961* (1961), p. 113.

[5] J. M. Clark once referred to contemporary economics as "an economics whose theories have become largely theories of what is sound and economically correct, rather than that of the forces determining actual events." M. Berger, T. Abel, and C. H. Page (eds.), *Freedom and Control in Modern Society* (Princeton, N.J.: D. Van Nostrand Company, Inc., 1954), p. 199.

This normative brand of economics is not restricted to the maximization of consumer advantage or to welfare notions more broadly. It is equally present in the field of planning in the construction of models which are viewed as the keys to a future wanted state of the economy. As the next paragraph spells out, to the extent that this analysis exhausts the economist's interest in planning, it

you want, then consumption and investment and the export-import balance and the government budget and a few other variables must behave in this way, or in these alternative ways. On the other hand, if you modify your objectives thus, then the necessary conditions will look like this. Make your own choices.

In the more disaggregated models, such as that for France, the technical-economic analysis also suggests the various rates of growth which must be elicited from the principal sectors of the economy if overall targets are to be realized.

But this coordination on paper leaves to the policy makers not only the choice but also all the problems of inducing the behavior which will establish the conditions postulated. The model says nothing whatsoever about whether the "necessary" savings and investment and import restrictions and wage policy are politically feasible—whether they can in fact be achieved, and whether therefore the model is a "realistic" one. It does not even pretend that the policies suggested by the system of relationships pictured are somehow better or more attainable than other policies which attempt to take into account political factors or values which have been left out of the model, but which cannot be left out of governmental operations. Any model, particularly of the econometric or mathematical variety, is necessarily more simplified and assumes more logically consistent behavior than is ever the case. In part this is due to the process of abstraction, but in major part it is due to the fact that it is a model of the system as a whole, treating it as an Adam Smithian "machine," with all the parts meshing or interlocking so that the action of any component produces calculable effects on others.

But the actual economy is not so integrated. It is composed of a large number of subsystems, each of which has its own somewhat divergent objectives, which can be made more or less compatible with any posited objectives for the system as a whole only by a process of pulling and hauling, bargaining and cajoling. The organization of the economy which is assumed in the technical-economic models must be

leaves out of account, in Clark's words, "the forces determining actual events." It leaves to others, if to any, an examination of the actions of government as *manager* of the nation's assets, coping with numerous power groups having sometimes competing and sometimes complementary objectives, and seeking to push and pull them into some state of coherence which is reasonably on the road to the generalized—and generally accepted—objectives of the economic system as a whole.

contrived through political action. The coordination which the one treats as a matter of logic, the other must treat as a matter of management.

Both types of coordination are part of the planning process. Technical-economic coordination performs, as we have seen, an advisory and guiding role. It is indispensable as soon as one has established objectives for the system. Political-organizational coordination performs the managerial task of bringing the parts into a functioning whole, without any more loss of efficiency in the system than is necessary to satisfy subunit objectives enough to induce them to perform as wanted.

In Western society the possibility of divergence between private and public goals is regarded as itself a value to be protected. Freedom on the part of subunits to go their independent ways, up to some point which cannot be identified by any system of equations, is even considered conducive to long-run effectiveness of the system by encouraging experimentation and innovation. But to the extent that inefficiency results from other causes than divergence of objectives, it is a loss without any offset. And to the extent divergence of objectives is sharp enough to lead to stalemate or greatly reduced economic effectiveness, it is the task of the government as manager of the economy to reduce the discrepancy. Its job is to attempt to formulate policies which achieve as much as possible of the goals of both the economic system as a whole and the subunit as a separable entity—a political balancing operation rather than a technical exercise.

This task is not based simply on ethical or philosophical values, but has an organizational imperative. Lacking hierarchical command over all the parts of the economy, the government can achieve its objectives only by inducing responses from the private subunits. That necessity places it in a bargaining relation vis-à-vis such subunits, and its power to elicit the desired action increases to the extent that the action is compatible with subunit goals as well as system goals.

This reconciliation of the goals of the system and its components is the chief purpose of political-organizational coordination. We have been through this before in Chapter 3 and will have occasion to return to it in Chapter 8, so there is no need to dwell on it here. Some divergence of goals is inescapable in a private-enterprise economy, but some coincidence of goals not only exists but can be increased by managerial (here governmental) action.

One outstanding example is provided by the relation of the French government to the *commissions de modernisation* which it calls into being and whose role in technical-economic coordination we have already seen. The fact that governmental representatives sit on these committees and that the government's Planning Commission elaborates the overall framework within which they operate, gives it no authority to compel "appropriate" decisions from the private industries or labor unions represented. These must be won in the course of a process that is set in motion during the preparation of each commission's report. Each commission initiates a form of bargaining with the government by specifying in its report the conditions which it "must" have if it is to be able to produce the results set forth. These conditions may relate to special financing arrangements, tax concessions (with respect to depreciation, for example), import or export privileges, or other matters.

Neither industry nor government is committed by the fact that its respective representatives sign these reports, including the statement of "essential" conditions. These constitute only recommendations for the consideration of the Planning Commission and other relevant agencies of government, each set of recommendations having to be weighed against those made by all the other commissions, so that governmental policy is reasonably consistent and within the limits of overall financial equilibrium. It is this *actual* elaboration of inducements, which involves a considerable maneuvering and negotiation of an informal nature, which constitutes the political-organization coordination without which the work of the commissions would remain only an exercise.

Political-organizational coordination, in any planning framework, also extends to a reconciliation of goals among the major interest groups, notably industry, labor, and agriculture. This is most evident in the case of the search for an "incomes policy."

ORGANIZATION OF THE TWO COORDINATING FUNCTIONS

The structure of the planning programs, differing from one country to another, reflects the way in which the several governments conceive of the process of political-organizational coordination in relationship to technical-economic coordination. In the Netherlands the Central Planning Board is responsible only for the latter, and it has perfected its econometric model of the economy to a level of sophistication which probably surpasses any other Western country. The task of political coordination is almost entirely outside its purview. In France, the Commissariat du Plan is concerned with both functions, in an *expert* capacity. It elaborates the model of the economy and also participates extensively in the deliberations, negotiations, and arrangements which are used to effectuate the expressed intention. In England, the National Economic Development Council performs both functions within a *representative* framework, composed as it is of an equal number of industry and labor officials, with a leavening of public and governmental representatives. Its activities thus far have not led it very far down the planning road, but as far as it goes, it has sought to join economic and political coordination in the same body.[5a]

To be sure, in any country no one authority can ever be charged with political-organizational coordination (in the way that technical-economic coordination can be delegated to a single agency), since by its nature this is something which is carried out through all the agencies of government. But this simply underscores that to be effective, political coordination requires not only a reconciliation of partially conflicting aims between firms in an industry and between interest groups and between private and public sectors, but also *within* the government sector itself. Bargaining goes on between the several departments and agencies of government as to the preferable policy vis-à-vis those whose responses must be induced, as to the preferable compromise, between system and subunit goals.[6] These intragovernmental differences of opinion and interest become additional elements to be reconciled, in a diffuse process which extends throughout the whole of society, linking the parts into a loose system—more or less successfully, depending in large part on the skill with which the managerial function of coordination is exercised.

The political-organizational coordination which attempts to relate performance to the standards of efficiency provided by the technical-economic models could conceivably take place on a system-wide face-

[5a] The above was written before the Labor Party took office in 1964. Subsequently a new Ministry of Economic Affairs took on most of the functions of the NEDC, which now appears to be concerned primarily with organizing industry commissions having the same ambiguous status as it itself has.

[6] In France in 1962, for example, there was a division of opinion between the Ministry of Finance (contra) and the Ministry of Industry joined by the Commissariat du Plan (pro) as to the advisability of an increase in the price of steel.

to-face, negotiated basis, resulting in a social-economic "contract." Perhaps the closest approximation of this is in the French planning program, where the projections of the *commissions de modernisation* become the basis for the final plan. But even here the plan is not viewed as actually committing anyone (except possibly the government ministries). The submissions of the twenty-five or so commissions do not represent even an implied agreement to work within the overall framework of the plan, since they are prepared by groups which have no operational authority (that is, by industries rather than by firms).

But even in the absence of such system-wide negotiated consensus there emerges—piecemeal and *ad hoc* and constantly subject to revision—what may be referred to as a "national budget." This is the equivalent of the budget in the firm, after allowing for the fact that it is not subject to hierarchical insistence on a particular performance. It represents the performance which can realistically be expected, guided by the technical-economic standards of potential performance but modified by political considerations, as necessary, to weld the relatively autonomous subunits into a functioning system.

THE INTERPLAY BETWEEN PROSPECTIVE AND ACTUAL

In the case of technical-economic coordination, we are interested in standards of efficiency applying to an economy seeking specified objectives. Only logical analysis is involved. In the case of political organization, it is the actual process of coordination which is relevant, however facilitated by standards or theory. At this stage it is not a normative exercise on paper which concerns us, but something which is realized in fact, however well or poorly. The contrived organization of the economy, however effectively carried out, is as much a part of the planning process as the standards which guide it.

This inclusion of the actual coordination of the numerous subunits in our analysis of planning may seem to blur the traditional distinction between planning and execution. This is indeed the case. The result is here viewed as part of the planning process no less than the intent. Moreover, it will be argued that the distinction between plan as intention, on the one hand, and action as the consequence of plan and something distinguishable from it, on the other, obscures the nature of the process and endangers its effective application. In this matter the business firm, in its conception of planning, has moved ahead of the public planners.

Time is a continuous stream, and any segmenting of it into discrete intervals—a quarter, a year, a quinquennium—is of course arbitrary and justifiable only as a matter of convenience. Economic activity is ongoing, just as is economic intention. Neither one starts or stops by the calendar. The sorts of changes with which economists are always wrestling—in technology, in population, in tastes, in resource location and utilization, in political alignment, and so on—necessarily affect economic activity, deflecting or diverting it in ways which had not been foreseen, or if foreseen, only as one of a number of possible courses of development.

But such changes necessarily have their effect on intentions too. The notion that a "plan"—the paper document setting forth objectives and technical-economic standards—can in effect stop changes other than those foreseen and incorporated in it, over the period of time for which projections are made, stretching from one to twenty years into the future, is too artificial to warrant comment. Yet that is the implication of calculating, at the expiration of such documents, by how much the "actual" has diverged from "plan," treating the degree of discrepancy as a measure of the success or failure of the planning process.

If change is continuous and not always foreseeable, and necessarily affects economic activity, then it affects too the nature of intentions, since the base from which they take their departure has been altered. And the modification of intentions in the face of change is no more a defect of planning than the modification of activity in the face of change is a defect of economic administration. We would criticize the business manager or public official who refused to alter course when circumstances have altered. We should be equally impatient with those who fail to alter intentions (and the technical-economic standards with which actual behavior can be compared) when circumstances have changed sufficiently to invalidate them. Otherwise, the standards of technical-economic coordination must be viewed, prospectively, as only some form of prophecy and judged good or bad on the basis of whether the prophecy "came true." The economist is cast in the role of seer—a most uncomfortable role since prophetic vision is not part of his professional equipment. Since few prophecies materialize, a "frozen" plan quickly becomes history before its terminal date. It remains a useful guide only for a short span, at its inception. One criticism directed at the Swedish five-year plan, prior to its 1963 modification into a "rolling plan" (one year dropped off as another is added), was that it became less and less useful with the passage of time, as unforeseen developments made its aging projections less and less relevant to contemporary economic activity.

As actual economic behavior departs from that which had been expected or intended, the departures themselves, and the reasons for them, become critical information feeding back into the planning process. If a divergence is for reasons which can be corrected, the original planning document—the standard with which the effectiveness of actual behavior is compared—can remain unaltered. It is the behavior which one seeks to modify. But if the variance is for reasons which supersede the assumptions on which the original planning document had been based, then it is the latter which must be changed, not—or not only—the performance.[7] Thus actual performance and intended performance constitute related and integral parts of a single process. Once "execution" is separated out from "planning," the conception of correcting intentions in the light of "feedback" from performance is lost and with it, the conception of planning as the *systematic* management of assets. One is left, instead, with the indefensible notion of planning as prophecy.

The very notion of a plan period, at the end of which actual performance can be compared with that expected, reveals its arbitrary character once we recognize the continuing interplay between intention and action. One plans as far ahead as needed in order to make effective decisions relative to assets and engages in continuing modification of intentions in the light of unfolding experience. Where plans are frequently adjusted, with what would one compare performance to determine its relative success or lack of it, if he wanted to—the oldest

---

[7] This was explicitly recognized in the 1947 Norwegian plan: "When the conditions and assumptions underlying the national budget change, and when better information is available and new experience gained, the plans will be modified to the extent required, and the economic policy, correspondingly modified." (Translation by Bjerve in *Planning in Norway, 1947–1956,* p. 39.) Norway has in fact incorporated revisions, when necessary, on a quarterly basis. Bjerve, who has been close to the Norwegian program throughout its existence, has questioned (p. 43) whether plan revisions may not at times have simply been *post hoc* validations of government actions—plan following actions rather than vice versa.

statement of intention, or the most recent? In the case of a rolling five-year plan, should results be compared with the projections made five years earlier, or last year's?

The conception of the planning process adopted here, then, necessarily involves a continuing interplay between intention and action—the adjustment of one's orientation to the future in the light of the new information constantly being generated by ongoing activity. To attempt to divorce these two aspects of the process leads to a lack of interest in an adequate reporting system (as we shall see has generally been the case) and an excessive interest in the technical-economic exercise, considered almost as an end in itself, as though a neatly articulated formulation will produce the results which are wanted if only men are intelligent enough to follow its lead, and if they are not—blame politics or self-interest, not the "planners."

The idea of planning as only a statement of intentions based on forecasts or projections and not as a process which includes as well a continuing inflow of current information on the strength of which both projections and intentions may be modified as necessary, has led to a misplaced emphasis on the importance of "reliable" forecasts, and—as a frequent corollary—a rejection of planning because forecast accuracy is obviously too much to expect.[8] Now, it is obvious that the more reliable a forecast is, for whatever period of time, the better a guide it is to policy, and the more applicable it is to the derivation of technical-economic standards with which actual performance can be compared. But to assume that because no one can foresee the future, therefore no one can plan for it, is a conclusion which none of us finds it possible to make stick. We all do plan, and necessarily so, for varying periods of time into the future, attaching such probabilities to our assumptions as appear reasonable in the light of what we know and modifying our expectations and intentions on the strength of what transpires with passing time. Accuracy of some "original" forecast is perhaps less important than its prompt correction whenever developments indicate its inaccuracy.

[8] Examples of this point of view are found in Everett Hagen's essay, "The Role of Economic Forecasting in Income Stabilization," in Millikan (ed.), *Income Stabilization for a Developing Democracy*, especially at p. 175, and George Terborgh's comments in *Employment and Unemployment: The Problem of the 1960's* (Washington, D.C.: U.S. Chamber of Commerce, 1961), pp. 77-79.

THE NEEDS OF A REPORTING SYSTEM

From this point of view, a reporting system which feeds in data as to what is actually going on in the economy, in as much relevant detail and as promptly as possible, is an essential element in an effective planning program. But surprisingly little attention has been paid to this need.

Every Western government has, to be sure, its statistical office, sometimes located in a ministry or department, sometimes an independent agency. Its functions are frequently directly connected with the national income accounting office, which is charged with preparing an annual—sometimes quarterly—statement of the nation's gross product and income. In this respect it performs the same function as the typical corporation accounting office which is responsible for preparing the firm's income statement and balance sheet reflecting the year's (or quarter's) operations. But this kind of statistical compilation is a long way from being the kind of data which is useful in the management of current operations. It is not timely enough, and it is not cast in a form appropriate to managerial needs. No business manager today would consider traditional year-end or quarterly statements sufficient for the firm's planning program. He would require a variety of daily, weekly, and monthly reports as well as those for the quarter or the year, all of which could be laid alongside the relevant budget projections to determine where performance was departing from intent.

At the same time, any manager in the upper reaches of the corporate organization who received all such reports would be inundated by them. Thus there has developed the practice known as "reporting by exception." Any manager in the hierarchy has passed up to him only those reports which indicate a clear departure from the budget plan. This screens out most of the data flow and focuses attention on those elements of the company's program which require analysis and possibly action.

Public economic planning in the West has yet to develop any comparable reporting system. Government officials, in their capacity as managers of the nation's assets, do not have available to them such a systematic and timely flow of relevant information, on the strength of which plans can be revised. There are a number of reasons why this is so. Perhaps the most important are the following:

1 Emphasis on periodic technical-economic coordination, often taken to be synonymous with planning, has lessened interest in a flow of information organized in such a way as to permit continuous revision. Governments move from a Fourth Plan to a Fifth Plan, for example; they do not engage in continuous planning.

2 There is some fear that performance reporting carries an inference that wherever variances occur, the government should intervene. If the men's clothing industry experiences a slump, should the government move in to do something about it? If the automobile output is greater or less than projected, does this carry the connotation that government should restrain or stimulate it? What is the purpose of a flow of data on economic performance if the government is not intended to react?

This fear springs from a failure to distinguish between specific and categorical objectives. Only in the case of specific objectives would the government be expected to move in with specific remedies. Where categorical objectives are involved—the level of consumption, of investment, of exports—departures of firms or industries from levels of activity which they had expected would not constitute "exceptions" to be reported as long as they were offsetting at the appropriate levels. If the output of shoes was down, the output of hats might be up. If investment in steel was up, investment in textiles might be less than anticipated. These variances would offset each other partially or wholly, at the level of the economy as a whole or of some major sector, which is to say at the level where they constitute a categorical objective for the system. Only insofar as they were nonoffsetting would an "exception" from intention emerge, calling government attention to the possible need for action. That is, only insofar as a condition of recession or inflation, of underemployment or overemployment emerged after all possible offsetting had taken place, and therefore general enough to be of some concern, would a government be called on to consider whether circumstances warranted corrective measures.

3 The need for an effective reporting system has been diminished by a lack of clarity as to plan objectives. The targets of the system have not been stated with sufficient precision to permit determination of when a variance has occurred.

This condition is true even of such a "planning" society as France. Officials there in the spring of 1964 were asking themselves what *were* the targets of the Fourth Plan, which presumably were about to be compromised in order to dampen inflationary pressures, and they were experiencing some difficulty in supplying answers. There was a general understanding that the plan was to stress social investment. But how much social investment? Were the figures built into the plan necessarily targets, or did they simply specify a general intent? Why treat as a "target" a figure necessarily subject to uncertain real content due possibly to faulty assumptions as to technological coefficients, possibly to changing international developments, possibly even to changing conceptions of what social welfare called for? What variables in the plan were really sufficiently "key" so that deviations from projections might be considered to jeopardize overall performance? Was the projected investment and output in steel really crucial, or in oil refining, or in electric energy? Should the number of housing units in the plan be viewed as a target, or did it really make any difference if perhaps 50,000 were shaved from the original figure?

In such an atmosphere of uncertainty as to objectives, the need for timely and detailed reports on performance evaporated. What difference did an "exception" make if the figure from which an "exception" was noted was itself a floating, vague, or indeterminate quantity? [9]

This understandable soul-searching, scarcely avoidable in some measure, can be carried to the point where it negates the value of a reporting system only if (a) there is failure to distinguish between specific and categorical objectives and (b) if the reexamination of objectives is covert rather than explicit.

a In the French plan, for example, it was never clear whether steel investment was viewed as a specific objective (as the Planning Commissioner once asserted) or simply as an element of a categorical objective which might or might not be offset by investment elsewhere. Lacking clarity on this point, the significance of variances in the steel investment total is likewise obscured.

b There is no reason why objectives should not be reexamined and changed, but if so, quite explicitly, so that a variance can

[9] The same consideration has been noted by Bjerve as applying to Norwegian planning: "The interpretation of deviations between ex ante figures of government variables and the corresponding ex post figures may in some cases be difficult because it is not clear to what extent the ex ante figures represent obligatory directives to governmental agencies and to what extent less imperative suggestions concerning policy." *Planning in Norway, 1947–1956*, p. 56.

be identified as such if it emerges. In the absence of such explicit change, but with some generalized sentiment that perhaps the stated objectives are only approximate or expressive of broad intent, it becomes difficult to determine whether an "exception" has or has not occurred.

4 Whether a variance, even if promptly identified and reported, has any operational meaning, is another question which has reduced concern for establishing a data-collection system. Suppose a divergence from a properly identified objective is ascertained. It may be only a temporary fluctuation, something which will be offset in time, perhaps next month, by a corrective fluctuation in the other direction. It is necessary to wait for a while before it becomes apparent that the variance is not a fluctuation but is cumulative. But if one must wait a while before the significance of statistical data can be established, then present collection procedures are perhaps quite satisfactory—always subject to some improvement, to be sure, but hardly to be dismissed as totally inadequate.

There is a good deal of validity to this position, but it is based on an assumption that a government must either respond to a variance by action, or do nothing. Actually, a variance is primarily an occasion for an inquiry as to why it has occurred. The inquiry may be sufficiently inconclusive that there is nothing to do but wait for further developments, but in other cases it will elicit explanations which, at a minimum, provide lead time for considering appropriate measures, whether or not they later have to be put into effect.

This approach makes possible prompter action when action appears called for, and, because prompt, the action may actually involve less government intervention than if the "exception" were allowed to persist and cumulate. M. Massé, the French Planning Commissioner, has commented that because of a variety of "uncertainty" factors, anticyclical measures tend to be delayed—and then when initiated are excessive, leading to the familiar stop-and-go effect. He has argued that a policy based on more modest actions, taken sooner, would improve the possibilities of both growth and financial equilibrium.[10]

[10] Massé report, p. 23. In the same vein, the value of prompt reporting in decreasing the scale of corrective actions has been noted by Prof. Phelps Brown, in "The National Economic Development Organization," *Public Administration*, Autumn, 1963, pp. 240–241. Speaking of the British economy's "propensity to lurch and sway," he comments: "...From the Napoleonic Wars until the Second

5   Another reason why less attention has been paid to the use of current performance reports as the basis for determining whether action needs to be taken to make a plan effective or whether the plan needs revision is the unreliability of the data. It is common enough for statistical agencies to revise their figures several times before they are considered "final." [11] Under the circumstances to use a preliminary figure as the basis for reporting "exceptions" may be to trigger responses purely on the strength of statistical errors, or in any event on the strength of data the significance of which is distorted by statistical error.

That aggregative statistical data are unreliable is not a proposition that requires debate. Everyone knows it to be true. To the extent they fail to reflect actual conditions, they reduce the value of reporting systems. That too is evident. But it is equally a matter of experience that with all their unreliability such data are essential to effective governmental operation. Poor data are better than no data. Poor data obtained sooner are likely—though not necessarily—to be better than good data obtained later, when it comes to corrective action. In any event, data collection systems are not fixed, but are subject to improvement. Recognition of the value of timely reporting and experimentation with the means of providing it can only lead to better results than are now

World War, Western economies passed through a recurrent alternation, occupying some nine years on the average, of higher and slower rates of advance, which at their extremes became boom and slump; this cycle was particularly marked in the rate of investment. A similar cycle of alternately quickened and retarded investment has run through the activity of the United Kingdom since 1952, though now the period is more like five years. This instability arises from a defect in the mechanism of the market. When producers respond, for instance, to a signal calling for a greater supply, they need to see the effect of their response as they go along, so as to be able to adjust its amount. But if the effect is fed back only with some lag, they have only expectations to go upon meanwhile, and these expectations are affected by the sight of what others are doing, and by contagions of mood. Then, when the feedback does come through, it may impose a correction, but how great a correction can in turn be known only after some lag. Hence a propensity to overshoot and undershoot: adaptive responses based on expectations in the presence of lags set up 'hunting.' "

[11] "... estimates of the size of the investments during any given year are gradually adjusted by the [Swedish] Institute of Economic Research according as better statistics become available and the methods of calculation are improved. If we follow in detail the estimates of the Institute of Economic Research year by year we find that considerable adjustments have been successively effected to the different items and that the same item may have been adjusted both upwards and downwards on the various occasions when the figures were revised." Jan Wallander, "Experiences of Long-term Planning in Sweden," *Quarterly Review of the Skandinaviska Banken,* April, 1956, p. 53.

possible. The statistic has always enjoyed a bad repute, but it has also always been in demand. Data which we are collecting and using now would, some years back, have often been considered neither collectible, nor, if collectible, usable. We have found how to improve—somewhat—our collection procedures and how to improve—somewhat—the reliability of the data we gather. There is no reason to believe that improvement in these two respects has come to an end.

For the reasons cited above, and perhaps others, no country in the West has yet developed a reporting procedure suited to a planning program. It is an interesting commentary that the existence of a planning process in France apparently has made virtually no difference in its statistical procedures. As one member of the staff of the Institute for Statistical and Economic Studies (on which the Planning Commission principally relies for its basic data) wryly commented in conversation, they are doing very little that is different from what the non-planning United States is doing—except the United States probably does it better! Despite its elaborate procedures for the periodic drafting of a technical-economic planning model, France has not yet moved to the conception of a reporting system, geared to managerial needs, which a planning process requires. There is no greater frequency of data collection, no adequate network of reporting agencies, no organization built up to provide a flow of accounting data suited to the needs of managing the nation's assets (in contrast to the traditional set of national accounts), nothing approaching reporting by exception.[12] The principal difference is that the results of statistical analyses now get discussed within the planning framework, though it is by no means clear that lines of information flows to responsible authorities have been formalized. There seems to be more concern with improving the basic data for the elaboration of plans that in organizing data for plan administration, though the former without the latter is relatively barren.

[12] Conversations in the Spring of 1964 suggested that at least some of the people involved in the planning effort harbored fears that reporting of this sort implied a degree of government intervention greater than the "market research" character in which they prefer to clothe their program. When it was suggested that if the plan figures mean anything, then at some level of specificity, even of a categorical nature, they must represent targets or else they are meaningless in any planning sense, the response was an uneasy resistance to this proposition from some, though ready concurrence from others.

7...
actions in the light of variances

In Chapter 2 we noted that when a firm's adverse budget variances affect the achievement of its profit target, but its poor performance is offset by superior performances in rival firms, this suggests that whatever the difficulty is, it lies within the firm, and the solution must be sought there. The same is true with respect to industries.

In the short run a firm's corrective actions will probably have to center on cost reduction, since this is most amenable to prompt managerial control. Fixed and semi-fixed costs will be pared to levels appropriate to lower outputs. Inefficiencies and waste which were formerly ignored or tolerated will be hunted down and rooted out, industrial engineers will be prodded for cost-cutting procedures. Current production will be reduced in order to work off excessive inventories. Managers have frequently testified to the amount of "fat" that can be cut from a corporate budget when the pressure is on.

In the long run, however, persisting poor performance, offset by the continuing superior record of competitors, cannot be met on the field of cost-cutting. Corrective actions must relate to sales—the improvement of the marketing organization and especially the upgrading of the product line. This too is within the power of a firm's management, though it is a more difficult and demanding assignment.

But when the poor profit showing of one firm or industry is not offset by an improved profit showing of others, so that all (or most) firms tend to experience adverse variances, then the cause of the difficulty lies not within the firm or industry but in the system as a whole. The same is true with respect to plus-variances which involve all (or most) firms in an upward movement. In these cases, where variances are nonoffsetting as between firms and industries, the corporate variances arise from cumulative movements in national economic activity, which, by modifying the economic base for business performance, lead to results which are more or less than businessmen had generally anticipated.

That same cumulative movement in national economic activity creates variances in the national budget, if the latter is based on a potential output at stable prices, from which the cumulative movement is retreating or which it is overshooting. It is only insofar as the variance in the national budget can be corrected (inflationary or recessionary effects controlled) that business firms recover the power to deal effectively with their own internal variances.

We define the national budget as the economy's potential output at stable prices, embodying whatever specific and categorical objectives may have been settled on. When such a budget guides government policy, then movements away from it set up variances. These in turn are one cause, and a major one, of corporate variances. Control of variances from the national budget facilitates control of corporate variances. Moreover, a business *expectation* that government will move promptly to correct variances emerging in the national budget creates an environment in which business investment and production plans can more safely be premised on national budget projections. Reciprocally, by encouraging such private conclusions from national premises, business firms help to validate the latter.

Nevertheless, corporate actions based on assumptions as to government economic policy would not by themselves guarantee that the aggregative national budget would be realized. Other influences are also at work: consumer behavior, local government programs, labor union actions, foreign trade balances, crop failures, and a variety of other forces help to determine whether variances from the national budget will emerge. Moreover, business decisions are by no means always forthcoming or, if forthcoming, "correct" even if perfect assumptions as to the national budget are made: other considerations bear upon their feasibility and profitability. Even if the business community were generally agreed—and correct—on the level of investment and output appropriate to an expected level of national income, actual investment and output would be almost certain to deviate from the appropriate level due to circumstances peculiar to the plans and capabilities of individual firms. As the effect of these several sources of possible variances from the projected national budget materialized, then the government would be put in the position of having to adopt measures to deal with the aggregative variance—or else forfeit the expectation which had been built up in the minds of the business community, an expectation which is important to the realization of its own objectives.

What actions a government might take in the face of variances from the national budget depends on a number of factors.

1   The clarity with which system objectives are identified influences the significance of variances, as we observed in the preceding chapter, and thus effects whether a government moves to do anything about them. The determination of what should constitute the categorical objectives of the system is not a matter of cataloguing resources and then "translating" these into some quantity of goods and services specified in value terms. Economic theory is involved: What are the key variables which determine overall performance and thus are essential to the objective of realizing the full potential of the system's assets? How do they interact? Is business investment one of them? If so, do all kinds of investment have the same significance, so that inventories and research can be added to plant and equipment, for example, or are some investments more strategic than others? What role

does aggregative consumption play? Is the government's budget to be treated only as a balancing factor, or do some of its expenditures—for transportation facilities and education, for example—have a more specific functional role? If the latter, in what way and over what period?

Only in the light of satisfactory answers to questions like these can system objectives be properly designated, and, once designated, be maintained with any degree of firmness. But such answers require theoretical development, which is never far enough advanced to supply all the knowledge needed, is subject to revision and correction in the light of changing institutions as well as improving methodology, and is always open to disputation and contention.

Nevertheless, the actions which a government takes in the face of variances depend on some—even implicit—theoretical assumptions with respect to the necessary mechanisms for achieving system goals, and these in turn become the basis for indentifying other (instrumental) targets. How much growth or employment it believes is possible without excessive inflationary pressure depends, for example, on some—even implicit—theory of how the economy ingests resources to turn out goods and services, which permits the determination of certain categorical objectives—investment and consumption, for example—which are named as such only because of their relevance to the larger goal.

These instrumental goals become such only at levels of aggregation which permit no offsetting. Investment in textiles is not made a goal, because a decline or increase in its amount can be offset by investment elsewhere without jeopardizing the aggregate investment requisite to the growth or employment objective. Similarly, aggregate investment in plant and equipment would become an instrumental goal only if it were believed that a variance in that category could not be offset by an opposite variance in other types of investment, such as inventories. "Bottlenecks" may impose targets of lesser aggregation: investment in steel or energy may become an instrumental goal if an increase in steel or energy is critical to overall production levels. But even here, the target investment in steel or energy is not made any more specific by designating types of steel facilities or areas of energy buildup, so that even these remain categorical with respect to the industry or sector.

By minimizing the specificity of system objectives and by

simplifying the theoretical models which guide its determination of which variables are strategic enough to be treated as targets, a government can reduce the demands on its managerial role. The limitation of the number of specific targets is a political matter insofar as social welfare objectives are involved, but a technical-economic matter insofar as it involves the simplification of theoretical models.

2   The action which a government will take in the face of variances from the national economic budget depends in part on their magnitude. Minor variances can be safely ignored: they may be nothing more than a statistical aberration, and in any event they do not constitute a serious enough departure from the norm to warrant intervention to improve performance, and they certainly do not call for plan revision.

But what constitutes a "minor" variance? Opinions are likely to differ. A rule of thumb is likely to be the safest way of avoiding excessive hesitation or excessive urgency. A deviation of some predetermined percentage in any of the key instrumental variables would trigger an immediate analysis of the cause, with corrective action as found necessary.

3   This brings us to the reason for the variance as itself a factor in influencing the government's response to it. Departures from expectations, even in the key variables, may represent only a fluctuation which will be righted in the next period or two—a case of offsetting over time. If investment was above the projected levels for last month, this may be offset by a decline in the next month. At the same time, to adopt a "wait and see" attitude may permit a cumulative movement to gain such momentum that when action is finally taken, it will have to be more drastic than if taken more promptly.

This dilemma is partly a consequence of present reporting systems. Although the instrumental targets, exceptions from which constitute an alarm system, are taken at the highest possible aggregative level (thus allowing for a maximum of offsetting), desirably there should be sufficient detail accompanying the reports from which the aggregate is derived to provide clues to the cause for its behavior. If investment rises or falls this month, the aggregate investment figure, standing alone, offers no explanation. It is only by going back to the sources of data— the firms themselves—that explanation can be found. A good reporting system would make provision for information shedding light on individual corporate variances significant enough to raise questions. Even in the absence of a regular flow of such information a quick survey is likely to suggest leads which could be pursued to establish whether the variance which has emerged in an instrumental target merits concern or even some limited action.

DEGREE OF CONTROL OVER THE SITUATION

Unless planning is simply an exercise, there must be some expectation (a) that the economy will do about as well as projected—some fluctuations will of course inevitably occur and can be ignored; (b) that if it does not, for reasons which are actionable, something will be done about it; or (c) that if it does not perform as expected for reasons about which nothing can be done, then an adjustment in the plan is called for.

As long as the national budget represents potential performance and incorporates the system's goals, both specific and categorical, we can assume that the government will bend every effort to realize the levels of output projected. Why abandon what has been carefully analyzed and found possible? If the plan has any significance, variances will stimulate further action to realize the full value of the nation's assets.

The actions which may be taken are exactly the same as those which we examined in Chapter 4. The same panoply of inducements and facilitating fiscal and monetary measures which may have been considered necessary as part of the original plan may be modified in degree in the light of actual performance. Tax concessions and interest rates, for example, may be moved up or down as the occasion seems to require. Or implements in the government's tool kit whose use had not been thought necessary may now be put to use.

The difficulty may lie not with the private sector but with the government itself. Policies which had been planned as part of the overall economic program may have been delayed or pursued ineffectively, particularly if there is some disagreement as to their value within the official circle. The finance ministry or treasury department or central bank may have indulged their usually more conservative instincts by bureaucratically delaying the introduction of stimulative actions which had been agreed on. A public works office or housing agency may have been instructed to put into effect "gradually" a reduction in the amount of construction which had been agreed on, overall, as necessary in the interests of financial stability, but may interpret "gradually" in a way that is favorable to its "constituents" in the construction industry even if unfavorable in its impact on the budget. In cases like these it is not a revision of policy as much as its enforcement that is needed. As a member of the staff of the French Planning Commission commented, when such instances come to the Commission's attention it "rings the bell of the Prime Minister" and acquaints him with the situation and its effect on economic performance.

Whether a modification or more effective implementation of government policies, the purpose is clear—to bring performance into conformance with the plan as projected. But there are some circumstances which in effect supersede a plan. Actions capable of bringing performance into line with intent may lie beyond the powers of government. This is particularly true with respect to the foreign trade balance. If exports decline because of a drying up of overseas demand, or if the price of necessary imports rises because of world market conditions, there is little that a government can do, at least in the short run. In such a case it is the plan which must be made to conform to the changed situation.

The fact that the government does not stand in an hierarchical relationship to the private sector, except in certain limited spheres, constitutes another major limitation on the power of government to make its plan effective. However assiduously it seeks the political-organizational coordination necessary to plan fulfillment, there are always times when such coordination fails. Perhaps business confidence is shaken over government handling of some matter, perhaps one not even connected with economic activity, with the result that investment plans are put on the shelf and no interest-rate or tax concessions can bring them down off the shelf. Or labor union dissatisfaction with the distribution of revenues leads to wage demands which are price-destabilizing. Or perhaps there is an unexpected change in government, due to vote of censure or an official death, or an international incident unsettles both producer and consumer expectations. In such circumstances as these the economic "inducements" which a Western government is free to employ are not so certain in effectiveness as to allow their user to play on people's reactions as on an organ console, producing a controlled harmonic effect.

For whatever reason, there are times, then, when the plan must be brought into line with "reality," which is to say that the government must settle for a poorer performance than had originally been intended. The *actual* performance of the economy—its inputs and outputs—balance at a level something less satisfactory than the *projected* balance. At times, to be sure, the reverse may be true— exceptionally favorable circumstances may burst on the scene, so that the inputs and outputs balance at a more advantageous level.

As the actual balance departs significantly from the projected balance, and revision of plans becomes necessary, objectives must be scaled upward or downward, technical-economic standards must be rewritten, new political-organizational lines of conduct must be worked out. There then emerges from such a reconsideration a new and *preferred* input-output balance which replaces the old plan— preferred over the former projected balance, where circumstances have become more favorable, preferred over the actual balance emerging where circumstances have deteriorated.

This preferred balance thus becomes the revised plan—the *new* projected balance of inputs and outputs embodying the modified system objectives. How long it will remain such depends on the same considerations we have just noted, but we can be sure that variances from it will soon enough emerge. They may be of a sort which can be corrected. An alteration in government policy, in the use of inducements vis-à-vis the private sector, may be all that is needed to bring performance back to the revised plan. But sooner or later circumstances will arise leading to variances too great for corrective action. The inputs of resources and the outputs of goods and services will again come into balance only at a level and with a composition differing from that intended. The actual balance will diverge from the projected balance far enough to destroy the usefulness of the existing plan.

Then once again the procedure must be repeated. A revised preferred balance must be drawn, a new national budget, which differs both from the actual balance and that previously projected. This becomes the new projected balance, the new plan, from which—in due time—the actual balance will again deviate enough to invalidate it, requiring a new preferred balance which becomes the official projection, from which actual performance will in time diverge, and so on into the future.

From this point of view, a revision of plans is nothing which signifies a failure of the planning process. Indeed, we should expect such revision as a normal part of planning. And yet, there is a danger in too sweeping an acceptance of this point of view. Frequent revision of plans may mean that the current plan is accorded little respect. If it is to be changed again shortly, why pay attention to it? It is in this respect that the reliability of forecasts and plans takes on significance: they need not be "accurate," in the sense that they are always fulfilled, to be of value, but they must be accurate enough to be able to stand for periods of time which both warrant and make possible the development of technical-economic and political-organizational coordination.

But it is equally true that excessive emphasis on the preservation of projections and plans, even in the face of changed circumstances, invalidates their usefulness. They cease to provide meaningful guidance to all the functioning parts of a complex system. Losing their significance as a basis for the coordination of the subunits, they throw decision makers at all levels back on their own improvisations. It is as though an army's military plan had been made obsolete by unforeseen developments, but no substitute plan was provided, forcing every commanding officer to rely on his own estimates and intuition as to what his fellow officers would do and on his own judgment as to what he should do under the new circumstances. For a plan to be effective it must be feasible, and to be feasible it must be revised when circumstances have invalidated it. But whether a plan remains workable, with changed implementation, or is beyond implementation and requires revision, is a matter of judgment, guided by the conflicting requirements of realism and stability.

THE TIME HORIZON

In examining corporate planning, we noted that in the short run the marketing, production, and financial structures are integrated into a functioning system, with each cueing the other and receiving cues. This is an ongoing performance, with incremental changes being made in various budget categories the better to achieve the firm's objectives. The marketing organization tends to take the lead in this short-run integrative exercise by controlling—insofar as control is possible—the flow of orders on which the whole operation rests. Short-run budget planning begins with estimated sales.

In the long run, however, a different initiative is required. Incremental changes are not enough. There must be innovative planning which creates whole new categories of activity, beyond the concern of those who are immersed in integrating the firm's ongoing activity. The business unit plans for these innovations not by building on present operations as much as by laying out an entirely new phased program which will reach the contemplated objective by some scheduled date. As time passes and the activities pointing in new directions become an increasing part of the overall activities, the former must be gradually integrated into the ongoing organizational pattern, the short-run planning. This process of innovating—changing the pattern of a firm's operations—while at the same time continuing "normal" operations constitutes a different dimension in planning from that which we normally associate with the coordinating functions based on existing, known relationships. To provide for it a number of companies have instituted separate departments of long-range planning.

The same considerations apply in the case of economy-wide planning. In the short run, principal energies are devoted to coordination of the two varieties which we have seen are parts of a single process, both concerned with projections of a largely incremental nature. From year to year and even from five-year plan to five-year plan, innovations that involve major structural changes in the economy seldom receive much explicit attention. And yet we know from experience that such innovations are necessary for the continuing vitality of a society. Private-enterprise economies have a safeguard in this respect, for by their very nature they diffuse the process of innovation among the private subunits, each of which is free—indeed, environmentally encouraged—to experiment with change. The concern of private corporations with their own long-run planning needs is some assurance that innovation will not be wholly neglected. The use of categorical public objectives in key variables such as investment and consumption gives scope for business invention even within an overall planning framework.

Nevertheless, such private innovation does not entirely meet the problem. The development of new products, with which business is chiefly concerned, does not answer the need for structural innovation of a social nature. As an economy moves into a state of productiveness which provides a constantly rising per capita income, the demand for goods becomes satisfied more readily than the demand for services, particularly of a social nature. We have already had occasion to observe that social investment is likely to play a more important role in a prospering economy which is already industrially advanced. But social investment in what? The desirability of long-range planning to increase the options, the better to satisfy anticipated demand, is as evident here as in the case of the firm.

This is not quite the same thing as the identification of specific objectives of the type we have previously encountered. The specific objectives of most economic planning are not so much innovations as extensions of present social capital—more schools, roads, hospitals, and so on. They are familiar enough to win political acceptance and to arouse relatively little controversy. Their cost can be estimated and tailored to meet budget requirements.

But the kinds of innovations for which long-range social planning is needed are the same kinds that preoccupy a good deal of business long-range planning—wholly new categories of activity, usually large in scale, so that they cannot be reached by increments of present activity, but only by initiating a new line of activity which eventually leads to the conceived result. Such ventures, because they involve large expenditures and are potentially disruptive of present organized relationships, cannot be lightly undertaken. They must be researched for technical feasibility, economic value, and social consequences. The eventual decision as to whether to proceed or not must be left to the political process, but the conception and investigation must first be provided for or there will be nothing for the political process to consider.

This additional dimension of public planning has so far been largely neglected. Most Western countries have departments of public works, or their equivalent, which have to a degree filled the breach, in some instances quite notably. But the systematic continuing consideration of an economy's long-range future, with the intention of directing the reinvestment of its assets into wholly new and more promising lines, always subject to public approval, has not yet been granted a major role in the planning process.

With few exceptions, the renovation of cities proceeds along relatively familiar lines, piecemeal and uncoordinated. It offers a more modern version of what it is displacing. There has been virtually no political consideration of "new" cities built on radically new lines, although there is a substantial literature dealing with the subject. Additional schools are constructed—the most modern, to be sure—but there is remarkably little examination of the desirability of restructuring the whole educational system in line with contemporary needs. Transportation networks of all sorts have become outdated, but we continue tinkering with incremental improvements, so that scarcely a highway is now completed which does not earn the engineer's contempt as "obsolete" before it is opened.

If public planning is to aspire to the systematic management of the nation's assets, with whatever degree of discretion is politically accorded it, it must follow the example of private corporations in establishing a separate and influential department of long-range planning.

In some instances so-called long-range planning has served as an excuse for present inaction. Distant dreaming creates "futuramas" without adequate consideration of the path and the timetable to get from here to there. But it is no less true that excessive preoccupation with the short run robs present efforts of their full effectiveness. A "path" is being laid, step by step, but with little consideration of where it is to lead. Long-run planning is needed to give significance to short-run activity, just as the latter is the condition for ever reaching the goals of the former.

GENERAL VERSUS PARTICULAR INDUCEMENTS

One issue which has aroused a good deal of feeling concerns the particularity of such actions as a government may take in the face of variances: is the solution adopted generally applicable throughout the economy, or is it selective with respect to industrial or geographical sectors? This issue also enters into the drafting of plans, but it is convenient to discuss it in the present context.

In the case of specific objectives it is clear that selective inducements are warranted. The fact that society has singled out certain identified goals from the more generalized targets of growth or employment gives license to government to accord preferential treatment to the objectives in hand—whether housing or education or nuclear development or regional redevelopment. There may be room for debate over the wisdom of specifying such objectives at all, but once specified, the use of selective instruments to achieve them is hardly in issue.

It is with respect to the categorical objectives that the question of general versus selective measures arises. If investment is a categorical objective, for example, should the amount projected be achieved by general fiscal and monetary devices applicable across the board, or is the government justified in determining that certain industries are more strategic than others, more underdeveloped than others, in greater need of modernization than others, and so on, and—without setting targets—granting them special inducements to ensure that they play a larger role than they otherwise would in the achievement of the overall categorical target? In seeking financial equilibrium, once again we ask whether the government should limit itself to imposing common monetary and fiscal restraints, or is there some advantage in attempting to identify the sources of greatest inflationary pressure and dealing with them more stringently?

The division of opinion on this score is marked, and also is marked with emotion. There are certain countries where a preference for general measures is strongly asserted, even in the face of exceptions from that policy. This is true in the United Kingdom, the Netherlands, and Sweden, for example, as well as in the United States and the German Republic. The basis for such a preference is that it avoids the danger of governmental favoritism. In a society that lives according to rules, it is desirable that everyone be placed on the same footing, and that none be granted special favors on the arguable ground that they are somehow making a special contribution to society. These are the societies, too, which place greater reliance on market mechanisms.

The argument for selective action is rooted in a belief that the market does not work so smoothly and ubiquitously that all sectors respond equally to general measures. Some industries which are important to economic expansion may not react to expansionary inducements with the same ebullience as other industries which are of no special significance, or may react more sharply to restraining measures. Special bottlenecks of a structural nature may emerge, such as shortages of natural resources or of certain skills, or the presence of oligopolistic sluggishness, or the inability of an industry to profit from the external economies which it could create, or the existence of special risks of technological obsolescence or of foreign competition, and so on. Some regions may become isolated from effective involvement in the system of markets; they may, in effect, get spun off from the rest of the economy, and the impulses linking them with it may require strengthening.

Selective measures are also advocated in the belief that the market does not always operate expeditiously enough to obtain the economy's objectives within a "reasonable" time. If growth is wanted, it may come more promptly if there is some central guidance through a system of inducements than if it is left to the dispersed intentions of a large number of individual business units responding to a general incentive. It can be "programmed" for swifter accomplishment. "In postwar Norway rapid reconstruction and development and considerable income equalization could hardly have been brought about simultaneously without resorting to a much more differentiated system of controls than that applied before the war." [1]

Several Western European economies have subscribed to this approach. In addition to Norway they include France, Italy, and to some extent Belgium. In Chapter 4 we noted some of the selective measures which they employ: differential interest and tax rates, loan guarantees, preferred access to credit, priorities in building licenses. Indeed, even those countries which tend to oppose particular measures in contrast to general have found themselves impelled to make some use of the former. The United Kingdom has power, through the Bank of England, to engage in selective credit policies, even though it has employed this authority sparingly. Its initial investment allowance has been used discriminatorily. In Sweden authorization for firms to draw on blocked investment reserves can be and has been used to counteract declines in particular industries (pulp and paper, building, engineering, and shipbuilding).[2] Its labor market policies have included such devices as encouraging the transfer of workers from sectors with unemployment to expanding sectors by travel grants, dual-residence allowances for up to nine months, and relocation subsidies. Selective training programs have also been widely used. With respect to industrial structure, its

[1] Bjerve, *Planning in Norway, 1947–1956*, p. 8. Bjerve also comments: "It has been recognized that the more ambitious the economic and social goals, the more numerous means of control are required in order to achieve these goals. Put differently, the more controls available, the greater are the possibilities of achieving a desired set of goals."

[2] In fairness it should be pointed out that Sweden has sought to refrain from the *regionally* selective use of investment reserves, however. On one occasion authorities in the south of the country, which was enjoying full employment, were fearful that a general release of investment funds to counter unemployment which was concentrated in the north might only serve to raise their wage rates. The Labor Market Board decided against confining the release of funds to the north, however, inclining to the position that if unemployment existed it should be met by creating jobs generally, relying on the mobility of labor to prevent a regional increase in the wage level. As noted in the text, however, it has not been at all reluctant to use other labor market measures selectively with respect to region.

Freedom of Commerce Board does not follow general principles in passing on pricing and market-sharing agreements, but adopts a rule of reason which necessitates particular applications.

In most economies agriculture and construction have been singled out for preferential treatment, in other countries the energy industries. The list of such geographical- or industry-oriented actions could be considerably lengthened. To be sure, good and sufficient reasons can always be advanced for such exceptions to the rule of general solutions, but that is no less true in countries which use selective instruments by preference. To some extent the issue appears to be not whether there shall be selective policies, but which policies can be selectively used to greatest advantage, with least adverse side effects. If fiscal and monetary measures are always general, then other actions will have to be selective. If fiscal and monetary inducements are used particularistically, then other selective actions may be unnecessary.

We may expect that there will always be pockets, regional or industrial, of high unemployment or, similarly, pockets of inflationary pressure. To move on one or the other of these with general fiscal or monetary policies invites excesses. Fiscal and monetary ease in the face of lack of use of full productive capacity and manpower might lead to heating up *parts* of the economy due to structural rigidities or differing reaction levels. Fiscal and monetary restraint in the face of inflationary stresses can have the opposite particularized effect.

Moreover, each of these policies carries a corollary that it is a matter of indifference which sectors respond weakly or sharply to the stimulus. Or to put the corollary as an independent proposition, general measures have selective effects. A change in interest and tax rates, for example, affects industries differently, and often predictably so. Easier or more difficult access to credit affects firms differently, again often predictably. Thus general policies do not escape being selective.

If, as we now know is entirely possible, there are sometimes pockets of unemployment and inflationary pressure coexisting simultaneously, then the adherents of general measures are reduced to a schizophrenic reaction which is almost certain to be translated into a do-nothing policy.

The conclusion to which one is driven is that if we are to seek price stability and financial equilibrium along with growth and full employment, then general policies are not enough—particularly if there are social priorities among sectors. Selective actions need not be restricted to particular types: there is no reason why inducements and restraints may not take whatever form is most suited to the purpose.

Selective devices tend to fall into two broad classes: rationing and inducements. The former involves choice from among claimants on the basis of some standard deemed appropriate. Access to credit in times when the demand for funds exceeds the supply is an example, or allocation of jobs or of admissions to medical training among an excess of applicants. The second type, inducements, involves special encouragement to take some wanted action (or less frequently, *not* to take some action). Among its common forms are subsidies, concessions, preferential tax rates.

Either form requires some criteria in its application, unless the fears of those criticizing selective measures are to materialize, and favoritism becomes the basis for selection. In the case of a planning economy, the criteria presumably are provided by relevance to the plan. To preserve the value of the categorical objectives—permissive with respect to the subunit, limiting with respect to the exercise of governmental authority—any selective treatment must be restricted to actions taken to effect the plan's targets, whether specific or categorical. In this event, however, the latter must be broadened to include an interpretive gloss.

1 *Specified* sectors—changing over time—may be extended preferential treatment *without setting target levels of production or investment.* The government does not undertake to reach any quantitative goals in these cases but *explicitly* gives favored treatment to certain sectors in adopting measures for the attainment of categorical objectives. (This only provides for what is now commonly done, with or without the categorical objectives.)

2 More important, regions or industries deviating from overall full employment rates by a given percentage for a given duration may be accorded special consideration, and price-wage increases more than a given percentage in excess of the average may be subject to official public scrutiny. Such a proviso would carry fewer dangers from abuse of government discretion that benefits from a limited extension of government discretion.

This broader construction of categorical objectives would not destroy their positive value of permitting private and local initiative in the achievement of subunit goals and of restricting the government's managerial role in achieving system objectives. On the contrary, it would provide a degree of flexibility reducing the need for a more assertive governmental role (such as would be necessitated by the use of general measures to achieve limited targets, in the same way that the "massive retaliation" policy of national defense proposed to do). It would make possible a higher overall level of achievement of the mixture of subunit and system, private and public, local and national goals.

8...
micro-macro relations and the problems of authority

If one starts with the firm as a planning unit and looks down the organizational structure, one descries subsidiary decentralized planning units with varying degrees of autonomy. In each one discretion is limited, ideally, only to the extent necessary to assure achievement of the objectives of the firm—the larger system of which it is a part. If one starts with the firm and looks up the institutional structure, the same thing is true except that he is looking through the other end of the telescope. The firm itself becomes a subunit in the larger economic system, its discretion limited as necessary to achieve system objectives.

Where lines of hierarchical authority extend through a system of relationships, power is vested on one level to determine the premises guiding subordinate levels and bounding their discretion. Even in the absence of hierarchical authority, lines of influence and pressure may achieve some of the same effect.[1] A large corporation may impose certain limitations on its dealers, who are legally and organizationally independent (as one corporation in the United States restricted the vendors of its products from negotiating directly with the Federal government or foreign importers). A large corporation may also impose certain limitations on its independent suppliers (as one large company has insisted that its smaller suppliers permit it to analyze their operations to determine actual costs and efficiency). Similarly governments can sometimes exert influence over private corporations even in matters where hierarchical authority is lacking.

THE SYSTEM OF DECISION-MAKING UNITS

If we look at the economy as composed of a large number of decision-making units, we find authority and discretion lodged in each unit, modified in some degree by its relationships with other decision-making units. The scope of its authority and discretion measure the extent to which it has the power to coordinate the operations of other units in the achievement of its own objectives, by setting premises which limit *their* discretion—just as its own is limited by premises imposed on it by others. In Western societies every private and local unit possesses some area of authority and discretion which is immune from hierarchical control, and at the same time is limited in its autonomy by its relation to a larger unit—ultimately the economy as a whole, managed by the central government, to which it is linked hierarchically. But even the central government exercises power only in certain respects and is denied power in other respects, since Western governments are governments of limited powers.

This last fact has tremendous importance for the economic planning process. In Western society there is no central repository of power, since power is dispersed throughout the society. The management of

---

[1] Hierarchial authority, influence, and pressure can all be subsumed under the general concept of bargaining power, as I have done in *A General Theory of Economic Process*. Here I have avoided introducing that concept since it would have required more elaboration than seemed necessary for present purposes.

General Electric can, quite literally, do things which the U.S. government cannot do, can run its corporation with an authority which the U.S. government cannot exercise. It determines what products it shall produce, at what prices, in what locations, by what methods, with an authority that is immune from governmental hierarchical control except in particulars which have been specifically sanctioned by representative legislatures—such as that working conditions shall not be hazardous to health, that wages no lower than a specified minimum shall be paid, that it shall negotiate conditions of employment with its workers, that it must pay taxes on its operations. As long as it meets these limited requirements, it possesses a residual authority with respect to its own affairs that is independent of government control. Further, within its own organizational boundaries it enjoys a degree of hierarchical control over its own far-flung subunits greater than the central government has with respect to it. It can, for example, close down a plant or shift people to other jobs and locations, actions which the central government cannot exact from it.

This means, as we noted in Chapter 4, that the central government is not capable of coordinating all the activities of all the subunits in the system in the achievement of system goals, as a matter of authority. It cannot dictate the responses which it wants, but must induce them. Even in so basic a matter as the organization of an industry it cannot impose its wish but must negotiate with the relevant private authorities: public and private power must be pooled to effect the results wished, and the results are necessarily a compromise where interests diverge.[2] The *économie concertée* involves a meshing of private and public interests, and is distinguished from the *économie dirigée*, which subordinates private interests to public.

THE RAGGED SYSTEM

The dispersal of power and discretion throughout the economy, and the consequent necessity of relying on inducement rather than direction as a basis for coordination, means that the economic system can

[2] French postwar reorganization of the steel industry provides an interesting example of this. John Sheahan gives an abbreviated account in *Promotion and Control of Industry in Postwar France*, pp. 68–70. Similar is the British reorganization of portions of its textile industry, as noted by Grove in *Government and Industry in Britain*, pp. 313–316.

never be as neatly and efficiently organized as, say, a corporation, which can direct how its subunits shall relate to each other and to the firm as a system. In the economy at large, some subunits will be integrated more effectively than others, and other sectors will be more loosely linked. The difficulties of effecting compromises with private and local units to elicit their closer collaboration in achieving system objectives guarantees that the government's effort in this respect will be confined to the more strategic sectors. Large-scale basic industry, for example, will certainly absorb its attention, and the large fabricating units only a little less so, but it will virtually ignore the myriad of small retail outlets. Their operations relate to categorical objectives, and the government can afford to be disinterested in the degree to which any individual units among their number contribute to the aggregative result.

Norway provides a nice example of this limited integration, since its size permits the planning process—inevitably complex in a larger country—to be seen more clearly. Government relations with the private sector embrace a spectrum. At one end are the heavy power-consuming industries, such as aluminum, iron and steel, and fertilizer, which themselves engage in a high degree of internal planning, and whose relation to the government, in the latter's managerial role for the economy, is subject to intensive joint planning. These basic industries are also the most susceptible to government influence because of its control over electric power. The intermediate ranges of the spectrum include important industries such as shipbuilding and pulp and paper, the firms which are less given to planning and with less extensive involvement in the economy, but which are important enough to be provided for in the national budget. At the other end of the spectrum are the numerous companies engaged in the production and marketing of consumer goods, whose activities are considered only in the form of an aggregative prognosis unless some special problem emerges and must be treated on an *ad hoc* basis.

There is here no tightly knit comprehensive planning, but an intentional concentration on strategic sectors with relatively little regard to the nonstrategic areas. While short-run variances from the annual national budget receive attention and may invite action, they are of secondary interest as compared with long-run structural adjustments which appear to be necessary to keep Norway competitive in the international markets on which it is heavily dependent. (In the basic sectors, ten-year planning has been undertaken, although four years is the farthest ahead that the government plans for the economy as a whole.) [3]

The picture of Norway's "systematic planning" which emerges is thus a good deal more ragged but a good deal more organizationally sensitized than one would get by considering its technical-economic projections. What develops is a rougher and more approximate integration, due to the necessity both of compromise and of scaling down the administrative load, than that which can be achieved by building a model on paper. Both conditions which lead to this more ragged but nevertheless calculated result are the consequence of the dispersal of power throughout the economy.

In this kind of a planning system, economic equilibrium with respect to both resource use and price level is nothing which is gained by automatic adjustments in markets, even over time. Market forces continue to play the leading role, but an equilibrium in the sense of a balance of pressure at an optimum level of operations is something which, if achieved at all, must be contrived. The results are necessarily rough and uncertain, occurring within the framework of a system of projected relations between gross but strategic variables. The relationships are forever becoming distorted and out of kilter—something which is not casually observable even to the trained economic eye, but which must be reported by a trained economic intelligence system. Adjustments must be made—imprecisely on a trial-and-error basis—as information (also imprecise) filters through the intelligence network.

[3] This ten-year planning exercise embraced (as of 1962) chiefly aluminum, pig iron, and fertilizer, with firms representing something like 15 percent of the country's employment and 20 percent of value-added. The nature of the expansion contemplated is indicated by the fact that in aluminum alone there is an expectation of moving from a base output of approximately 180,000 tons to some 700,000 to 800,000 tons over the decade. The special planning group is estimating the manpower which will be required for the contemplated expansion, surveying the financial needs, and also giving special attention to plant location as a means of meeting some of Norway's problems of regional imbalance. The plans which are emerging can be more or less "firmed up," since the government can enter into contract with private industries for financing and water power concessions (in an approach somewhat comparable to the French quasi-contract). Moreover, the government can enter into negotiations for foreign capital investment, both to supplement domestic investment and to induce from domestic firms the kind of performance which it believes necessary.

The whole process could perhaps as well be described as a moving, controlled disequilibrium, in contrast to the static equilibrium of so much economic theory.

Western planning aims to be systematic, by definition, but by the nature of Western society it is at best a ragged system which emerges.

THE RECONCILIATION OF OBJECTIVES BY AUTHORITY

In Chapter 2 we examined the fact that the objectives of any subunit in a firm necessarily diverge from those of the firm as a whole, since these derive from different functions and interests. The objectives of each must be accommodated in some degree to maintain their functional relationship. The restrictions contained in whatever premises are imposed on a subunit are designed to facilitate and ensure the reaching of the objectives of the larger unit. Within the discretion remaining, the subunit is free to serve its own interests. From time to time the premises limiting discretion are redrawn—tighter when the goals of the superior unit appear to be sacrificed by excessive subunit concentration on its own ends, and looser when the absence of subunit discretion obliges it to conform to rules so rigidly as to reduce overall efficiency. But however the premises may be specified, there is an inescapable divergence between the objectives of the firm as a whole and its various subunits.[4]

In Chapter 4 we noted the same phenomenon in the economy considered as the overall system, with individual firms and local governments as the subunits. Public and private objectives, and national and local objectives, necessarily diverge. The more they can be reconciled, the more effectively does the system function as a system. Such reconciliation of objectives is in fact the role of political-organizational coordination, which we examined briefly in Chapter 6. It is now time to

[4] This is perhaps most clearly evident when a firm seeks to identify the interests of system and subsystem by establishing the latter as "profit centers," thus presumably conforming to the same motivation as overall corporate management. But what is profitable to the subunit may not be profitable to the firm (for example, the purchase of a component part more cheaply from an outside supplier, reducing variable costs to the subunit but increasing them for the firm). And what is profitable to the firm may not be profitable to the subunit (for example, redesigning a product in a way that reduces the latter's contribution). Much ingenuity has been spent on ways of making the two "profit" objectives compatible, but a gap must always remain when the two are in fact different.

explore more fully this integration of the micro units into a functioning system, pursuing its own goals.

There are two principal ways in which this can be brought about.
One is the reconciliation of objectives by the exercise of authority;
whatever hierarchical power exists is drawn on to restate the premises
under which subunits operate so that they are less free to pursue their
own ends at the expense of system goals. The other is by compromise;
both system and subsystem goals may be modified to make them more
compatible. Some sacrifice of system objectives may actually increase
its overall effectiveness. Let us first consider the use of authority and
the problems which it presents.

Of course, as long as we are dealing with "ragged" systems the need
for government intervention in the economy and for a reconciliation
of public and private (or local) objectives is very much lessened. Government actions are limited to those which are strategically necessary.
As long as the economy is moving relatively smoothly, there is little
occasion for the exercise of central authority since any divergences
between micro and macro goals are of little consequence. The premises
controlling the subunits are loose and permissive.

Nevertheless, planning is not the same thing as no planning. As long
as the system is planned, public and national objectives are posed
which at some point must be controlling over private and local. As
long as the system is planned, whenever performance varies from intent tensions are set up which invite governmental "corrective"
action:

> If a central authority draws a blueprint—even a technically per-
> missive one—for the economy as a whole, then the ability of the
> millions of independent units within the economy to make their
> own plans is in some degree restricted. They may be legally free
> to go their separate ways, but if enough of them do so and the
> working of the overall plan is threatened, the central authority
> may well be tempted to seek and find means of applying corrective
> pressure.[5]

As a staff member of the French Commissariat Général du Plan
remarked privately, those who think that freedom of business action is
paramount are quite right in fearing the Planning Commission as an

[5] "What Place for Planning in the Free Economy?" *Morgan Guaranty Survey*,
June, 1962, p. 9.

agent of control. The *purpose* of the Commission is to modify that paramountcy by asserting public goals alongside private ones.

To be sure, a conflict of objectives is equally likely to occur between purely private firms. Two rivals may each be seeking a larger share of a market which they divide between themselves. But the difference between this kind of goal conflict and that between business firm and government is that no hierarchical relationship appears in the former. Neither can gain its objective by asserting an authority over the other. In the government-business relationship, however, even if the government does not have present authority to subordinate private to public goals, it has access to such authority through the legislature. It can seek a revision of the premises controlling the actions and limiting the discretion of the subunits whose objectives conflict with its own. It is the possibility of such an authoritative "reconciliation" of objectives that bothers us when it comes to planning. As manager of the nation's assets, the government establishes certain goals. As manager of a bundle of private assets, the firm does likewise. When these conflict, the issue is not decided between two equals, but between superior and subordinate, between one with access to hierarchical ("sovereign") power and one without such a weapon.

In general, however, Western society—because it seeks dispersal of power—does not accord its governments such ready access to authority as to permit them to command the obedience of private units to a public program. If governments have access to sovereign power through the legislature, private and local units also have access to that same body to urge—with votes—limitations on the grant of such power. Since there is no central repository of power, but on the contrary power is dispersed, any new grants of governmental authority involve creating something which does not exist, or—even more difficult—taking away a discretion lodged in numerous subunits to confer it on the central administration. If the loss of discretion is "viewed with alarm" by those now possessing it, such a transfer is not easily accomplished. In general, then, private actions may be enjoined, but they cannot be compelled. Inducements must be provided if firms or households are to take certain preferred courses of action.

Admittedly, the line between inducement and authority may be a very fine one: refusal to take the bait may mean, in effect, that one goes hungry. Where access to credit is involved, or differential tax rates, or subsidies, a firm which is not "induced" may find itself at an impossible competitive disadvantage. Even if it is not compelled, it is coerced, and there is little comfort to be found in the distinction. Moreover, even if the government moves to implement its plans principally by coaxing, the sphere of governmental operations may widen if the private and local sectors do not respond.[6]

Without trying to compound a case against government per se, as though it were an evil which we—like the idealistic anarchists—would like to be rid of, we should note one further abuse of authority which is sometimes charged to it in connection with planning. It is said that a planning government tends to foster a concentration of private power in the hands of trade associations, large corporations, and national labor unions which are willing to accommodate it. These can be made the instruments for "coordinating" (coercing) the actions of smaller firms and local unions. The French industry-based *commissions de modernisation*, on which the planning program heavily rests, involve for the most part the existing private power centers, further adding to their control over their memberships and others. The secretary-general of one industry association suggested that while the French plan provides a basis for industry self-government, this can be used for the self-interest of the industry, particularly its larger firms. Where the industry is enabled to gain concessions as the price of its cooperation, there is a readiness to comply with, and a reluctance to criticize, government leadership. Private power concentration thus becomes an accompaniment to public power.

This relationship also holds in reverse. As Professor Perroux has succinctly noted, "Monopolies in France and Europe are gaining in strength. They create *both* supra normal profits and innovations. The Plan which develops and depends on them cannot at the same time attack them. It does not possess the means to discriminate between their positive and negative effects." [7] Thus a kind of "unholy alliance"

[6] The Fourth French Plan includes a paragraph to the effect that in the face of private inaction, where some action has been called for by the plan, the government may first undertake a study of the matter to ascertain the reasons for the nonperformance, and then if necessary it may intervene by a variety of methods, including the taking of an entrepreneurial role itself if that should seem to be necessary. This paragraph was added at the insistence of the trade unions, and plan officials concur with trade unionists in attributing importance to the addition.

[7] F. Perroux, *Le IVème Plan Français* (Paris: Presses Universitaires de France, 1962), p. 22, as translated by Malcolm MacLennan in *French Planning: Some Lessons for Britain* (London: Political and Economic Planning, 1963), p. 346.

may grow up between government and the major private power centers.

These several attacks on planning as something which (a) enhances government authority over private and local units and (b) enhances the power of major private power centers over smaller units are not without merit, but they go too far. The first line of argument implies that in the absence of planning, government controls would be reduced. But that is a non sequitur. It is an open question whether more governmental intervention, and of a less predictable nature, might not be required by lack of system than by system. The second line of argument starts by admitting that the large corporation, the trade association, and the national labor union even now have the capacity to limit the discretion and autonomy of lesser units, asserting their own objectives over those of their constituent parts and using their hierarchical authority to "reconcile" such divergences of goals. While stressing that government may reinforce that existing power, the argument neglects the equally plausible alternative that government may constitute a countervailing power against the authority of the major private centers. Effective political-organizational coordination of the system can lead in either direction—to strengthening the associations at the expense of their constituents or strengthening the constituents at the expense of the central associations. This is in part the same issue we confronted in examining the relevance of institutional structure to economic planning (in Chapter 5), where it was noted that under given circumstances a vitalization of market forces or a greater reliance on organized administration ("rationalization") might be warranted. The issue is not clear-cut.

But perhaps the most telling consideration is that while the exercise of authority in a planning program may limit discretion in certain directions, it increases discretion in other directions. It creates alternatives which would not have existed in the absence of planning. There is no point in urging on unemployed workers or near-bankrupt firms the loss of their individual freedoms if they consent to a measure of planning for full employment or growth. Consumer sovereignty may be better preserved, it can be admitted to make the point, by allowing individuals to spend a larger share of the GNP (say by reducing government outlays), but the size of both the GNP and their share of it may be smaller as a result; they will be free to choose what they want with what income they have, but the lower income which they have will itself limit their choice. A lack of coordination of the parts resulting in a poor overall performance can create a tyranny of circumstance over individuals, an absence of effective choice, greater than is contained within the exercise of such government authority as may be needed for planning. A failure of the government to intervene can be destructive of private discretion no less than its intervention.

Individual action is not inherently better than collaborative action, in economic affairs no less than in political or military. To take but a single example, the private sector today would be a puny thing indeed without the legal device of the corporation—a device resting on governmental sanctions for its effectiveness. Governmental authority gave private initiative a new organizational alternative which vastly expanded its range of possibilities. That the corporate form also opened up a new avenue of governmental regulation does not negate the value of the alternative which had been legally created; the continuing flow of new incorporations attests to that.

To argue against government intervention in economic affairs is to ignore the real contribution that governments can make. To be sure, the question of purpose and effect remain to be settled, in every instance, but governmental intervention can scarcely be condemned in principle.

By the same reasoning, economic planning cannot be rejected on the grounds that it limits individual discretion. It can extend individual discretion no less than curb it. It is not the principle, but the specific measures which should be subject to critical scrutiny.

As we move away from the individual, in any social direction, we move away from "individual" freedom—even in the case of family organization. But the kind of "freedom" from which we move away is that of a Robinson Crusoe before the advent of Friday. Every form of social organization inhibits individual freedom in some respects, but most of us do not, for that reason, choose to retreat to the solitude of Walden Pond.

It is possible to overemphasize the authority role in economic planning, just as in the case of the household or the business firm. Authority is essential, some forms of control are inescapable, as long as one accepts the fact that the larger social unit has valid objectives which diverge in some respects from those of its component parts. But authority and control are only part of the picture. Collaboration for purposes which are mutually compatible and which can only be obtained through compatible behavior, is the central feature of the social landscape.

THE AUTHORITY OF KNOWLEDGE

Governmental authority is the most obvious limitation on private and local discretion in the planning process, but there are subtler forms as well.

In addition to the authority that derives from position in an hierarchical order there is an authority that comes from possessing a special knowledge or expertise which is needed by others but is beyond their competence. This "authority of knowledge" has become important enough in the contemporary world to challenge some of our traditional views of organizational structure. The notion of a necessary "supreme authority," probably originating in military organization, carried over into affairs of state through the concept of "sovereignty," and into corporate activity through the designation of "top" management, continues to play an important part in organizational theory, but in practice its role has diminished.

In corporate operations increasing complexity and specialization have brought in a constantly expanding number of "experts," both in substantive and methodological matters. These functional specialists tend to become the "final" authority in their own mysterious areas of competence. Although usually "staff" people report to a "line" officer (again the military terminology) who carries formal authority and whose position places him at the top of an organizational ladder, in practice their nominal superior often has little basis for appraising their judgments and recommendations. Line executives may retain the illusion of making decisions on the strength of information and analyses supplied by subordinates—the normal and traditional procedure—but in fact there is a difference: the executives have no way of judging the analysis or recommendation. They are not likely to be able to talk the language of the specialist or comprehend his formulation of the problem or the techniques with which he approaches it. They are left with the option of accepting or rejecting and little basis for doing either.

Of course the views of one expert may be checked against the views of another, just as one geologist's conclusions with respect to the presence of ore deposits may be subjected to review by another geologist. But there is a difference between such a check on single occasional decisions and on a stream of operating decisions affecting everything from short-run routine to long-run strategic matters. The inherited notion of an organizational hierarchy pyramiding to some peak authority is being wrenched and strained by the fact that authority is dispersed throughout an organization among numbers of experts carrying out specialized tasks, working together more or less as equals, in an organization which is integrated by a generally accepted plan rather than by a commanding officer. The old hierarchy remains relevant for many routine decisions, where the executive's experience and acumen still give him the confidence and ability to coordinate the subunits through the exercise of his own authority. But in an ever-growing number of decisions of a more complex nature the hierarchical lines are losing their appropriateness. A new authority of knowledge has superseded the old authority of position. The "top line executives become not so much decision makers as legatees of action spelled out by staff." [8]

This development is not confined to the corporation. In the private sector it has affected the labor unions as well, whose formal officials have often ceded jurisdiction to specialists over such areas as pension planning, supplementary unemployment benefits, health insurance, and even the allocation of leisure time.[9] More important for our present inquiry, it is to be found as well in public administration.

There are some who view planning programs as enlarging this specialist bureaucracy whose expertise gives them an authority over others which was not specifically intended. A small number of technicians constitute the planning corps, a concentration of knowledge authorities whose technical-economic manipulations are beyond the comprehension of the politicians and administrators. The former make recommendations as to policy which are influential on the latter, even though the basis for the recommendation is only vaguely understood.

The same phenomenon is of course found in nonplanning countries

[8] Prof. Charles Summer, in Steiner (ed.), *Management Long-range Planning*, p. 78.

[9] George Brooks, former research director of the Pulp and Sulphite Workers Union and now professor of Industrial Relations at Cornell University, has called attention to this development in the course of condemning it in his article, "What Will Collective Bargaining Look Like in Twenty Years," in *The Next Twenty Years in Industrial Relations* (Cambridge, Mass.: M.I.T. Industrial Relations Center, 1957), pp. 3–21. It seems more appropriate to view it not as a breakdown in organizational structure, but as only another manifestation of the impact of specialized knowledge, imposing a need for new organizational forms. We shall examine this issue more fully in the following chapter.

as well. Senator Fulbright called attention to its effect on "popular" government in the United States. "Unless we become a nation of statesmen-scientists, we can kiss goodbye to our whole traditional constitutional system for responsible power. It will be done for, because only a handful of experts will make decisions for the rest of us, and we will have no exact basis for knowing whether they decided well." [10]

Nevertheless, economic planning undoubtedly provides additional scope for the play of this unconstituted authority. Public objectives—such as a rate of growth, or a level of employment—depend for their achievement on policies which are at least partially derivative from technical and theoretical formulations understood only by experts, policies which at times may collide with private objectives, for example by invoking credit restraints or limitations on wage increases. In this event the "reconciliation" of public and private objectives is partially effected by an authority which is even more difficult to grapple with than formal governmental power—an authority of knowledge.

This threat, if it can be called that, is a source of valid concern, but the fact that it is not peculiar to the planning process or even to economic matters reveals it as a more general problem that cannot be met simply by denying a place to planning—in the economy any more than in the corporation. It is part of the so-called revolution of knowledge which is having its impact on many aspects of contemporary society.[11] New knowledge has always been a revolutionary instrument, destructive of established methods and procedures. The problem of "containing" the authority of expertise and of making it appropriately responsible is a genuine one, but its solution must come through the devising of new methods for making use of specialist knowledge which take explicit account of the authority which that knowledge confers on the user and which erect appropriate safeguards against its abuse, as against the abuse of any authority.

THE DISCIPLINE OF LOGIC

In addition to limitations on private discretion which flow from the formal authority of government and the informal authority of special

[10] Speech on the U.S. Senate floor, August 21, 1958.
[11] As I have suggested in "Retooling the Mind," *Atlantic Monthly*, September, 1964.

knowledge, there is a third type which might be branded the "authority of the system" or the "discipline of logic."

To the extent a coordinated effort is necessary to achieve public objectives, this imposes a logical even if not a legal dicipline on those involved. Since it is the relationship of the parts to each other which produces the end results (as in the working of a machine), a sense of order, system, or "team play" urges each of the parts to perform its intended function—even without external compulsion. Even when there is some resistance to the planning program, the knowledge that its outcome depends on each part's playing its role, so that "sulking" destroys the game for everyone, exerts a strong pressure to conform. As M. Massé, the French Planning Commissioner, has commented:

> The logic of "indicative planning" consists in integrating all these interdependent effects, thus extending to a nation-wide scale the market surveys made by each single firm. The Plan gives to each branch of activity some reassurance that it can obtain its supplies and dispose of its products without running into shortages or gluts. This only materializes if everybody plays the game. The promise that such conditions will rule acts merely as an incentive: it is not binding on anybody.[12]

How businessmen may be induced to "play the game" by the logic inherent in plan formulation has been nicely illustrated by one of the industrialists who has participated in the French planning process. His remarks came during the discussion period of a conference devoted to European planning programs.

> MR. STEIN—Let us assume that the Plan envisages in some industry a 10 per cent growth of its productive capacity, and that the investment plans of firms in this industry would bring about an expansion on the order of 15 per cent. Would the Commissioner know what was happening? What would be the attitude of the Commission with regard to these firms, especially as concerns fiscal exemptions?

> M. DE CLINCHAMPS—I am going to answer by quoting an example:
> A while ago I said that in the industry I know best, the paper industry, the work group had succeeded in setting a certain higher

[12] From "The Guiding Ideas behind French Planning," in *Economic Planning in France* (London: Political and Economic Planning, 1961), pp. 219–220.

rate of production and, correlatively, a certain level for investment.

On my initiative, management in all the interested firms was informed. Next, I asked the general delegate of the Association of Paper Producers to make a study of all the investment plans of our fellow members. The fact that I am both the President of the work group of the Plan and President of the Association has perhaps facilitated matters. At any rate, 98 per cent of our fellow members answered—this of course under the seal of professional secrecy. We did not know whose plans were involved, only that they existed. We took the precaution of distinguishing between two kinds of projects: projects that had already given rise to a first order, and projects that were still somewhat hazy, that could not be realized immediately.

When we cast up the total for the year 1965 it appeared that we had a production capacity 30 per cent in excess of what the market required, taking into consideration imports and exports.

I then suggested to our general delegate that he ask the manufacturers to meet around a conference table to look at the situation together. It took a few weeks before we had their approval, but they agreed and the meeting took place.

I must, in passing, congratulate my fellow members; they gave the most precise information about types of machines ordered, dates when they were to be put in use, the nature of the paper to be manufactured, etc. We did not manage to arrive at a collective decision. But three points of view emerged:

The *first* was a general one: it was agreed that we would go on keeping each other informed and that for this purpose we would meet each six months, with a view to re-examining the situation to be sure we were not mistaken in our prognostications, for after all things might not be as bad as they appeared to be.

The *second* one was that of the pessimists, who said to themselves: "Why set out upon investments representing several billion (old) francs, while we take the risk of derailing the paper industry's economic machinery?" In the event, two of my fellow members temporarily delayed the date of making their investments.

Finally, the *third* attitude was that of the optimist who, on the very eve of the meeting, put in the order for his equipment, so as to be the first one to have it.

This little story is interesting because it shows very clearly the extraordinary freedom that remains inside the Plan, and the quality of the available information. No one doubts, among my friends, that if we had acted individually, we would probably have had 30 per cent excess capacity which would have been a real catastrophe, especially in our industry.[13]

Except for the optimist, the several reactions which M. de Clinchamps describes were all responses of individuals seeking to fit their activities into a framework which seemed to call for something different from what they had been individually intending. Even the optimist could remain an exception only because he was alone: if all participants had held firm to their original positions, any remaining optimism would have been substantially diluted. Without the assertion of governmental pressure to scale down investment plans, members of this industry undertook to do so on their own—because the "logic" of the system drove them in that direction. They felt the need to conform their own behavior to what the system—as described by the planners— seemed to call for.[14]

Here then is another subtle kind of authority, which exerts compulsion simply by describing the relative positions of all the players and the rules of the game, without actually assigning roles. The *inner* compulsion to conform takes over. But this of course is nothing peculiar to economic planning. It is a social process which has long been recognized—by Adam Smith perhaps more clearly than by most of his professional posterity. The market economy too has its own internal consistency and discipline of logical relationships, though of an even subtler variety than simply "playing the game" by acting on a target

[13] CEPES, *French and Other National Economic Plans for Growth*, pp. 69–70.

[14] A similar example was provided by the Commission for the Iron and Steel Industry for the Fourth Plan. Demand projections for steel tubing indicated that excess capacity would result if all firms carried through their investment plans. Without any pressures being put on them and without interfirm discussions, but purely as a result of this statistical confrontation, four or five companies abandoned their expansion plans.

It is not wholly clear why any particular company might react in this fashion. If, say, eight companies had been planning investment in this category, all of them might have been so influenced by the statistical evidence as to cancel investment plans, leaving capacity deficient. Even if discussions were initiated, it is not clear why some firms would give way to others unless as a *quid pro quo* for preference in some other type of production, or—what seems the most likely reason—unless some firms were much less farther advanced in their investment planning, perhaps even without final approvals or financing. The revelation of investment plans— the industry confessional, as it is sometimes called—would seem to be most effective on firms least committed to expansion programs, where overcapacity seems probable, or those farthest along in their investment planning where capacity appears to be inadequate for future needs.

laid down in a written plan. It is a coherence which is constantly shifting—the coherence of broken-field running in the mosaic of a football game, where the runner must relate himself meaningfully to the shifting players around him, some of whom are cooperators and some of whom competitors, all conforming to known rules.

The difference between the logical discipline of planning, on the one hand, and the market, on the other, is that market logic assumes a framework of fluid movement and full utilization of all resources (no team members or equipment idle on the bench). But that assumption has been demonstrably false, so that the logic has lost much of its compelling force to integrate the economic system as a whole. Planning logic, in contrast, seeks a contrived result and then attempts to implement the movement and utilization of resources to that end. It draws up a blueprint so that the parts of the economy can see that a particular set of relationships among themselves will contribute to the overall result. The logic of such a demonstrated synthesis encourages conformance without compelling it.

Such a discipline of logic has sometimes been attempted even without system-wide planning. The wage and price guideposts designed by the U.S. Council of Economic Advisers are intended to encourage individual managements and unions to conform to the prescription because of the logic of the design, through an appeal to each to adopt policies which if adopted by all would give rise to an internally consistent set of price relationships. The resistance by business and labor to the logic is partly attributable to the fact that it was a logic not relevant to their own requirements, as we noted in Chapter 5, but was also in part an expression of resistance to a species of authority in a country that as yet is opposed to economic planning.

As usual, there are two sides to the issue. Let us assume that a plan does generate its own logical pressures for conformance and thus reduce the need for formal governmental authority. From one point of view this represents an insidious influence because less apparent. From another point of view reliance on voluntary concurrence is more compatible with Western social philosophy.

But however one may regard this aspect of it, the logic of planning is actually much less disciplinary than it is often made out to be. The parts of the economy are much more numerous than the lines in any blueprint. The latter is at best a sketch, leaving large areas of uncertainty and the discretion which uncertainty brings with it. Only a detailed blueprint would generate the internal compulsion to conform which would warrant concern and justify opposition. Western planning tends to eschew detail as a matter of preference. There is no clear indication of what is expected of each subunit, so there is little to which any one could conform even if amenable. This is the chief significance of the categorical objectives, which we shall have occasion to consider again in just a moment.

THE ADEQUACY OF NATIONAL AUTHORITY

Planning in any unit almost always raises problems that can be resolved only in some larger unit. Short-run planning in the corporation, for example, begins with estimates of final demand for its products. While this is partly within its own control through such devices as product design, advertising, marketing organization, and price, it is also largely dependent on aggregate economic activity, about which it can do nothing. Only economic planning in the national unit can provide the firm with some degree of assurance as to what GNP will be next year or five years later. Thus it is almost always the case that authority in any given unit is insufficient, by itself, to control its own performance. Outside influences intrude with disturbing effects.

Planning in a national unit is no exception to this generalization. There are difficulties of controlling exports, foreign investment, and to a lesser extent imports which render governmental authority—so often feared as excessive—inadequate to assure the results which are sought. This is especially true when a country is party to international agreements which limit its discretion in dealing with international pressures —conventions such as the General Agreement on Tariffs and Trade, and treaties such as those governing the Common Market and the European Free Trade Area.

No country can ensure that its exports will be maintained at a preferred level. If customer countries choose to buy less, its aggregate level of activity will be depressed, and the synthesis which was put together on the basis of an expected overall level of performance will be invalidated. If other countries choose to buy more, its rate of activity may be accelerated with unfavorable effects on the price level: it may "import inflation," as Germany in 1964 complained was the case due to stepped-up purchases from its Common Market partners whose own price levels had already risen high enough to make German prices look like bargains.

On the capital front, of what value is it for a government to seek to control "excessive" investment in, say, automobile production if foreign producers are free to enter and invest at will? Or to limit access to credit if domestic manufacturers can raise capital abroad? The latter can be all the more readily facilitated if foreign producers are invited in as "partners" in domestic enterprises, so that capital expansion can be arranged through them, as an "internal" matter.

These problems of international economic relationships which are beyond the control of national governments leave them, like the business firm in an unplanned economy, with a greater need for flexible planning. Just as the flexible corporate budget enables the firm to adjust its scale of operations quickly, in the face of an increase or decrease in its sales, so flexible national budgets enable a country to make more promptly such adjustments as a change in its foreign trade position seems to require. The lack of sufficient authority to control all the variables affecting its performance does not mean that planning is made useless.

At the same time, to those who resist the notion of governmental authority in an economic planning process, the circumstances just posed raise a frightening prospect. If problems cannot be met in one unit because of a lack of authority, pressures are generated to transfer them to a larger unit where authority is adequate. The notion of supranational planning, with some measure of control over national economic affairs, is one which would whiten the hair of most American businessmen, but it is widely and often sympathetically discussed in Europe.

One school of thought believes that it would be desirable to extend the French system of indicative planning to the Common Market as a unit. Others believe that industry-wide exchanges of information and rationalization of organization and production, comparable to that already achieved in the European Coal and Steel Community, must precede any larger attempts at planning. Some have suggested expanded regional economic planning in Western Europe, along lines largely ignoring national boundaries, within the framework of a supranational plan. Already the EEC is taking a modest step in the direction of intermediate-term projections of economic activity for the Community as a whole and has brought pressure on its constituent governments to undertake measures to restore financial equilibrium as a necessary condition to assuring equilibrium in their joint relations. Further actions in this direction can be expected, responsive not to any ideological quest for the expansion of authority within a larger system, but to the search for an adequate authority to deal with a range of problems beyond the competence of any single country to deal with.

THE RECONCILIATION OF OBJECTIVES BY
COMPETITION AND COMPROMISE

The objectives of any unit necessarily diverge, in some respects, from those of any other unit, in part as a consequence of a condition of scarcity which does not permit the satisfaction of all appetites (a condition most frequently pertaining to lateral relationships, where hierarchical organization is absent), and in part as a consequence of the necessity of coordinating the activities of subunits into a workable system (a condition usually applying to social organizations having some hierarchical elements). Thus, for example, the conflict of objectives among nations, in the absence of any larger supranational unit, arises primarily from scarcity conditions: imports are reduced to conserve foreign exchange, or are increased because they are cheaper in one country than another. But if a supranational unit were established, such as we contemplated a paragraph back, the conflict of objectives would be partly transformed into one arising between the individual countries composing such a unit and the larger unit itself; the former would be concerned solely with their own individual interests, while the latter would have to take into account the impact of individual performances on the system as a whole. In the first case, where no coordinating unit existed, resolution of differences would come through competition. In the second case, where a larger unit had been called into being, resolution of differences would come through the exercise of authority or through administrative compromise.

Conflicting objectives between the subunits and the system constitute the basis for public-private and national-local differences in national economic planning. Both sets of problems can be subsumed under the micro-macro rubric. We have just examined the uses and limitations of authority as an instrument for resolving such differences of objectives. Now we shall turn our attention to competition and compromise, as alternative devices.

Before doing so, however, it would be well to remind ourselves that micro and macro objectives are not wholly conflicting but have important mutual elements as well. Indeed, if the mutuality were not more important than the conflict, there would be no rationale for planning. But to the extent that the conflict component can be reduced and the mutuality component expanded, the planning process becomes more effective—hence our concern with methods for reconciling differences in objectives.

One way of reducing the incompatibility of system and subsystem objectives is to divide the former into specific and categorical objectives, as we earlier noted. The categorical objectives represent simply an aggregative level of certain kinds of activity, from whatever source deriving.

Government can give rather free rein to the operations of the private sector in these classes of activity, limiting them only by certain minimal premises such as those dealing with health hazards, monopolization, and misrepresentation. The individual subunits pursue their own objectives vigorously and competitively, without respect to the system, but collectively their efforts help to achieve system goals. Indeed, the freedom of private firms and local governments to innovate and experiment provides a dynamic element which over the long run furthers, rather than conflicts with, system objectives.[15]

The opposition of system and subsystem interests can be minimized by the specification of system objectives at as categorical a level as possible. Government action with respect to these objectives is needed only when the aggregative performance falls short or exceeds the target amount by a large enough margin to be considered serious. The assurance that some action to support overall performance will be taken when needed provides a firmer basis for private business plan-

---

[15] On this latter point, Prof. Albert Hirschman has suggested that it is both a weakness and strength of private initiative that it ignores external diseconomies (marginal social costs) and innovates even when this creates hardship for others, such as those whose capital and skills are made obsolete by the innovation. This indifference to the immediate social consequences of private actions seems harsh, but it also makes possible developments which in a longer run add up to a greater social good. If private initiative were restrained by the need to obtain governmental approval, the approving authority—at least in democratic societies—would be more disposed to take into account the external costs of the proposed action, with the inescapable consequence that innovation would be slowed. *Strategy of Economic Development* (New Haven, Conn.: Yale University Press, 1958), chap. 3.

Presumably some combination of private and public initiative is preferable—the former because it ignores external diseconomies (but, economies as well) and the latter because it takes external economies (as well as diseconomies) into account.

ning. Thus private actions cumulate in public goals, and public actions underwrite private goal seeking. Here the mutuality element comes more clearly into focus.

The same mutuality of interest is evidenced in the related matter of productivity. This elusive concept has at least two meanings: at the micro level it is the familiar measure of input-output efficiency, an efficiency which is largely engineered by private management and is perhaps most nearly described by the notion of the production function. It is an important determinant of a firm's rate of return on investment, that portmanteau objective we encountered in Chapter 2. On the macro level productivity is a measure of the effectiveness with which the government as manager of the economy makes full use of the economy's assets—whether manpower and industrial capacity are fully employed or partially idle—in realizing as high a level of GNP as is realistically feasible, a public categorical objective.

But each of these is partially determined by the other. The efficiency with which a firm produces depends in part on its capacity utilization, which is in part a matter of the economy's effectiveness, a governmental responsibility. And the economy's effectiveness, in the sense of the GNP which it is capable of producing, depends not only on the degree of utilization of its assets but also on the efficiency with which producing units operate, which is a managerial responsibility in the firm. The management of the firm and the management of the economy interact to increase each other's productivity, the better that each may realize the private or public objectives for which it is separately responsible. Such mutuality of interest between private and public sectors is encouraged by the aggregative nature of the latter's goal, which gives free rein to the competitive goals of the individual firms composing the former.

The categorical objectives are thus important for two reasons. First, as we noted in a previous chapter, they are important because they make possible the achievement of the specific public objectives: general levels of economic activity must satisfy present consumption demands sufficiently to permit the siphoning-off of resources into investment for general growth as well as specific social goals. The specific goals, which help give tone to a society, can be planned only because the overall aggregate permits. Second, the categorical objectives are important because they provide the conceptual justification for private discretion within a system of planning. The offsetting nature of the activities of numerous firms and households reduces the risk that the exercise of private discretion will jeopardize public objectives and reduces the administrative demands on central government.

DECENTRALIZING SOCIAL OBJECTIVES

The more detailed the blueprint and the more specific the objectives in national economic planning, the greater the potential conflict between micro and macro units. One method of reducing this conflict is by decentralizing the specific social objectives. In Chapter 2 we noted the long-run need of the business firm to innovate and to create new markets in order to find outlets for its investment funds. In Chapter 3 we noted the growing emphasis on social investment, as private consumption becomes better provided for. Scarcely a country in Western society is not contemplating a relative expansion in social services in the years ahead—not in response to any governmental desire for added power but in response to needs felt by society itself, insofar as the political process can register such an expression.

It has been customary to think of this as a movement from the private sector to the public sector, but this is necessarily the case only in a demand sense, not with respect to supply. By definition it constitutes a movement from private to social consumption, but it does not necessarily connote a movement from private to public production. A business firm can produce for governments no less than for individual consumers. If business comes to look on governments as *markets*, and to recognize that social demand provides an opportunity for developing wholly new product lines geared to those markets, then its field of operation is expanded. Opportunities are opened for research and development leading to new kinds of products and services.

Once this is realized, attention can be directed to ways of making this new market for private business ventures as effective, competitive, and innovative as possible. One area for examination is the relative roles of central and local governments in the provision of social services. We had occasion earlier to observe that central governments were coming to play an increasingly dominant role in this respect. The atrophy of local governments has been remarked by a number of observers in different countries. There has been good reason for the more important role of the central government in providing social services. In a national economy standards of social services can hardly be left to local administrations, with widely varying degrees of fiscal and professional competence. So central governments have become the collecting agents for revenues and the disbursing center for expertise. It is logical enough.

But to the extent that there is an increasing centralization of governmental provision of social services, the less satisfactory a market does this become. Even when the government buys rather than produces, it appears on the scene as a monopsonist; business firms are invited to compete against each other for such contracts as the central government lets; the successful bidders become more heavily dependent on the central government as a buyer, more subject to its influence, more clearly drawn in as a subunit of its own extensive organization. Moreover, centralization of decision making contributes to loss of adaptability to changing or varied circumstances. There is an almost exact parallel here with the weaknesses of corporate centralization.

If we regard local governments as the equivalent of corporate departments or divisions, then there is the same gain to be had from decentralization in the one case as in the other. But aside from the increased efficiency that comes from decentralization, there would be a further gain for which there is no parallel in the corporate case, arising from the fact that decentralization of public-service functions to local governments would be chiefly with respect to a *purchasing* rather than a *producing* function, thus helping to create a market rather than expand a hierarchy.

The central government could continue to collect and redistribute revenues and could specify minimum standards to be met in the provision of the social services for which revenues were allocated. These would constitute the premises binding on local governments and guaranteeing that the specific objectives of the economy as a whole were reasonably met. But within these premises local governments would be free to exercise their discretion, to innovate and experiment in line with local preferences.

From the point of view of building a market for the private provision of public services, the important consideration is that there would be a proliferation of purchasers of the same type of service, as a large number of local governments would form the demand side of the market in contrast to a single central government. Private suppliers would cease to become dependent on any one government: the loss of a contract in one locality might be compensated by the gain of a contract in a different locality. We could presume that with a growing but diffused demand for such services, the number of firms competing would also increase. What would be the difference to a firm whether it sells its product to individual consumers, to other corporations, or to local and state governments? Thus more buyers and more sellers would help to create a more competitive market, with all its attendant advantages. We need only accept—could we not say welcome?—a variety in the provision of social services in respects which do not threaten system objectives.

The number of types of services for which local governments could contract, in line with certain prescribed national standards, is probably much greater than we sometimes tend to think. There is no reason why it could not extend to general education, recreation and youth development programs, health, housing, and cultural activities. At the level of the state or province it could include highway construction and some regional redevelopment activities.

One important consequence of such reorganization of public markets would be that it would encourage business firms to direct their research and development activities to social as well as individual wants, to develop new product lines more nearly meeting public needs, thus expanding their own potential investment outlets. The result would be to harness private initiative and innovation in the service of organized society no less than of the individual.

The potentialities are suggested if we consider public education in the United States as a prototype. This is carried on as a state and local function (but without national standards). Architects, construction firms, furniture and equipment suppliers, and textbook publishers, among others, compete among themselves in this specialized and diffused market. Local governments do not supply these goods and services themselves but purchase them from private profit-making institutions. In particular, the flow of improved textbooks to the school market is directly traceable to the competition of publishers to best each other, and the result is more varied and updated instructional materials than if the schools—or a central ministry of education—undertook to provide this important ingredient of the educational system on their own initiative. One might reasonably argue that overall educational objectives might be better served if minimum national standards were provided for, but even with that modification the same principle of local discretion in meeting national standards would permit the operation of an effective market.

Thus private and public objectives can be made more compatible by improving the market relationship of the public to the private sector. An increase in the public budget designed to provide more adequately for social services and investment would carry no more adverse connotation to private business than a decision by consumers to put more of their expenditures into, say, housing than clothing. One early example of such a business reorientation is provided by the Reynolds Metals Co., which in 1960 established a subsidiary, Reynolds Aluminum Service Corp., headed by a former U.S. housing administrator, primarily to contract for construction projects in urban renewal programs. Such business ventures may encounter difficulties at this early stage of market organization, but this is entrepreneurship in the pure Schumpeterian sense of opening up a new market.

"PRIVATIZING" PUBLIC OBJECTIVES

There are, of course, some public services which cannot be disaggregated to the local level. These must be carried on by the central government directly. Included in this category are national defense, technical assistance to foreign countries, development of transportation systems other than road transport, noncommercial research programs, resource development, underseas and space exploration, and certain forms of power development.

In the case of such activities, public and private objectives can be brought closer together by what may be termed the "privatizing" of public objectives—the contracting with private enterprise for their development and operation. There is seldom any reason why the government need carry on such activities itself, even if its initiative is required to set them in motion.

The extensive system of contracting which has been developed by the U.S. Department of Defense is indicative of how reliance can be placed on private firms for the effectuation of public programs. Even the conduct of research and development with an eye to the more effective meeting of public needs can be undertaken, on a competitive basis, by private corporations. It would be interesting to see, for example, what varied proposals a half-dozen large firms might come up with for the economic provision of more suitable transportation between the cities on the U.S. East Coast, from Boston to Washington. Whatever system was selected could then be privately constructed under government contract, and arrangements made for its private operation—either on a subsidized ownership or management fee basis. The important consideration is that from start to finish it would rely on private inventiveness and organization to provide a public need. In the process the economy would make more effective use of one of its prime assets—its private business firms.

Such a system of economic administration by contract—something which the United States has pioneered and brought to a more advanced state of organizational effectiveness than is generally appreciated—is even the potential basis for a new type of economic system. It differs from historic capitalism, which stressed private organization to meet private wants, with the latter assumed to be overriding. It differs from socialism, which relies on public organization to meet both public and private wants, with the former assumed to take precedence. The system of administration by contract depends heavily on private organization to meet both public and private needs, neither of which has any special claim to dominance but which can be mixed in any proportions desired. Its advantage lies in the dispersal of authority throughout society, accompanied by an instrument for its effective coordination for the achievement of system goals. It permits the realization of public wants without a concomitant expansion of the governmental establishment. It encourages private initiative by offering it a wider scope for its application.

A BALANCE OF PUBLIC AND PRIVATE OBJECTIVES

Despite such devices for diminishing the conflict element of the micro-macro relationship, differences in objectives are bound to remain. They can never be wholly eliminated. Where governmental authority is unequal or undesirable as the instrument for arbitrating the remaining divergences, the only alternative is outright compromise. Regardless of whether it has "sovereignty" on its side, the government is reduced to bargaining with private and local units for the performance which it seeks. Sovereignty is not always adequate to secure compliance: governmental measures have been often enough ignored by subunits which believed they could get away with such behavior, or to whom the penalties for noncompliance appeared less than either its potential rewards or the penalties (losses) associated with compliance.

The bargaining which goes on—widespread and continuously—between the central government and the system's subunits is embedded in the complex political processes of democratic society.[16] In the course of bargaining each bends the other closer to its own objectives. The inducements offered become part of a bargain which is voluntarily entered into. The sanctions which a subunit can impose on the central government—in terms of nonperformance, opposition to programs, and political opposition—influence the inducements which are offered.

It would be quite erroneous to assume that these sanctions in the hands of private firms and local governments are weak and ineffective relative to some massive central power. They frequently play an important part in shaping public programs, as is recognized when business accuses government of pandering to the unions, and labor unions charge the central administration with responding to the dictates of big business, and rural areas complain that the city political machines pull the strings to which the national government jumps, and urban interests charge the Federal legislature with being excessively solicitous of the farm bloc's welfare. Most such charges have a degree of validity, since the groups indicated constitute subunits whose performances are essential to an overall program, performances which must be elicited by appropriate bargains. The resulting compromises lessen the attainability of public objectives as spelled out in any technical-economic models, but they increase the likelihood of their realization in larger degree than would be the case in the absence of compromise.

In Western society public objectives are not overriding. There must be a high degree of compatibility between them and private objectives in order for planning to be effective. Compatibility—the reconciliation of micro and macro objectives—ultimately becomes a matter of bargains rather than fiat, of compromise rather than the exercise of sovereign power, of agreement (with its element of inducements shading off to coercion) rather than of formal authority.

[16] I have tried to spell these out, insofar as they relate to economic decision making, in *A General Theory of Economic Process*, chap. 14.

9...
economic planning
and political institutions

Government's systematic management of the nation's assets in a planning program has its impact on traditional political institutions. Perhaps it would be more accurate to say that the planning process makes more evident, more explicit, political changes which are already in process.

REPRESENTATIVE GOVERNMENT AND
THE PROBLEM OF EXPERTISE

First, let us revert to a problem which was introduced in Chapter 8. Special knowledge carries with it an authority of its own. This fact, which is important in government's relations with the private and local sectors, is also relevant to the relationship of the executive arm of government with the legislative branch. In Western societies, parliaments or legislatures are elected representative bodies composed of people drawn from all walks of life, many of whom are expert in certain fields (principally law) but few of whom are expert in the technical field of economics. The consequence is that economic plans, drafted by specialists, tend to be removed from the subject area which representative legislators can discuss intelligently. They can accept or reject but they cannot do a very competent job of modifying the administration's formulations.

The French Fourth Plan is highly instructive in this respect. More than two years of detailed and expert preparation had gone into the drafting of the four-year plan which was finally presented to the Assembly and Senate in the summer of 1962. As we noted in an earlier chapter, it had begun with an econometric exercise, in which several alternative statistical projections had been poured through the matrix of an input-output table detailed to twenty-eight cells. The alternatives had been examined by the professionals in the Planning Commission and subsequently by subcommittees of the Economic and Social Council, among whose members were a number of professional economists. After selection of a growth target, projections were further refined into a sixty-four-cell input-output table, which formed the basis for the discussions which took place in the twenty-seven *commissions de modernisations*, including both the horizontal (industrial) and vertical (functional) commissions. The results had been reviewed by the central Planning Commission, consolidated and again made internally consistent, and then approved by the Superior Council of the Plan on which industry and labor representatives sit and by the Economic and Social Council. And only then had it been presented to the French Assembly, the nation's principal representative body, for approval.

The response in that sensitive body was almost predictable. For hours its members laid bare their frustration at being presented with a technical and complicated document, into the devising of which had gone so much ingenuity, skill, and compromise, with a request for their endorsement. What they were being asked to endorse filled volumes of statistical and policy analysis, all of which was—to a degree which they did not really know, but which they were told was very substantial—functionally interrelated, so that the whole formed an integrated system. What could they do? Could they at that stage begin picking the design to pieces? Could they quibble with certain of the assumptions on which the program was based, conscious that to do so would mean the rejection of the whole monumental exercise, including the labors of some 3,000 members of the several *commissions de modernisation?* And how could they have any feeling of assurance that so destructive an act, if they did engage in it, might be based on nothing more than their own misunderstanding of what was involved?

A member of the Conseil Supérieur du Plan, who reported that that body was subject to the same frustrations and misgivings, ventured an interesting analogy. As a youth, he said, when he visited the Louvre the museum still included in its collection numerous pictures which were certainly not masterpieces and which even with his limited knowledge he could competently criticize as to color and composition. But when it was decided that the Louvre's collection should be limited only to "great art," selected on the strength of the judgment of outstanding art critics, he lost the confidence of his own judgment. And so it is with the plan, he went on, concluding his analogy. When economic policy is subjected to the judgment of a great many experts, whose efforts are devoted to the articulation of a master design, interlocked in all its parts, what effective role is left to the inexpert critic?

Out of the vigorous debate which ran through the night and into the early morning there finally emerged a compromise between the Planning Commission and the National Assembly. A distinction was drawn between plan objectives and plan execution. It was agreed that before the detailed elaboration of the Fifth Plan got underway, the Assembly would be consulted on the objectives to which the plan would be directed, and informed of the implications in the choice of one set of objectives (including a planned rate of growth) over alternatives.[1]

But such a compromise is necessarily only a partial solution. As we are all aware by now, all ends are means, and all means become inter-

[1] Approximately the same story was repeated in Belgium only a short time later. In the first program presented to the legislature appeared this admission (author's translation): "It will be necessary in the future to enlarge the program beyond the problems of production and their determinants. Besides the economic objectives, the great social objectives—the preoccupations in terms of which national welfare is more and more expressed—have to be taken into account. The Government will take special care that a more extensive discussion precedes the determination of the next program so that the basis for a democratic acceptance, necessary to its realization, will be enlarged."

twined with ends, so that for a representative legislature to content itself with defining a few major objectives of a national plan, endorsing the work of experts in the means of achieving those objectives, still leaves to the executive arm of government an enormous area for relatively autonomous decisions. In the field of economic policy, the representative function of legislatures is subjected to considerable strain. The specialist authority of administrative experts is a major challenge to it.

THE BASIS OF REPRESENTATION

If the technical-economic aspects of planning challenge the traditional representative function of Western legislatures, that function has been exposed to further assault based on the importance of political-organizational coordination to achieve the planning program. As we have noted repeatedly in previous pages, the essence of Western planning lies in inducing responses from private and local institutions which, while achieving their own independent objectives, simultaneously realize public goals. A national economic program thus depends on a close working relationship between central government and the micro sectors, a working relationship achieved through understandings, compromises, and bargains. This means that the private functionaries of the industrial sector in fact assist in the making of public economic policy, however that fact may be disguised by the use of special or advisory commissions or unofficial bodies.

Since this is the case, new fuel has been added to the old arguments for functional rather than geographical representation. Even those who sympathize with the legislature in its contest with the executive are sometimes ready to downgrade the former in their effort to control the latter.

Again France provides a pertinent example, although the issue is by no means peculiar to that country. While the government has sought to picture the planning process as a paradigm of economic democracy, in which large numbers of citizens participate, the same process has been branded as "technocratic" by a considerable number who believe that trade unionists in particular, but small businessmen and farmers as well, have been effectively if not nominally excluded from the program. Present procedures, they argue, are dominated by the civil service bureaucracy linked with the major trade associations. Critical statistical information, on which the whole planning process rests, is kept confidential within this "clique," it is said, so that effective participation is denied to all except a small coterie of experts and officials. This dominance of a small corps, referred to as the technocrats, can only be partially broken by requiring them to leave the choice of major economic objectives to the legislature. That is good as far as it goes, but it does not go very far. Since the attainment of the national objectives defined by elected representatives depends so crucially on the whole intricate apparatus by which private actions support public goals, there must be a more adequate representation of those private interests whose supporting actions are needed. In addition to citizen representation through the legislature, there should be a more inclusive producer representation through functional agencies. It is this revised planning procedure, rather than what now exists, which is commonly referred to as *planification démocratique.*

Numerous suggestions have been offered as to how this can be accomplished. Some would expand the role of the labor unions in the *commissions de modernisation.* Others would give more decision-making authority, in contrast to the present advisory role, to either or both the Conseil Supérieur du Plan or the Conseil Économique et Social, in both of which the labor unions and professional people are represented. Some would carry the elaboration of the plan down to the level of the individual firm, involving something akin to a workers' council in local consultation with management.

If some aspects of the French movement for "democratic planning" suggest a more tightly controlled economy (even though the number of people involved in imposing the controls is increased and their base broadened), this should not divert our attention from the widespread support for *some* form of functional representation in Western economies. That growing support has directly paralleled the growth of planning programs.

One group of experts which undertook to review the development of planning programs in the West reached this tentative conclusion:

> The broad outline of this overall [economic] policy must be endorsed by the interested parties to be successful. It is not sufficient that it has been decided by the Government nor even accepted by Parliament; it must have been subject to some measure of agreement among the main groups whose decisions affect the working of the economy. At first it may be sufficient to decide on policy

in consultation with these bodies but more frequently the idea is encountered that it is necessary to go somewhat further to the point where policies are actually formulated by government representatives in conjunction with leaders of industry and of the trade unions. In other words, it is not enough that the government should implicitly translate the aspirations of the majority of people in the country; there is apparently a belief that it must get the main bodies whose decisions influence the economy not merely to acquiesce in but actually to commit themselves to particular policies.

Even in Britain, a country with firmly entrenched parliamentary traditions, the establishment of the National Economic Development Council can be regarded as a first tentative step in the direction of such functional representation, raising delicate problems of its relationship to Parliament. "I want," said the Chancellor of the Exchequer, in calling it into existence, "both sides of Industry to share with the Government the task of relating plans to the resources likely to be available." [2]

Sweden has moved along this same informal route. As Prof. Hans Thorelli has noted, the emergence of powerful pressure groups in industry and labor has led to talk of a "usurpation" of Riksdag authority: "The government frequently finds itself prompted to enter formal or informal agreements with these organizations, later presenting the Riksdag with what is more or less a fait accompli." [3] In 1963 a Council for Economic Planning was established, with a composition roughly comparable to Britian's NEDC, lacking formal authority but capable of representing the opinion of powerful functional groups.

Sweden has for some time been accustomed to tackling complex or controversial issues by appointing commissions to prepare recommendations to the Riksdag. As many as a hundred commissions may be at

[2] The delicate question of whether this does not involve NEDC more than Parliament in determining at least major aspects of the country's economic policy has been sidestepped by keeping the situation appropriately muddy. Three government ministers sit on NEDC, including the Chancellor of the Exchequer as its chairman. The decisions which NEDC reaches can thus be coordinated with government policy, without binding the government. Admittedly it would be awkward if an NEDC decision in which the Chancellor of the Exchequer had joined should be overridden by the government. But formally NEDC has no policy-making power and is only advisory. Thus it has not taken from Parliament any authority in the field of economic policy, since theoretically it has no authority. (The above constitutes a description of the NEDC relations prior to the advent of the Labor government in 1964.)

[3] Hans Thorelli, "Overall Planning and Management in Sweden," *International Social Science Bulletin*, vol. 8, no. 2, 1956.

work at any time, most of them staffed by civil servants. In perhaps 20 percent of the cases functional representatives will be included, as notably in the tax reform commission which over a period of several years surveyed the mechanics of shifting emphasis from direct income to indirect excise or value-added taxes. Here too, as in France, the legislature is likely to be presented with an expertly researched and conceived proposal ready for adoption. One consequence has been to generate a growing feeling of indifference to their role by the parliamentarians themselves.

EXPERIMENTS IN REPRESENTATION

Besides the experiences in France, England, and Sweden, other Western countries have experimented with various forms of functional representation. We can appropriately leave out of consideration, in this context, the U.S. National Recovery Administration and other proposals of the thirties. Postwar experimentation has all been of European origin, except for the NEDC-like Economic Council of Canada set up in 1964.

The Netherlands is probably the outstanding case. In 1950 a Social and Economic Council was established, its forty-five members appointed by the government and drawn in equal part from the labor unions, industry, and the professions (so-called public members). It owed its origin to a belief which, according to government account,[4] gained ground between the First and Second World Wars and flourished thereafter—that some combination of economic freedom and economic regulation would produce better results than unrestricted freedom. But—an important addendum—as much as possible, regulation should be self-regulation, under the watchful eye of government. This view blossomed into the Industrial Organization Act of 1950, which is composed of two parts. The first provides for the creation of the Council, an advisory body designed to promote the interests of trade and industry, broadly speaking, and of the nation as a whole—in our terms, to suggest means of reconciling the objectives of system and subunits. It advises the government on all major economic issues, and its advice is not treated lightly.

As a second part of the act of 1950, provision was made for the

[4] *Digest of the Netherlands: No. 1, Constitutional Organization and Political Life*, 1958, pp. 57–60.

establishment of industrial boards and commodity boards, known as horizontal and vertical boards, respectively. The industry boards, which can be established by royal decree, are composed of equal numbers of employers and workers representatives. Commodity boards can be organized only by an act of parliament. Either decree or act specifies the areas of the board's competence, which may include some or all of the following: the production, sale, and use of goods and services; research; industrial modernization and rationalization; competition; wages and working conditions; training programs; data collection. As of 1958 thirty-one industrial boards had been established and fifteen commodity boards.

In recent years the significance of the boards has tended to diminish somewhat, while the Economic and Social Council continues to enjoy a role of major importance in the determining of economic policy. It has been referred to as a kind of economic parliament. The Central Planning Bureau services it with information and analysis, and the director of the CPB is a member of the Council. Care has been taken to insist on the supremacy of parliament over the Council, but in view of the latter's influential role candor would require the admission that power in economic matters, even if it has not been formally delegated, is nevertheless shared.

The Norwegian experiment with functional representation proved somewhat less successful than the Dutch. As an aftermath of the war, a Coordination Council was constituted in 1945, composed of representatives of major interest groups. Its function was to review the national economic budget (only then coming into use) rather than to assist in its initial preparation, with a view to ensuring that the government's proposed program reflected the will and won the support of the major groups which would be responsible for its success. Inside of six or seven years it fell into disuse, however, victim of an incompatibility between functional and political representation. In the Storting, Norway's parliament, the Labor Government's chief opponent was the Conservative Party, whose backbone lay in the financial and industrial communities. The latter interests came to the conclusion that the Coordination Council was being used by the government as an instrument for securing the equivalent of a commitment from them to the national economic budget, as proposed or amended, even though this was not the supposed intent of the Council's review, and, further, that they were then being saddled with certain responsibilities for achieving the plan, which they did not propose to accept. The review function was being converted into a policy-approving and executing function which was not to their liking. In parliamentary debates the government sometimes sought to silence Conservative criticism of economic policy by using the argument that Conservative business representatives on the Council had approved it. To ensure that political opposition remained vital, business interests withdrew from the Council.

A need for some functional review of national economic budgets has continued to be felt by the Norwegian plan authorities. Discussions have been revived within the last few years looking to the establishment of a revised form of the old Coordination Council. In 1963, as we noted in an earlier chapter, informal bargaining among all the principal interest groups (including business, labor, and agriculture) led to a national wages and prices policy.

Belgium initiated an experiment with functional representation in economic policy matters almost coincidentally with its venture into programming. In 1960 a royal decree established a Committee for Economic Development, whose members are major officials of the chief interest groups (labor, industry, trade, and agriculture) along with five governmental ministers (Economic Affairs, Social Affairs, Labor, Agriculture, and Finance). Although this tripartite body is, as customary, advisory only, the nature of its membership suggests that few major pieces of legislation are likely to pass Parliament without carrying its approval. In addition, there is a Council on Economic and Social Affairs, composed of representatives of major economic organizations who may co-opt other professionals; government representatives are not included. This older body is also advisory and plays a lesser role than the Committee for Economic Development.

Functional representation is by no means a new concept, and the institutions which have embodied it are by no means all of recent origin. But the postwar surge of economic planning in the West has given a vitality to the process which it has not had in many years, and there is no indication that this is a temporary phenomenon. The rationale for such an agency is implicit in the planning process as it has developed in Western society. But new institutions create new problems. The relationship of these new bodies to the familiar legislative bodies, geographically representative, remains to be settled. Despite the practice of labeling them "advisory only," if they function effectively they will be almost sure to withdraw from traditional parliaments some of their authority in economic affairs. Is it possible to operate with a bifurcated system of representation, in which economic policies originate in one "parliament" and all other matters in another "parliament"? Even the determination of what is economic, and what not, may prove sticky, especially in the hands of a government which uses a body over which it has appointive power (because "advisory") to bring into line an elective legislature in opposition to it.

Is it possible that the economic element has now so permeated all forms of social activity that new, functionally representative, "legislatures" intended to act only in that field, may in time come to take over all legislative matters? Or, on the contrary, can traditional parliaments (even with their usual cumbersome size) muster sufficient strength so that even if they are driven to cede actual authority in economic matters to "advisory" bodies, they can assert their authority in non-economic areas where their competence is at least as great as that of other persons? We might listen in twenty years from now to see how this exciting encounter is turning out.

As we shall shortly see, however, the chances are that the conflict will be somewhat less dramatic than would at first appear. A head-on collision between two systems of representation is unlikely to emerge. It is much more probable that our historic legislatures will simply become less and less effective, at least in the realm of economic policy. The executive branch will gather more and more authority into its hands, treating with those functionaries in the economy whose roles are important to political-organizational coordination.

THE TIME FACTOR IN PLANNING AND THE LEGISLATIVE PROCESS

The time element enters into the planning process in two important ways. First, corrective actions must often be taken promptly, in the face of variances from the national budget projections, if greater deviations and more sweeping remedial measures are to be avoided. This involves the short-run end of the time spectrum. Second, results which are wanted at some more distant point in time must be initiated now, the amount of lead time depending on the magnitude and "roundaboutness" of the project. This involves the long-run end of the time spectrum.

The exercise of traditional legislative powers to review proposed executive actions comes into conflict with these two requirements imposed by the time element. Prompt executive action in the face of variances—such as characterizes business planning—is not possible when the legislature insists on its customary right of approval. The 1964 reduction in the U.S. personal income and corporate tax structure provides a dismal example. On October 4, 1963, Walter Lippmann wrote: "The President first announced his plan to seek a reduction of taxes in order to stimulate the economy on Aug. 13, 1962. That was over a year ago. A tax bill passed the House last week. But the Senate has not even begun to hold hearings. . . . I do not see how a modern government can be conducted successfully if, on a major issue such as fiscal policy, the Executive is refused for more than a year a debate and a decision." [5] It was half a year later, more than one and one-half years after the presidential request, that the tax reduction was finally approved.

One solution to this legislative restraint on prompt economic adjustment is a conditional grant of executive discretion. In Sweden and the Netherlands, emergency budgets can be drawn upon by the government under certain circumstances enumerated by the parliament. In England the government has sufficient authority to initiate changes in tax rates on its own motion. These provisions, and others comparable to them, all have one thing in common: they involve a transfer of authority from the legislature to the executive. However hedged about, executive initiative is augmented and legislative control is reduced.

The long-term time factor provides difficulties of quite a different sort. In some Western countries, legislators are elected for specific terms of office; in other countries a term of office may be shortened by a governmental call for new elections. Legislatures thus "turn over," and each new legislature inherits full authority to act as it sees fit: it is not bound by prior legislatures except as it chooses to honor their commitments. This makes difficult the initiation of long-term projects. An undertaking requiring perhaps ten years to complete will normally have to be financed by a succession of appropriations voted by a number of legislatures, sometimes not even with the same party majority. What has been initiated in one parliamentary session may be scuttled, modified, reduced, or redirected by a subsequent legislature.

France has sought to meet this problem by a device known as "pro-

5 "The Furtive Filibuster," *New York Herald Tribune*, October 4, 1963.

gram laws," first made use of in connection with the Second Plan in 1956. That document noted:

> Of all the criticisms levelled against the present policy regarding public investment the one most frequently voiced ... concerns the insecurity of the credits voted. ... It is thus necessary to establish programme laws which will guarantee to the bodies responsible for their execution a fixed amount of funds for the duration of the plan. They will constitute a "super-budget" which the authorities will be forbidden to interfere with in the preparation of the annual budgets.[6]

Among projects which have been covered under such super-budgets are housing, railway electrification, nuclear energy, airport development, telecommunications, agriculture, school equipment, and merchant shipping. This device does not wholly resolve the problem, however. Limited to the plan's duration, it can anticipate expenditures for a given project by no more than four years (five years beginning with the Fifth Plan). Thus a program dealing with educational expansion, such as was incorporated in the Fourth Plan, looking ahead some twenty years and requiring not only buildings and equipment but also teacher training, does not enjoy immunity from attack by a subsequent legislature which may have quite different ideas as to where priorities should lie. Commitments which should be made now in anticipation of needs some two decades hence may thus not be made, or be made with a degree of caution which undercuts the objective.

The problem is of course more than a legislative one. The executive branch of government may not rest in the same hands, or even with the same party, over a period of time sufficient to bring a program to completion, so that specific objectives of a long-term nature initiated by one government may be subjected to surgery by a subsequent government. On the whole, however, the dangers to realization of long-term plans are less likely to come from executive action than from legislative inaction, due to a reluctance to appropriate funds for distant objectives or to be bound in current budgetary matters by past decisions with which it had nothing to do.

The realization of successful long-term planning in the public sector is thus likely to involve some further relinquishment of control by the

[6] English translation from PEP, *French Planning: Some Lessons for Britain*, pp. 373–374.

legislature to the executive, in the form of acquiescence in a more positive commitment of public funds to projects which can be brought to fruition only over a span of years. Already this is being done more than has been true in the past. The magnitude of many current programs, the extensive period of preparation often required, and the need for a phased program all work in that direction. The acquiescence may be grudging, and formal review powers may be reserved, and appropriations may still be put on a short-term basis, but the tendency is clear.

RELATION OF PLAN AND GOVERNMENT

In the period since World War II, planning has typically gone on in a planning commission, which is either independent or a subdivision of the ministry of finance. The planning commissioner or director often enjoys less than cabinet status. For a time the plan was not even viewed as controlling the actions of the several ministries, though this is now changing. It is often only advisory to the prime minister, who may follow it or depart from it as seems wise to him. Thus a distinction has grown up between the plan and governmental policy. The former is not equivalent to the latter; the government is not bound by its own plan.

Even in a country as committed to planning as France this has been the case. The plan emanates from the Planning Commission, which is only one of the agencies of government, without power over other agencies or ministries, whose views have to be reconciled with those of other officials even after the plan has been formally adopted. (Only since 1963 has it been requisite on the ministries to make their policies conform to the plan.) The government does not necessarily stand behind the Planning Commission, but may listen to other advice and make independent decisions in matters of economic policy.

This conception grossly confuses the planning process with the planning office—a confusion which frequently has its parallel in business administration. The planning office and the planning documents which it prepares are neither the planners nor the plan guiding government in its systematic administration of the nation's assets. The only plan which can be effective is one which motivates the government itself and which instructs all its branches and agencies. Such a plan can emanate only from the highest authority—the president or prime minister, not from a planning commissioner who has no responsibility to a constituency.

Governments whose chief officer leaves the planning function to some appointed commissioner, without himself impressing the stamp of his authority on the program, have not understood planning. Unless the government as an entity is committed to a program which guides its actions, and scrutinizes all variances with a view as to whether corrective action or revision is called for, it remains a hodgepodge of competing ministries or departments, without overall objectives which clarify their respective roles, improvising without forethought.

Any program which purports to direct the assets of a nation to the accomplishment of public as well as private goals cannot devolve on a minister or commissioner of planning, any more than planning in the business firm can be left to the controller, even though these may be the officers in charge of pulling the pieces together. The planning function cannot be delegated by a chief executive to a subordinate, since whoever is capable of performing that function *becomes* the chief executive by virtue of that fact.

A plan is presumably not directed simply to a random assortment of production advances which collectively add up to some rate of profit or rate of growth. A plan stands for specific as well as categorical objectives, some of which are more strategic than others. The question of priorities is critical and can receive its appropriate answer only from the chief executive, who alone has the authority and the influence adequate to win agreement on them and induce cooperation in achieving them. Insofar as the parts of the economy—or the company—can be induced to pull together to realize defined goals, it will be through his prestige and power, playing on the partially independent and partially mutual goals of the subunits, down to individual citizens and employees.

The realization of this need for the integration of the planning program in the office of the chief executive, so that the plan which emerges and which must be continuingly remade serves its purpose of systematizing the operations of government and the economy, is only now beginning to make its impact in Western economies. It is well understood in France, even though advocated chiefly by those who are in opposition to the present government, whose President is above planning and whose Premier tolerates it. In England the Labor Party, in opposition, included in its platform the centralization of budget planning in the office of the Prime Minister rather than in the Treasury. In 1964, in power, it did something less than this (though something more than its predecessor) by locating the planning function in a new Ministry of Economic Affairs. No country has as yet acted to identify its economic policies with its planning program, though the tendencies lie in that direction.

EXECUTIVE INITIATIVE

The reliance on specialist knowledge beyond the comprehension of the usual legislator, the necessity of inducing a cooperative working— functional—relationship between the macro (system) and micro (subsystem) elements in the economy via bargains and compromises, the importance of prompt short-run reactions to variances from the economic budget and of dependable commitments to long-run objectives, the surer coordination of the numerous arms of government—these are all developments which move in one direction: the increased importance of executive vis-à-vis legislative authority and discretion.

That movement may be decried by those who fear the concentration of governmental power in the executive office, and who look to the legislature as the traditional champion of the rights of the people as a defense against concentration of authority. But the rising importance of the executive in Western society is not attributable to any calculated attempt by ambitious schemers to seize power for their own aggrandizement, any more than the same phenomenon, occurring in the business firm, has taken place for that reason.

The reason has been neatly put by a devoted defender of private rights, Bertrand de Jouvenel: "If there are important goals of government which should be achieved, and if the ways to achieve them cannot be boiled down to routines prescribed by the legislative to the Executive, then *the law is consequently devalued and the Executive upgraded.*" [7] Complexity and the time factor rule out the "prescribed routines." The "important goals" which Western societies are demanding of their governments, particularly with respect to growth and

[7] "On the Evolution of Forms of Government," in de Jouvenel (ed.), *Futuribles I* (Geneva: Librairie Droz, 1963),p. 91. [Italics in the original.] This is the most perceptive essay on current political trends in Western society which I have encountered.

employment, require administrative flexibility and expert knowledge. If those goals are to be achieved, the legislature can no more afford to limit the discretion of the government as chief economic executive than a corporate board of directors can afford to limit the discretion of its management in the achievement of a desired rate of return on investment.

The British Parliament, that august institution, already shows the effect of this circumstantial compulsion. "Today, the role of Parliament is much reduced; as a collective body, it sanctions, but it does not initiate. The government controls the course of business because it can usually rely on its majority in the House of Commons to force ready-made policies through or to block the adoption of policies with which it does not agree." [8]

To avoid the stalemate which now at times emerges between an executive who seeks to exercise initiative, and a legislature which seeks to assert its role of final authority—the kind of deadlock of which Lippmann wrote with respect to the U.S. tax debate of 1962–1964—some have suggested that the legislative role should be restricted to one of veto. The executive would propose, and if a majority of the legislature did not oppose within some prescribed period, the proposed action would stand approved. [9]

Whether the legislative role should be formally reduced to one of control by power of veto is not in issue here. We are only concerned that the development of planning programs in the West constitutes an additional factor elevating the status of the executive over that of the legislature. The systematic management of the nation's assets is not simply an economic matter but inevitably has political consequences as well.

Stress on the technical standards of efficiency, an appeal to norma-

[8] Grove, *Government and Industry in Britain*, p. 152. He comments (p. 141): "The British political system (unlike the political systems of most other Western democracies) is characterized by the almost complete dominance of the Executive in policy-making as well as in the direction of day-to-day business, by the correlative weakness of the Legislature, and by the monolithic character of the two great political parties which makes for a high degree of party discipline in Parliament and a unified approach in matters of party policy."

[9] Such a procedure has been recommended by Prof. Michael D. Reagan in "Toward Improving National Planning," *Public Administration Review*, March, 1963. De Jouvenel, while not so explicit, is favorable to the general intent: "This means at the very least that legislative initiative passes to the Executive." *Futuribles I*, p. 91.

tive models as a guide to judgment, and the administrative manipulation of inducements understandably raise suspicions and fears on the part of those who recognize that reliance on expertise threatens the representative function, and who are committed to political institutions which (in contrast to organized efficiency) preserve private spontaneity and innovation and emphasize subunit discretion rather than system goals. But if such suspicions and fears are logically enough derived, they are nonetheless incompetent to stem the changes now in process. Concentration of efforts on preserving subunit discretion is doomed to failure at the point where income changes in the subunits are nonoffsetting, leading cumulatively to recession or inflation. At that point the discretion of subunits is as effectively thwarted as though it had been curbed by authoritative decree. The preservation of subunit discretion *requires* the efficiency of the system. It is not a case of system versus its components, but their interaction in the achievement of objectives which, to the extent they diverge, must be reconciled if they are to be achieved at all.

The price of organization is a limitation on individual discretion, whether the unit of organization is the economy or the corporation. The price of nonorganization is lowered efficiency in the achievement of one's goals. Each brings with it a gain and a loss of freedom, but the freedoms differ. Organization brings with it a gain of freedom in the sense of added power (efficiency), while at the same time reducing freedom in the sense of discretion. Nonorganization adds to one's discretion, but the meaningfulness of its exercise is reduced by inability to exercise control over one's environment. It is difficult to defend the dogmatic assertion of one against the other, but by imaginative analysis and inventiveness in social relations we may reduce the amount of one freedom which must be traded for a gain in the other.

Although the business form can scarcely be regarded as a guide to good government, its evolutionary development is at least instructive. Power in the sense of discretion has moved steadily from the corporate board of directors, where it is formally placed, to management. The board retains control principally by its power of review and veto.

Management has moved steadily to systematize the administration of corporate assets in the achievement of more explicitly defined goals. It has made use of specialists to provide technical standards, but has not hesitated to compromise those standards when necessary to effect political bargains essential to effective organization. Its role as innovator is given more stress, and greater attention is paid to the anticipation of long-range changes and to participation in creating long-range changes.

All these developments have their appropriate analogues in government's management of the economy. But there is one further aspect of corporate management where analogy is less certain; at least we may so hope. Managements of large corporations have developed means for perpetuating themselves in office, and sometimes for naming their successors. There is surely no need to detail here the specifics of how widespread stock distribution and control over the proxy machinery make this possible.

We can hope that the democratic processes in public political life will be sufficiently vigorous to preclude a comparable result. We can hope, but we cannot be sure. The national executive's access to the media of popular expression, particularly television, permits a buildup of his familiarity if not popularity that creates an enormous hurdle to any would-be opponent. Even when the term in office is limited, the same media can be used to popularize a successor. His position in the seat of central power facilitates the organization of a following which, even if numerically a minority, is potent because organized.

There is nothing inevitable about the accretion of power in the hands of the central executive as an individual, in contrast to the growth of power in that office, with the office turning over to successive occupants. Opposition too can be organized and is not necessarily impoverished. Rules to curb the abuse of executive authority and to institutionalize contests over its exercise can be made effective. But the warning is there.

In any event, whatever danger lies in the growth of political power, it is not attributable solely to planning. Planning contributes its share to the process, but has the virtue of simultaneously producing results which enhance the power of the subunits. Planning relies on their contributions and contributes to their strength, endowing them with considerable bargaining power in the political process. In Western planning as in the market system, public efficiency depends on private efficiency.

Finally, the notion of the coherent system, the integrated economy, the managed society, can certainly be overdone. If we are to escape the authority of the experts and rely on more dispersed and representative controls over the exercise of discretion, we must be content with a more "ragged" system. The parts will have to be related to each other in a manner which must be contrived, in order to achieve major objectives, but we can afford to have the relationships a good deal rougher than they appear in the models of economic deportment from which they take their departure, and by which the degree of sacrifice of efficiency (and the costs which that entails) are measured.

index